HINDSIGHT AND INSIGHT

HINDSIGHT AND INSIGHT

Focalization in Four
Eighteenth-Century French Novels

William F. Edmiston

The Pennsylvania State University Press
University Park, Pennsylvania

Library of Congress Cataloging-in-Publication Data

Edmiston, William F.
    Hindsight and insight : focalization in four eighteenth-century
French novels / William F. Edmiston.

        p.   cm.
    Includes bibliographical references and index.
    ISBN 0-271-00731-1
    1. French fiction—18th century—History and criticism.   2. First
person narrative.   3. Narration (Rhetoric)   I. Title.
PQ648.E3   1991
843'.50923—dc20   90-7844
                                                                              CIP

It is the policy of The Pennsylvania State University Press to use
acid-free paper for the first printing of all clothbound books.
Publications on uncoated stock satisfy the minimum requirements of
American National Standard for Information Sciences—Permanence of
Paper for Printed Library Materials, ANSI Z39.48–1984.

For Diana Guiragossian Carr,
who first taught me to love the eighteenth century

CONTENTS

PREFACE

Two major problems loomed before the eighteenth-century French novel-ist: how to guarantee the "historical" authenticity of the story he wanted to write, and how to lure the reader into sharing the subjective experi-ences of the hero. Both problems arose in the attempt to induce belief. During the first half of the century, the most common solution to these problems was that of the autobiographical convention, according to which a narrator authenticated his story by his own personal involve-ment in it. By identifying himself with his hero, a narrator increased his own storytelling authority. The story needed to appear to be a history, for reasons that have been well documented by scholars such as May (1963) and Mylne (1981b). At the same time, the history presented in the form of memoirs was a personal one, allowing the narrator to establish an intimate relationship with the reader and to involve the latter in the events that he personally experienced. Eighteenth-century novelists thus turned toward the memoir format because it responded well to their aspirations. On the one hand, preterite narration lends a historical quality to the memoir-novel, which presents itself as nonfiction; on the other hand the narrator's existential involvement is assured through his personal participation in the recounted events. First-person historical narration is thus a kind of compromise, "the only form which grants that freedom of subjective interpretation while preserving the objective per-spective of history" (Stewart 1969, 18–19).

The autobiographical convention thus introduced into the eighteenth-century novel a subjective point of view belonging to the narrator-hero. It allowed the reader to probe the psychology of the hero and to follow events as he experienced them, while providing hindsight from the narra-tor who was less immediately involved but no less subjective. Despite the obvious advantages of this first-person perspective, the memoir-novelists' attempt to disguise their fiction as history imposed upon them some severe restrictions—a set of rules that we might call "memoir-novel logic." The narrator was to approach his story with only the kinds of information that an actual autobiographer could report. He could give no details that were logically outside the realm of his experience. He could not recount events that happened without his knowledge. Most important, he could not delve into the mental machinations of surrounding characters without reasonable justification. The impossibility of providing any psychological insights into the secondary characters constituted the major disadvantage of the genre. It is for this reason that Showalter (1972) refers to the eighteenth-century novel as a "blind alley" as far as technique was concerned, until the novelist was freed from the "bondage of the first person" (192).

These limitations, however, were merely theoretical. Infractions of the rules abound. As Scholes and Kellogg (1966) have observed, "the novelist's determination to have the benefits of eye-witness narration without accepting its limitations has been indefatigable" (259). Whereas narratorial hindsight proved useful for commenting on the life of the hero, providing insight into the other characters was an equally important concern. In order to gain this insight, novelists were apparently willing to break the rules and to sacrifice "historical" credibility in more or less obtrusive ways. In undertaking this study, my original aim was to compare the theoretical ideal with the actual practice of several French memoir-novels of the period. This task required research into the question of point of view, which revealed several problems.

The concept of point of view in fiction has been an important preoccupation in narrative study since Henry James, and it has generated a great deal of confusion in its various applications. Genette (1972) attempted to put an end to this confusion by separating the function of point of view from the function of narration and by coining the term "focalization" to designate the former. Since then Genette's new term has been widely accepted and yet criticized, amplified, redefined, and used in numerous ways, thereby begetting more confusion. There is clearly a need for this concept in literary criticism, although debates over its terminology and application may leave the reader bewildered. In an appendix to this study, I have traced the evolution of the concept of focalization by contrasting various theories that have appeared since 1972. I hope this will be useful to readers who have not followed the debates, and that it will provide the theoretical justification for my own concepts and terminology.

What I found was that the theories of many narratologists were inadequate to accommodate the kinds of focalization found in first-person fiction. Like earlier students of point of view, more recent theorists of focalization have tended to pay little attention to personal narration, as though the choice of a first-person narrator immediately limited the point of view to that of the autobiographer-historian. There has generally been a failure to recognize that such a narrator has several focal possibilities at his disposal, the more so since his text is not a true autobiography but a work of fiction. In saying this I do not wish to imply that an authentic autobiographer like Rousseau was entirely bound by historical convention whereas his fictional counterparts were not. We know that Rousseau, too, took liberties. Autobiography, writes Lejeune (1975), claims fidelity to an extratextual referent, by means of an agreement that Lejeune calls the "referential pact" (35–41). Here again, however, the reader may find that this pact is not always strictly maintained. Indeed, it is possible that no true autobiography conforms entirely to the logic of retrospection, perhaps because focal infractions are inherent in the discourse of personal narration. In any case, what I am suggesting here is that the eighteenth century's best novelists—who had no extratextual referent to begin with—were quite innovative in their integration of focal manipulations with the rigors of memoir-novel logic. They were not historians, and the point of view adopted by their narrators is not limited to that of hindsight. In *Transparent Minds*, Cohn (1978) demonstrated that the range of narrative devices for representing consciousness is as much available to first-person as to third-person narrators. It will become apparent that Cohn's ground-breaking work has had a great influence on my own thinking. I hope to show that the focal options at the disposal of a personal narrator are precisely those that are open to an impersonal one (memoir-novel logic notwithstanding). They contain elements of all three components of Genette's triadic typology. Clearly, a revision is in order. My introduction proposes a concept of focalization that is applicable to personal narration and relates focalization to the various modes of represented discourse. This working definition should prove both clear and useful to literary critics.

Finally, and to return to my original goal, I have analyzed the functions of discourse (in the sense of Benveniste [1966–74]) and the types of focalization in four major memoir-novels of the French eighteenth century, the period of the rise of this form and of its greatest production. Each of the novels studied—Crébillon's *Les Egarements du coeur et de l'esprit*, Marivaux's *Le Paysan parvenu*, Prévost's *Manon Lescaut*, and Diderot's *La Religieuse*—is the subject of one chapter. These novels have been chosen because they are widely read today by students of Enlightenment fiction, and because each provides an interesting and different case-study for the problems of focalization. The eighteenth-century

French novel, long regarded as rather primitive and inferior to the great novels of the nineteenth and twentieth centuries, has recently undergone a rehabilitation thanks to new methods of critical analysis. My study continues this trend by showing that focal manipulations are nearly as old as first-person fiction itself.

I have taken the liberty of translating into English the quotations of French theorists and critics. All translations are my own, while page numbers refer to the original French texts found in the bibliography.

I am grateful to the University of South Carolina for granting me sabbatical leave, which enabled me to devote time to this project, as well as financial support in the form of a Research and Productive Scholarship Grant and a grant from the Venture Fund. I also wish to thank two friends, Meili Steele of the University of South Carolina and John Duffy of Indiana University, for their willingness to read portions of my text and to offer constructive criticism. Parts of this book have appeared in the *French Review* (63: 45–56) and in *Poetics Today* (10: 729–44), and are reprinted here with permission of the publishers.

INTRODUCTION: FOCALIZATION AND THE FIRST-PERSON NARRATOR

[1] Cette idée, qui n'était pas sans fondement, la pénétra de douleur: elle voyait une femme sans moeurs, sans jeunesse, sans beauté, lui enlever en un jour le fruit de trois mois de soins: et dans quel temps encore, et après quelles espérances! (*Les Egarements*, 167)

[2] Elle apprenait pourtant par là l'infidélité de son mari; mais elle ne s'en souciait guère: ce n'était là qu'une matière à plaisanterie pour elle. (*Le Paysan parvenu*, 21)

[3] Elle ne pouvait espérer que G...M... la laissât, toute la nuit, comme une vestale. C'était donc avec lui qu'elle comptait de la passer! Quel aveu pour un amant! (*Manon Lescaut*, 147)

[4] La nuit suivante, lorsque tout le monde dormait et que la maison était dans le silence, elle se leva. (*La Religieuse*, 237)

There is nothing in the above passages to indicate that they have been taken from retrospective personal narration. Not only is there no evidence of a first-person narrator, but they also contain features usually associated with what is often called an "omniscient, third-person" narrator. Even without a context, we can easily discern evidence of psychological penetration of the characters in [1] and [2], of the expression of a character's point of view in [1] and [3], and of the description of a scene that no character witnessed in [4]. These functions are theoretically denied to the first-person narrator, who can relate only what he or she has experienced directly. They are aspects of *focalization*, a term that has come to supplant that of "point of view" among structural narratologists.[1]

The fact that our four passages are taken from eighteenth-century French memoir-novels points to the inadequacy of recent theoretical debates on the concept of focalization. If we examine these theories with an eye toward retrospective personal narration, we find that a major revision is necessary. Romberg (1962) claimed that "all theoreticians of the novel are in agreement about the internal point-of-view of the first-person novel" (30). This is no longer the case today, yet Romberg's statement is symptomatic of the general dismissal of point of view as an area of little interest in texts in which narrator and character are the same individual. Since most theorists define internal focalization as the presentation of events by a character within the fictional world, many of them locate personal narration in this category, presumably because a first-person narrator (FPN) is a fictional character. This definition seems most unsatisfactory because it equates, for purposes of focalization, a FPN with a focal character who perceives but who does not narrate. It should be obvious that the personal narrator in fiction, like his autobiographical counterpart, has at least two possibilities at his disposal. He has his own subjective point of view, and he can also, because of the duality of the subject, adopt the point of view of the hero, his earlier incarnation.[2]

Before pursuing these and other possibilities in our four novels, we must sketch the criteria of focalization as they apply to personal narration. First, a word about terminology is in order. My definition of focalization will be that of Genette (1972, 1983), i.e. a restriction on perception. Following Cohn (1981), I will use the terms *external* and *internal* *focalization* to designate the vantage point of the narrating self and that of

1. In her poststructuralist study of point of view, Lanser (1981) points out several drawbacks to the formalist-structuralist approach to point of view, notably its tendency to deal with surface structures, whereas much of the material that shapes textual perspective operates on the level of deep structure (39–41). I agree with Lanser that focalization is only one aspect of point of view, which also includes the diegetic authority of the narrator, his attitude toward the characters, his spatiotemporal locus, his ideology, and so on. I will take these other aspects into consideration as well, but I wish to concentrate on focalization.

2. The element of subjectivity results from the explicit presence of an identified speaker, whose entire text is presented as a speech event, a subjective monologue (Tamir 1976, 418; Doležel 1967, 541–552). The duality of the subject results from the element of retrospection: the present is detached from the past, creating two referents for the personal pronoun, each with its own spatiotemporal situation (Lejeune 1975, 16; Starobinski 1970, 257–65). In literary terms this duality means a refraction of the subject into the narrating self and the experiencing self.

the experiencing self. It seems better to base this opposition on the diegetic locus of the perceiving subject rather than on Genette's criterion of psychological penetration, as the FPN always has access to his own mind and must always remain, theoretically, outside the mind of other characters (see Appendix). Therefore these terms will refer only to the subject of perception, whom I will call, following Bal (1977), the *focalizer*. The verb "to focalize" will mean "to be the subject of perception," as in "the narrator allows his younger self to focalize a certain event."

A FPN can present his story from essentially three vantage points. The first is that of *internal focalization*. The narrator can place the focus in his experiencing self, a participant inside the story, and allow the latter to focalize characters and events just as he perceived them at the time of events. The focalization is delegated to the experiencing self, and the narrating self remains silent, provides no correction, and withholds all subsequent knowledge ("I believed," "I was convinced," etc.). Spatially, the subject's vision is limited to proximal objects, those found in his immediate environment. Psychologically, he is limited to his own thoughts and remains outside those of other characters. Any supposition on his part about the thoughts of others requires the use of modal expressions ("it seemed to me," "she looked angry," etc.). We can say that the experiencing self is the focalizer when a narrative statement contains nothing more than what he could have perceived or known at the moment of event. In such cases we follow him through the story as though events were being unfolded before our eyes. This is analogous to Benveniste's *histoire*, for there is no evidence of the speaker (narrator) and no reference to the act of speech.[3] Internal focalization thus corresponds to what Cohn calls "consonant self-narration": a consonant narrator momentarily identifies with his younger self and draws no attention to hindsight (1978, 153–61).

The second vantage point is that of *external focalization*. The narrator can view events and characters from his present vantage point, as an observer in his here-and-now, outside the story he is recounting. External focalization is retrospective and thus provides a broader perspective than the internal type. It corresponds to Cohn's "dissonant self-narration": the dissonant narrator maintains his distance from his younger self and emphasizes hindsight (1978, 145–53). Temporally speaking, the narrat-

3. Benveniste's famous distinction has been reformulated by Simonin-Grumbach (1975). For Benveniste, discourse (*discours*) contains shifters, or words whose specific meanings depend upon a given speech event, whereas historical narration (*histoire*) excludes all shifters (1:239–45). For Simonin-Grumbach, discourse contains references to the speech situation (*énonciation*), and historical narration contains references to the narrated situation (*énoncé*), whereas shifters are common to both (100–103). See also Genette (1969, 61–69).

ing self is virtually unlimited, as he knows what has transpired since the moment of event and can provide subsequent knowledge. He can therefore intervene and manipulate the reader through *discours*, which posits the existence of a speaker, an addressee, and a time and place of the communicative act. The narrator's utterance can be foregrounded through his discourse, when he describes himself, communicates his present thoughts, or refers to the narrative instance ("as I have already told you"). The narrator's presence can be signaled not only by discursive elements, but also by lexical items that the hero would not have used, and by grammatical elements that establish a present–past polarity. He can provide evaluative commentary ("Foolishly, I entered the room") as well as corrective commentary ("I did not know," "I could not have realized"). External focalization is nonetheless a restriction on perception: the narrator is external to the diegesis of his story but not to the fictional world in which he still lives. Spatially, he is still limited to proximal objects, those that the experiencing self could have perceived, and it is this limitation that leads many a FPN to spying and eavesdropping. Psychologically, he must remain outside the thoughts of other characters.

The temporal distance that separates the FPN from the story he recounts is a tremendous advantage, however, in that it affords him the occasion to acquire subsequent knowledge. His retrospective stance allows him the possibility of presenting objects that are spatially distal as well as proximal. In other words, he may not need to resort to eavesdropping in order to learn what happened when he was not present ("As I learned later, she had told him privately that she was in love"). Similarly, on the psychological plane, his subsequent knowledge of the characters allows him to reconstruct their thoughts and to present them more or less as narrative facts—something we all do when we tell a story. Uspensky (1973) observes that we ordinarily use two methods in constructing our narratives: we can relate only our firsthand observations, or we can reconstruct the state of mind of those involved and the motives that governed their actions, even though these are unobservable (81–84). The technique of presenting characters from the narrator's present vantage point ("as I see them now" as opposed to "as I saw them then") is especially conducive to psychological reconstruction or supposition. The reader might expect these suppositions to be justified to a certain degree, and consequently too much knowledge might jeopardize the plausibility and credibility of the report. The boundary between perceptual possibility and impossibility is often nebulous. Soelberg (1982) defines it as follows: "The I-narrator can report only the knowledge of the narrated-I, either his knowledge at the moment of event, or—as long as he specifies it—a knowledge that he has acquired later (I have since learned that . . .). To tell what the narrated-I has never learned, or could never have known, is to transgress the convention" (91). Precision of the type "I have since learned" is not always necessary, however, because of the retrospective stance, and indeed may appear clumsy if used to excess. It might be better to say that the narrator's information must be justified explicitly or justifiable implicitly. Otherwise we are faced with an infraction. Nonetheless, the narrator's temporal distance serves as a camouflage when he yields to the temptation to provide the thoughts of others or to recount events that he did not witness.

In a "neutral" sentence, one devoid of discourse or evaluative commentary, it is often difficult to distinguish between internal and external focalization: "I entered the room," as opposed to "Foolishly, I entered the room" or "As I said earlier, I entered the room." An attempt to distinguish between the narrating self and the experiencing self in such a case is probably futile because the subject of perception is simply not significant. The distinction is clearer, however, in sentences dealing with mental activity, depending on the presence or absence of corrective elements. These may be withheld for purposes of maintaining interest and suspense. The same is true for statements regarding other characters. Generally speaking, psychological insights will be restricted in internal focalization ("She looked at me as though she knew the truth") and less limited in external focalization ("She knew I was lying"). Ambiguity can still prevail, however, as an internal focalizer may present another's thought as fact, while an external one may still be ignorant of what others were thinking at the moment of event.

The third vantage point is that of *zero focalization*. There are occasionally times when a FPN clearly steps out of bounds and provides information he could never have known, either spatially or psychologically (Genette [1972: 221] cites an example from Proust: Marcel's narration of Bergotte's dying thoughts). If we continue to define focalization as a restriction on perception, we may call such passages nonfocalized, unrestricted to the perception of even the retrospective FPN, who then resembles an omniscient narrator. Genette's term *paralepsis* will be reserved for this type of focal infraction, in which the narrating self says more than he could possibly know.

The opposite type of infraction, *paralipsis*, belongs at the opposite end of the spectrum. It can occur in two ways. The first, in which the narrating self says less than he knows, is actually quite conventional and may not in fact deserve the term "infraction." It occurs in internal focalization, every time the narrator refuses to tell the outcome of an episode in advance, every time he allows the perspective of the experiencing self to dominate. This kind of "hyperrestriction" means simply that the narrator becomes consonant with his younger self, who is allowed to focalize in ignorance of what the future holds.[4] A more extreme type of paraliptic infraction occurs when the narrating self withholds vital information that even the experiencing self possesses. This is sometimes done in order to trick the reader, as in a detective novel, but it rarely occurs in the autobiographical or memoir-novel. In the latter genre, important information is more often provided when it becomes important for the story, obliging the narrator to inform the reader about something the experiencing self already knows ("I forgot to mention that I had seen her three times"). Nevertheless, this hyperbolic type of paralipsis should be included in a typology of focal positions available to the FPN. These positions may be schematized as follows, progressing from more to less restriction (NS = narrating self, ES = experiencing self):

paralipsis	*internal*	*external*	*paralepsis (zero)*
NS < ES	NS = ES	NS = NS	NS > NS

In summary, NS may say less than ES knows (paralipsis); NS may say only what ES knows (internal, including conventional paralipsis); NS may say what NS knows (external); and NS may say more than NS could know (paralepsis, nonfocalized). It should be noted that as the narrator progresses from more to less restriction, the reader gains information about the characters.

The concept of the FPN is thus in serious need of revision. Stanzel ([1979] 1984) makes a most important remark in this regard. As conceived by many theorists, the FPN's role is to present only his own experience, whereas in literary practice the FPN often claims authorial privileges: "Many first-person narrators go far beyond transcribing that which they have experienced themselves by letting the narrative arise anew from their imagination" (215). As a teller of fictional tales, the FPN has many options that are not available to a true autobiographer. We can speak of his "infractions" because these are useful for characterizing and categorizing his narrative presentation, but they should in no way be interpreted as judgments on aesthetic value. On the contrary, they repre-

4. Glowinski (1977) refers to this phenomenon as the "paradox of narration": a narrator rarely deviates from chronology or displays all his knowledge from the outset; rather, he reveals the story step by step (105). Although this is a possibility open to the FPN, it is certainly not a necessity. Indeed, the freedom to depart from chronology, says Ci (1988), is a sign of the narrating self: "For, as soon as an intradiegetic character becomes a narrator, he has at his disposal exactly the same narrative options that are open to an extradiegetic narrator" (21).

sent a novelist's willingness to transgress the rules of memoir-novel logic in order to achieve certain aesthetic effects, as we shall see.

I shall now attempt to relate focalization to the three forms of represented discourse of the characters.[5] The first to be considered is that of *direct and indirect discourse*. The most obvious way in which a FPN can allow the experiencing self and other characters to present their respective points of view is to allow them to speak for themselves, by quoting their speech in direct discourse (DD). Each change of speaker involves a shift in focalization.[6] DD is almost always marked graphically and is often introduced by inquit phrases (e.g., "She blurted out: 'I know you are lying to me' "). DD combines two speech events, each with its own deictic field, and two distinct perspectives, that of the reporter in the frame, and that of the reportee within the inset. All shifters within the inset refer to the situation of the narrated event, not to that of the speaker. Indirect discourse (ID), on the other hand, contains an embedding structure, so that the exact content of the speech, as well as its perspective, are ambiguous. Attribution in ID can be problematic (e.g., "She blurted out that she knew I was lying"). Nothing tells us whether this indirect report represents a verbatim transposition or a paraphrase on the part of the narrator. In his typology of reported discourse, McHale (1978) distinguishes between "indirect content-paraphrase . . . without regard to the style or form of the supposed 'original' utterance," and "indirect discourse, mimetic to some degree" (259), which gives the illusion of preserving aspects of the style of an utterance. The word "illusion" is important to note, for the degree to which the illusion is created is always regulated by the reporter. In either case, the two perspectives are not neatly distributed, and the reporter always taints the reportee's utterance. Traditionally, DD and ID have been considered to be perspectivally determinate—with the reporter excluded from DD and the reportee excluded from ID—whereas ambiguity is characteristic only of free indirect discourse (FID).[7] Sternberg (1982) calls this view the

5. Throughout this study I shall use the terms *discourse* and *discursive* (Benveniste) to designate the speech that emanates from the narrator in his communicative act, while the term *represented discourse* (Doležel) will designate the speech or thoughts that emanate from characters in the narrated events.

6. For a study of the formal criteria of shifts in focalization, see Berendsen (1981). When marked by *verba dicendi* ("I said," "she thought," and so on), the shifts are obvious. But delegation of focalization may not be marked at all, and only later does the reader realize that the narrator has been effaced. In this study we shall be more concerned with these unmarked shifts, the subtle ways in which the FPN yields focalization and which are not so noticeable.

7. Ifry (1987), for example, states that in ID the focalization by the hero is mediated by the narrator, who expresses the hero's point of view in his own terms, whereas in DD there is no influence of the narrator (491).

"direct speech fallacy" and shows that perspectival ambiguity is common to all varieties of reported speech. In DD, the reporter may manipulate the effect of the inset by means of the juxtaposed frame. In ID the inset, however it may be paraphrased, still reflects the reportee's point of view by adhering to his attitudes and to his range of information (68–74). Sternberg's arguments concerning the indeterminacy of ID are more convincing than those concerning DD, especially in personal narration. A FPN may present lengthy dialogues between the experiencing self and other characters. By means of the frame he can always insinuate his own point of view and provide the corrective commentary of hindsight, but we must agree that dialogue does give access to the unmitigated point of view of the characters. ID is much more indeterminate in that its report by the narrator need not reflect the latter's point of view. On the other hand, in ID the narrator is always in control in one important sense not mentioned by Sternberg. Whether his indirect representation of speech consists of a summary in his own words or a more literal report (and it is true that we cannot always know), he is nonetheless preventing his characters from speaking for themselves. Extensive use of ID will have an effect on the way a given character is perceived by the reader.

The second form of represented discourse is *self-quoted monologue*. As defined by Cohn (1978), self-quoted monologue involves the narrator's quotation of his own past thoughts, on the pattern of "I said to myself: 'I have nothing to fear.' " It is signaled by quotation marks and inquit phrases, without which these thoughts could be confused with the narrator's present thoughts (161–65). Such markings are necessary because both the narrator's discourse and self-quoted monologue use the first-person pronoun and the present tense, which are doubly anchored deictically. They point to the utterances of both the narrating self and the experiencing self, to both *now* and *then*. Self-quoted monologue resembles DD in that it contains a frame and an inset. The focalization of the inset is clearly that of the experiencing self, yet it creates only an illusion of consonance because it is presented and marked off by the narrating self in his here-and-now. The tags betray dissonance, especially if they are qualified tags (e.g., "I thought to myself, *naïvely:* 'I have nothing to fear' "). The result is the juxtaposed views of narrator and character. A second similarity with DD is that self-quoted monologue poses problems of credibility: how can a FPN recall his exact thoughts, which were not even verbalized, and the verbatim conversations he had with others? Glowinski (1977) states that theoretically only two types of quotation are allowed in personal narration—indirect speech and typified speech—neither of which is a literal reproduction. Literal quotations bring the speaker close to an omniscient narrator (109). Ifry (1987) contends, on the contrary, that quoted dialogue and self-quoted monologue are suspect only in a true autobiography, and not in the autobiographical novel (491). Cohn (1978) remarks that extensive use of self-quoted monologue stretches the limits of credibility further than use of quoted dialogue (162). Perhaps this is true, but in either case the law of literary convention is in force.

The thoughts of other characters are, strictly speaking, off-limits to the FPN. While quoted monologue of another (e.g., "She thought to herself: 'I know he is lying' ") would seem to constitute an infraction, supposition of another's thoughts through ID is rather common and far less obtrusive (e.g., "She knew that I was lying"). The important question here is not to what degree the character is focalizing, but whether or not the narrator has transgressed his focal limits and moved into the domain of nonfocalization.

A third form of represented discourse is *narrated and self-narrated monologue*. One of the most controversial issues in contemporary narratology is the one surrounding the concept of free indirect discourse.[8] FID has been considered as a reporting device, one of several means of reproducing the speech or thoughts of another, as well as a transitional device through which the utterance of a character is experienced by the narrator. McHale (1978) points out that FID cannot function unless it can be recognized by the reader as "the intrusion of some voice other than (together with) the narrator's" (264). McHale alludes here to one of the central elements in the controversy, the vocal or perspectival ambiguity of FID. The problem may be stated essentially as follows: does FID represent only the perspective of a character, or is it bivocal, combining the voices and perspectives of character and narrator? Stanzel ([1979] 1984) places FID on the modally neutral ground between narrator and reflector, and describes it as "the combination of the speech, the perception or the thought of a fictional character with the voice of the narrator as the teller" (219). Doležel (1973) states that it is a transitional narrative device resulting from the neutralization of the opposition between a narrator's discourse and a character's discourse (20). Ginsburg (1982) identifies three kinds of possible utterances in FID: (1) a statement may be bivocal in that it contains elements of both narrator and character, yet no one person could have uttered it; (2) a statement may be wholly attributable to either narrator or character, in which case it is undecidable; (3) the utterance can be attributed to neither narrator nor character

---

8. It is not my intention here to discuss the theories concerning the formal criteria of FID, but instead to deal only with its implications for focalization. For a review of these theories, see McHale (1978) and Ginsburg (1982).

(135–36). In short, it is often difficult if not impossible to determine whether a statement in FID represents an objective fact provided by the narrator or the subjective point of view of a character, especially as there is no apparent transition between such a statement and the surrounding narrative context. In her review of Stanzel, Cohn (1981) criticizes the latter's dual-perspective concept, since Stanzel's "(seemingly) narrator-less reflector pole corresponds so closely to the (seemingly) narrator-less linguistic structure" of FID (172). According to Cohn (1978), passages written in FID rivet our attention on the protagonist, not on the narrator. She calls FID "narrated monologue" and defines it as "the technique for rendering a character's thought in his own idiom while maintaining the third-person reference and the basic tense of narration" (100), that is, while simulating the discourse of the narrator.[9]

It was long assumed that FID could be found only in third-person texts. Hamburger ([1957] 1973), for example, states categorically that in personal narration it can occur "neither with reference to the third-person characters nor to the first-person narrator himself" (316), for its existence would transform first-person narrative into fiction.[10] On a formal level, Ginsburg (1982) claims that FID excludes the first person (142), as does Simonin-Grumbach (1975, 104). Cohn (1978) has amply demonstrated, however, that "self-narrated monologue" can and does occur in personal narration, when the perspective is figural (internal focalization) and the emphasis is on the experiencing self. In such cases the narrator momentarily identifies with his past self, gives up temporal distance and cognitive privilege in order to narrate his past thoughts. Self-narrated monologue, says Cohn, is sometimes used as a dramatic device to convey past uncertainties and agitations: "There are sometimes curious moments in autobiographical novels when the narrator makes statements

9. Cohn seems to have later modified her earlier definition of narrated monologue, moving toward the position of ambiguity and dual perspective. In her original definition she states that narrated monologue, like quoted monologue, "reproduces *verbatim* the character's own mental language" (1978, 14). Later she protests that when FID is applied to the expression of nonverbal thoughts, it cannot be considered to be a simple quotational device, hence the ambiguity: "[I]s it the language of the narrator (in which case it would be part of the narrative), or that of the character (in which case it would be a quotation)?" (Cohn and Genette 1985, 103).

10. For Hamburger ([1957] 1973) first-person narration is not fiction at all but a "feigned reality statement" (336), and for this reason she excludes from this genre all fictionalized forms of third-person subjectivity such as dialogue and FID, because these make the feint more obvious. Characters, she says, can never be portrayed objectively, i.e., outside of their relation to the first-person narrator, nor can they be subjects as they are in fiction. Hamburger's theory fails to consider the fact that the speech event is *feigned*, as she says, and that it is just as fictional as a third-person narrative. See Tamir (1976, 422–23).

about past events that are immediately belied by what happens next, or asks questions that are clearly answered on the following page of his text" (166). If a FPN says, "There was a knock at the door. It could only be my wife. Why had she come back?," he may know *now* that it was *not* his wife at the door, but he suppresses this information in order to create empathy with his younger self. Stanzel ([1979] 1984) suggests a reason for the lower frequency of FID in first-person narratives. Having admitted the dual perspective of narrator and character as the essential feature of FID, Stanzel points to the lesser frequency with which such dual perspectives occur in first-person as opposed to third-person texts. This difference reflects the fact that "here a dual perspective does not result in a true doubling of the perspective because the narrating self ultimately retains an existential link with his earlier, experiencing self" (221).

Unlike Cohn, Genette maintains that FID can be verbal as well as psychological, and that the result is no less ambiguous. In a sentence such as "I announced to Mama my intention to marry Albertine: I was decidedly in love with her," there can be ambiguity concerning attribution of speech to the narrating or to the experiencing self (Cohn and Genette 1985, 107). Stanzel ([1979] 1984) agrees and points out that FID can also be used by a FPN to render the speech of other characters, as his knowledge of that speech is not restricted. Only the narrator's own thoughts, however, can be reproduced by FID, and Stanzel insists that the effects produced are quite different. Concerning the speech of others, he says, FID offers the possibility of characterization as well as providing indirect commentary on this speech: the speech is viewed with detachment from the more mature perspective of the narrator, whose voice is also heard as he remembers the scene. The technique thus creates distance and irony. As a rendition of the narrator's earlier thoughts, Stanzel says that FID promotes empathy with the experiencing self more frequently than irony. Whereas Cohn (1978) believes that the perspective of the narrating self disappears in self-narrated monologue, Stanzel feels that it is suppressed but still present, so that a dual perspective arises between the narrating and experiencing selves. The effect of FID is thus to direct the reader's empathy and detachment (221–24).

We shall retain Cohn's terms, but like Genette and Stanzel we shall extend their definitions to include the verbal as well as the psychological, especially as it is not always possible to distinguish between the two. We must agree with Cohn, however, on the subject of perspective. By definition, self-narrated monologue means that focalization belongs to the experiencing self. It fixes our attention on the moment of event without signaling the distance between event and narration. It is true that the perspective is indeterminate in Genette's example ("I was decidedly in love with her"). This sentence could represent either a fact presented by the narrator ("I" now) or the misguided opinion of the experiencing self ("I" then). Indeed, the reader may not be certain. But unless it can be recognized and interpreted as the latter, as McHale (1978) says, it cannot be called self-narrated monologue. The device owes its effectiveness precisely, and paradoxically, to this resistance to detection. The difference between Cohn and Genette on this issue could perhaps be resolved by the statement that FID represents the perspective of a character, although this may not always be recognized by the reader. Hence the ambiguity.[11]

It is the maintenance of the basic tense of narration that makes self-narrated monologue less obtrusive than self-quoted monologue, which is nearly always marked and set off from the narrative context. The narrated monologue of other characters may, once again, represent their speech (which the FPN is at liberty to reproduce) or their thoughts (which should logically be off-limits). Narrated monologue offers to the FPN an unobtrusive means of allowing the reader access to the minds of other characters, yet the ambiguity permits doubt. We may be faced with focalization by other characters, or with focalization of the narrating self who is making unsignaled hypotheses about the psychological activity of others.[12]

Genette states that he prefers his modal triad of "narrated speech" (narrator's summary) / "transposed speech" (ID and FID) / "reported speech" (DD) because such a progression reflects a diminishing degree of the narrator's intervention into the discourse of a character, and therefore a diminishing degree of distance between reader and character (Cohn and Genette 1985, 107). I shall argue that, in terms of focalization, the progression should be DD / ID / FID, in order to reflect (1) a diminishing degree of distance between the narrating and experiencing selves, or a tendency toward consonance, and (2) a diminishing degree of obtrusiveness regarding focal shifts.

DD and self-quoted monologue present the clearest case of focalization: the reported words or thoughts are those of the experiencing self, while the surrounding frame belongs to the narrating self. Genette (1972) states that this is the most mimetic and least distant technique. As we have seen, however, only an illusion of consonance is created

---

11. Vitoux (1982) speaks of a phenomenon he calls "free indirect focalization," by which he surely means FID with ambiguous focalization, or narrated monologue (363). I see no need for this term as I maintain that focal ambiguity disappears as soon as FID is recognized as such.

12. Cohn (1978) does not discuss the possibility of narrated monologue of other characters in a first-person retrospective novel. It exists, as we shall see.

through direct representation, whereas dissonance is evident in the narrator's frame. Paradoxically, then, DD highlights the distance between the narrating and experiencing selves, and the reader is aware of the neat demarcation between them. Whether the intended effect is empathy or irony, a narrator uses DD to delineate clearly what he said or thought *then*. In ID the focalization may well be that of the narrator, who summarizes and transforms his own earlier speech or that of others. But the inset may also be somewhat mimetic, reflecting the point of view and even the vocabulary of the reportee (e.g., "He said he hoped that this sordid little affair of mine would put an end to my childish self-indulgence"). When ID is used to represent thoughts instead of speech, the focalization is more ambiguous. In some cases the narrator's frame dominates the inset, correcting its content (e.g., "Foolishly I imagined it could only be my wife"). The narrator thus calls attention to his retrospective stance and maintains his distance. In other cases the frame may be so neutral as to allow more focal autonomy to the experiencing self through the inset (e.g., "There was a knock at the door. I thought it could only be my wife, and I wondered why she had come back"). While the narrator in this example is summarizing what he thought and wondered, the perceptual horizon is that of the experiencing self, and the distance between them is reduced. It may be that focalization by the experiencing self will become evident only by means of information provided on the following page. The distance can be reduced even further in ID when the narrating and experiencing selves agree, so that the frame appears to confirm the information of the inset (e.g., "I knew that it was my wife and I realized why she had come back").[13] In FID, finally, the frame disappears altogether, and with it go all traces of the narrating self, who identifies completely with the experiencing self. All distance between them is momentarily abolished, so that self-narrated monologue is a device more readily adopted by consonant narrators than by dissonant ones. The shift in focalization is not marked graphically and is therefore not readily noticeable. The decrease in obtrusiveness and in distance also explains why a FPN is more attracted to narrated monologue as a technique for penetrating the consciousness of other characters. Technically, of course, any such penetration constitutes an infraction on the part of a FPN. In practice, however, it is done all the time, and narrated monologue provides the best vehicle in that it is the least obtrusive:

13. Genette points out that narrative statements such as "I knew," "I divined," and "I understood" coincide with the "I know" of the narrator. Indirect discourse of the character alternates without contrast with the narrator's discourse, because the two instances share the same truth (1972, 260–261).

DD: She thought to herself: "I hate him. He has always been so mean to me."

ID: She thought about how much she hated me, how I had always been so mean to her.

FID: She hated me. I had always been so mean to her.

The last example could be a supposition on the narrator's part, or it could be focalized by the character herself. Because it reads as a narrative fact, unsubordinated and indistinguishable from the narrator's discourse, it abolishes the distance between narrator and character. Although it constitutes a case of mind-reading, it is nonetheless the least obvious sort of infraction, and indeed it will not be noticed as such by most readers. As Chatman (1978) says, "the absence of the tag makes [FID] sound more like the character speaking or thinking than a narrator's report" (210).

Every speech act, says Lanser (1981), implies a point of view, "a relationship between the speaker and the context, the listener, or the content of the communicative act" (64). This is especially true in personal narration, in which the speaker is identified as a specific human being. In the following chapters we shall look first at the narrative situation and the way in which the narrator sets up his or her discourse with the reader, establishing a point of view in Lanser's sense. We shall then concentrate on perception and attempt to characterize the narrator based on his or her focal choices. Finally, we shall consider the ways in which the narrator delegates focalization to the experiencing self and to others.

1

LES EGAREMENTS DU COEUR ET DE L'ESPRIT: SELECTIVE FOCALIZATION

The narrator of Crébillon's *Les Egarements du coeur et de l'esprit* is an older man who has recorded the experiences of a two-week period in his youth and his relations with several members of his society. Despite the constraints imposed upon him by convention, he often takes liberties with his focal limitations and gives information that he cannot naturally possess. More important, he also chooses to ignore his temporal advantage and to withhold information that he should possess. In viewing certain characters in the novel, the reader follows the consciousness of the narrator and is thus privy to all the knowledge of the experienced older man. At the same time the reader's understanding of other characters is limited, and strictly so, to only the knowledge of the young Meilcour. This selective focalization, focal variation between the narrating self and the experiencing self, creates a certain confusion in the mind of the reader. This confusion is essential to understanding the puzzlement of the poor hero trying to cope with an ambiguous and often false society.

Narrative Situation

In his opening pages a personal narrator must establish his speech situation, either explicitly or implicitly. In oral language, discursive elements refer to the one who speaks and to the spatiotemporal coordinates of "I" and "you," whereas in written language these elements depend upon a situation for their interpretation. As Ginsburg (1982) points out, the formal description of "I" as the individual who produces the present instance of discourse is "insufficient in the novel because unless we are furnished with some information about this instance of discourse, we are still at a loss as to who the 'I' is" (143). Written discourse supposes a speech situation common to the one who writes and the one who reads, which permits them to refer to the same referents without ambiguity. Strictly speaking, of course, the time and place of writer and reader cannot be common to both (Simonin-Grumbach 1975, 89). Nevertheless, the temporality of the narrator is converted into that of the reader (Benveniste 1966–74, 2:76).[1]

With his first sentence, the narrator of *Les Egarements* both begins his historical narration and refers to his here-and-now, combining temporal distance and proximity. He thus creates a tension between difference and similarity that will characterize his entire text: "J'entrai dans le monde à dix-sept ans, et avec tous les avantages qui peuvent y faire remarquer" (69). In the opening paragraphs we learn that the narrator's family name is Meilcour, that he is noble and rich, and that his father is dead.[2] We do not know the degree of temporal distance that separates Meilcour-narrator (MN) from the there-and-then of Meilcour-character (MC), but his use of the present tense ("peuvent") indicates that the two share the same world, a society that has not changed in the interim. MN tells us that his mother took pleasure in giving her son a modest education and he finds her unique in that regard. Despite her efforts, however, he admits that MC was a conceited young man. The present tense reflects MN's thoughts at the moment of speech ("Ce projet, je crois, serait entré dans l'esprit de peu de femmes"), while the *passé composé* indicates what has transpired since the moment of event ("à ce que l'on m'a dit," "[Madame de Meilcour] que je n'ai pas vue galante sur son retour," "par la suite, je n'en ai pas été moins fat"). The narrator also

---

1. I am of course aware of the distinction that needs to be made between the "reader" and the "narratee," the latter being the one whom the narrator addresses textually. I agree on this point with Genette (1983): "It is absolutely legitimate to distinguish in principle between the narratee and the reader, but one must also admit cases of coincidence" (91). The narratee of *Les Egarements*, like that of *Le Paysan parvenu*, is an extradiegetic and unspecified individual who becomes readily confused with the implied or virtual reader, and the same is true even of *Manon Lescaut* and *La Religieuse*, in which the narratees are specific characters. Moreover, as Genette (1983) says, no author can address a real reader but only a potential one (103). My use of the term "reader" will therefore designate this potential reader.

2. According to Sgard (1975), in the beginning of the text a novelist often creates complicity with the reader by defining the norms of reference, the social ideals (young, handsome, rich, etc.) that lead us to suspect disillusion and downfall (18).

reveals a kind of sententiousness that pervades the novel, one that puts forth a series of universally accepted truths ("il est ordinaire, lorsque l'on pense ainsi, de s'estimer plus qu'on ne vaut").

The moment of speech and the moment of event are linked existentially by the identity of the narrator and by his general observations about a society that the reader is expected to recognize: "L'idée du plaisir fut, à mon entrée dans le monde, la seule qui m'occupa. La paix, qui régnait *alors*, me laissait dans un loisir dangereux. Le peu d'occupation, que *se font communément* les gens de mon rang et de mon âge . . . m'entraînait vers les plaisirs" (69–70).[3] While the reference to the moment of event ("alors") distinguishes it from the narrator's present, the two are joined by the narrator's acknowledgement of the similarity of conduct in young men of this rank and age. What is beyond all doubt is that MN is quite different from MC. The former insists, here and throughout his text, on the latter's lack of understanding: "Sans connaître encore toute la violence du penchant qui me portait vers elles [women], je les cherchais avec soin" (70). MC was seeking a happiness that MN refers to as "ces douces erreurs de l'âme," and through self-narrated monologue MN affords us a glimpse of his early confusion: "ce choix était-il déterminé, comment l'annoncer à l'objet qui m'avait fixé?"

Temporal distance is thus emphasized by the narrator's acquisition of social awareness, and at the same time reduced by his recognition of the similarity of society then and now. The narrator has changed, as he has grown older, but his use of the achronic present testifies to the fact that young men in society have not. The sameness–difference dichotomy also seems at first to be divided along lines of gender. The narrator's sententiousness becomes increasingly aligned with a masculine point of view: "On s'attache souvent moins à la femme qui touche le plus, qu'à celle qu'on croit le plus facilement toucher." From the impersonal "on," clearly referring to men, MN moves on to use the first and second persons in the same way ("il [respect] devient un outrage pour les femmes, et un ridicule pour *nous*"; "assurément elle *vous* croyait," 71). It becomes clear that the narrator, progressing from "on" to "nous" and "vous," is addressing a male reader and excluding women, who are relegated to the third person. So sure is Meilcour, in fact, of his male readership, that it bears upon his narrative choices: "Je passe sur les

---

3. While the reader is expected to share a certain knowledge of society, the narrator leaves nothing to chance. Bennington (1985) is quite right to observe that while the formula "un de ces X" looks like an ostensive deictic gesturing beyond the text, it is usually backed up with diegetic support. In fact, everything is explained and nothing is presupposed as already known (127). Emphasis here and throughout is my own, unless otherwise indicated.

sentiments qui m'occupèrent cette nuit-là. Il n'y a pas d'homme sur la terre assez malheureux pour n'avoir jamais aimé, et aucun qui ne soit par conséquent en état de se les peindre" (164). Whereas men remain the same, now as then, women, together with the prevailing concept of love, have changed a great deal.[4]

The narrator refers several times to the past moment of his story, to "la façon dont *alors* elles [women] pensaient," and to "ce qu'*alors* les deux sexes nommaient Amour," admitting that MC had little understanding of these things, and aligning his past ignorance with the perversity of women. He also posits an earlier moment, a pre-story time: "l'amour, *jadis* si respectueux, si sincère, si délicat, était devenu si téméraire et si aisé . . ." (71). The moral corruption of "alors" (story time) is described and deplored by general reflections in the imperfect tense, and then contrasted with the purity of prehistoric time, of "jadis" or "autrefois": "Si nous en croyons d'anciens Mémoires, les femmes étaient *autrefois* plus flattées d'inspirer le respect que le désir." The narrator evokes the moral purity of a forgotten age, a literary commonplace used to foreground the perversity of story time. In an ironic twist, however, this forgotten past is likened to an equally virtuous present, the here-and-now of narrator and reader: "ce qui, dans un siècle aussi sage que *le nôtre*, surprendra peut-être plus" (71). The commonplace has now been reversed: whereas women were then perverse, they are now virtuous, so much so, in fact, that the story about to be narrated may be startling.[5] This reference to the "siècle sage" must not, however, be taken too seriously, as it forms part of the narrator's ironic stance. MN's claim— that the women of his youth, "celles de mon temps" (72), were more compromising than those at the time of narration—is belied by the first-person pronoun that joins the two moments, both of which belong to the same individual. Moreover, by his own admission the two types of women cannot be separated so neatly: "Il ne faut cependant pas inférer, de ce que je viens de dire, qu'elles offrissent toutes la même facilité. J'en ai vu qui, après quinze jours de soins rendus, étaient encore indécises. . . . Je conviens que ce sont des exemples rares." Finally, MN often explains the conduct of his female characters by making sententious generalizations about women (e.g., "j'ai remarqué que les femmes les plus aisées à vaincre sont celles qui s'engagent avec la folle espérance de

4. Segal (1986) points out that *Manon Lescaut* is also a text profoundly directed at a male readership, and that there is no place for a female, "unintended" reader (xiii–xiv).

5. Gaubert (1975) sees a parallel between the temporal divisions of prehistoric time / story time / narrating time and the evolution of Meilcour: the hero (pure, outside of society), the rival of Versac (corrupt, inside society), and the narrator, detached from society, who judges the other two incarnations (50).

n'être jamais séduites," 95), thereby indicating that they are the same now as they were then. Women have not changed; rather, it is Meilcour who has grown to understand them. The claim to the "siècle sage" disappears from the novel after the opening pages. Here it must be read as a mockery, an intertextual bow to the long tradition of cynicism against women, an inversion of the conventional purity of a forgotten age. The parody is intertwined with that of another literary tradition, according to which the narrator both foresees and forestalls disbelief:

> Les moeurs ont depuis ce temps-là si prodigieusement changé, que je ne serais pas surpris qu'on traitât de fable aujourd'hui ce que je viens de dire sur cet article. Nous croyons difficilement, que des vices et des vertus qui ne sont plus sous nos yeux, aient jamais existé: il est cependant réel que je n'exagère pas. (72)

The irony here is unmistakable: the present is so virtuous that the past becomes unbelievable, which leads MN to make a conventional protestation of truth—the first and only such attestation of veracity to be found in the novel.

To summarize, we can say that the temporal distance that separates MN from MC is foregrounded only by the self-references to earlier conceitedness and ignorance of society. It is Meilcour, not the social mores, who has changed. Conversely, distance is reduced by indications that MN and MC are linked existentially, and by general observations that the reader is expected to recognize since he shares the same world. There are, however, no signs of the narratee. If we except the oblique "vous" of generalization ("elle vous croyait") in which "vous" = "on," direct address is rigorously absent from Meilcour's text. Reference to his narrative function (e.g., "comme je l'ai dit," 96) is extremely rare.[6]

Dissonance and Hindsight

A major characteristic of MN is his differentiation between his present self *now*, as a narrator, and his younger self *then*, as a character in the

---

6. Curiously, two references to MN's narrative function occur at the end of his text, when MC has finally seduced Lursay, and the narrator admits reluctantly that the hero was pleased about his conquest: "Je l'avouerai; mon crime me plut . . ." [I will admit it; my crime pleased me . . .] (246); "Je l'avouerai même à ma honte, quelquefois je me justifiais mon procédé . . ." [I will admit it, even to my shame, sometimes I justified my devices . . .] (248).

story. MN's vision of MC is typical of the dissonant self-narration inherent in the memoir form. This dissonance is established from the beginning by MN's use of the tenses of discourse, distinguishable from those of historical utterance yet intermingled with them. It is a distinction based on self-knowledge. Older now and wiser, he is constantly able to impose his narrative authority and to expose the follies of his youth. He punctuates his narrative with references to what he did not know then: "J'ignorais, entre beaucoup d'autres choses," "je ne pouvais m'imaginer" (75); "J'étais trop jeune pour sentir" (95); "Je n'en savais pas assez" (119); "je ne savais pas encore," "Je ne connaissais pas assez," "j'avais trop peu d'expérience" (181); "J'étais trop jeune pour ne pas croire aimer" (245). Like a tireless refrain, MN takes pains to point to MC's youth, to his inexperience with women, and to his ignorance of society. The reader must agree with him when he says, toward the end of the novel, "j'ai trop parlé de mon peu d'expérience; on voit trop par ce récit combien je lui devais d'idées fausses, pour avoir besoin de m'arrêter sur ce sujet plus longtemps" (202). Because he does not associate himself too closely with the young Meilcour, the narrator is able time and again to provide ironic commentary that lays bare the hero's naïveté.

One technique used to highlight this naïveté is to juxtapose MC's perception with MN's dissonant commentary. On occasion the hero's understanding is correct but incomplete: "Quelque peu que mon ignorance me laissât deviner, je compris qu'elle [Lursay] était moins éloignée de me répondre que la première fois que je lui avais parlé" (101). Here the verb of perception ("je compris" instead of "je crus") lends narrative authority to MC's judgment. Sometimes this judgment is valid but misunderstood, and the narrator provides its significance: "En lui donnant la main pour la ramener à son carrosse, je crus sentir qu'elle me la serrait: sans savoir les conséquences que cette action entraînait avec Madame de Lursay, je le lui rendis" (102). More often, however, the juxtaposition reveals the hero's judgment to be erroneous: "Je croyais ne pouvoir jamais me déguiser assez bien à ses yeux [Germeuil]; et, par une sottise ordinaire aux jeunes gens, j'imaginais, qu'en me regardant seulement, les personnes les plus indifférentes sur ma situation, l'auraient pénétrée" (104). This time the verbs of perception ("Je croyais," "j'imaginais") are contrasted with the narrator's reference to youthful stupidity. Although the modal verbs in a past tense already serve to distance the speaker from his earlier perceptions, their effect is usually intensified by the surrounding dissonant commentary.[7] A single qualifier can provide

---

7. Modality concerns subjective expressions that reveal the speaker's attitude toward the content of his utterance. Any expression that qualifies a declarative statement with

such commentary: "et commençant à avoir mauvaise opinion des femmes aussi *sottement* que je l'avais eue bonne, j'examinais Mademoiselle de Théville" (151). Dissonance between the narrating subject and his naïve object leads the reader to submit to the authority of the experienced Meilcour.

Self-quoted and self-narrated monologues allow for focalization by MC. Here again, however, these devices can be followed by the dissonant commentary of MN. On one occasion, for example, MN quotes the nocturnal thought of MC (in italics):

> *De quoi puis-je me plaindre,* me disais-je à moi-même? *Ses rigueurs [Lursay] ont-elles droit de me surprendre? M'étais-je attendu à me trouver aimé, et n'est-ce point à mes soins à me procurer cet avantage? Quel bonheur pour moi, si je puis un jour la rendre sensible! Plus elle m'oppose d'obstacles, plus ma gloire sera grande. Un coeur, du prix dont est le sien, peut-il trop s'acheter?* Je finis par cette idée, et je la retrouvai le lendemain. Il semblait qu'elle se fût accrue par les illusions de la nuit. (89)

The last sentence of this passage has a corrective value that signals the folly of youthful reasoning. In self-narrated monologue, on the other hand, the focal shift is more subtle because there are no inquit phrases. Even so, the narrator can intervene to point out the hero's ignorance:

> Je ne l'eus pas plutôt quittée, que ce rendez-vous . . . me revint dans l'esprit. *Un rendez-vous!* Malgré mon peu d'expérience, cela me paraissait grave. *Elle devait avoir peu de monde chez elle: en pareil cas, c'est dire honnêtement qu'on n'en aura point.* Elle m'avait serré la main: je ne savais pas toute la force de cette action, mais, il me semblait cependant que c'est une marque d'amitié, qui, d'un sexe à l'autre, porte une expression singulière, et qui ne s'accorde que dans des situations marquées. *Mais, cette vertueuse Madame de Lursay, qui venait de me défendre seulement de la deviner, aurait-elle voulu? . . . Non, cela n'était pas possible.* (102)

Momentary consonance alternates with dissonance here. Focalization shifts back and forth between the narrating self ("mon peu d'expérience," "je ne savais pas") and the experiencing self ("Un rendez-vous!"

---

doubt, belief, supposition, possibility, and so on, is said to be modalized. In terms of focalization, modals create distance between the narrating self and the experiencing self but often shift emphasis to the latter.

"aurait-elle voulu?") in order to differentiate between what MC did and did not understand at the moment of event.

Another technique for accentuating MC's ignorance is to contrast his perception ("what I thought then") with a maxim ("what I know now"). Bennington (1985) shows that because the sententious proposition is formulated in the present tense, it is easily assimilated by the narrative instance and it thus implies knowledge (123–24). Merging with MN's discourse, the maxim acquires the force of a universally recognized truth: "Avec un homme expérimenté, un mot . . . un regard, un geste, moins encore, le met au fait, s'il veut être aimé" (76). Here the contrast between an experienced man and the naïve hero is implicit. In the following example the ignorance–knowledge comparison is explicit: "J'avais si peu d'usage du monde, que je crus l'avoir [Lursay] fâchée véritablement. Je ne savais pas qu'une femme suit rarement une conversation amoureuse avec quelqu'un qu'elle veut engager" (83). While the first sentence illustrates the technique of juxtaposition, the second reveals the hero's ignorance of a truth about women that the (male) reader is expected to acknowledge. This second example is more typical of MN's sententiousness, however, in that it points less to the evolution of Meilcour than to the universally recognized qualities of women. It offers the more common contrast between "what I thought then" and "what we all know now about women."[8]

Meilcour-narrator is not always so sure of himself. At times he calls attention to his present uncertainty about his past self: "L'on me pressait d'accepter, mon embarras augmentait, et je crois que, faute de savoir que répondre, je me serais laissé reconduire, si Madame de Lursay . . . ne fût venue à mon secours" (121). This uncertainty can be viewed as an inability to express now what he felt then: "Je ne sais quoi de si touchant et de si doux brillait dans ses yeux [Hortense]" (113); "Je ne saurais exprimer la révolution qui se fit dans tous mes sens" (121); "Je ne pourrais exprimer que faiblement le désordre que cette vue me causa" (142). All of these uncertainties involve Meilcour's reactions to the love-interests of the novel. They do not alter his lucidity toward the role that vanity has played in his life: "Dès lors, j'avais sans doute dans le coeur le germe de ce que j'ai été depuis" (111).

According to memoir-novel logic, it is well within the natural capabilities of the autobiographical narrator to provide information about other characters that he may have acquired, and opinions about them that he

8. Bennington (1985) points out that the narrator sometimes aligns his sententiousness with a truth recognized by other characters. Since Lursay cannot educate Meilcour directly by referring to their own situation, she proceeds indirectly by means of the sententious mode, erasing from her statements all marks of the subject of their enunciation (105).

may have formed, since the moment of experience. In fact, the reader is given such information on two of these, Versac and Senanges, both of whom are to play a major role in Meilcour's education. The narrator announces their importance by means of proleptic intrusions:

> Versac, de qui j'aurai beaucoup à parler dans la suite de ces Mémoires. . . . (129)

> Personne ne pouvait lui [Versac] ressembler; et moi-même, qui ai depuis marché si avantageusement sur ses traces . . . (130)

> Madame de Senanges à qui, comme on le verra dans la suite, j'ai eu le malheur de devoir mon éducation . . . (145)

> [I]l ne me vint pas dans l'esprit que ce serait elle [Senanges] qui me formerait. (146).

The presentation of these two characters leads MN to make rare references to the spatiality of his text ("la suite") and to the temporality of his readers ("on verra"). Paradoxically, these prolepses are never realized textually, as the novel remains unfinished. Story-time never joins the time of narration, so that we are never permitted to see exactly how these characters affected Meilcour's life. Nevertheless, we are given a glimpse of impending events that the hero could not have known. The prolepses demonstrate further the narrator's willingness to guide us, to prevent us from being misled about the future of MC's relations. With these aids, the reader has an understanding superior to that of the hero.

The attitude of the narrator toward Versac is quite clear and is often contrasted with that of the ignorant hero. The initial description of Versac belongs to MN and not to MC: "Adoré de toutes les femmes qu'il trompait et déchirait sans cesse, vain, impérieux, étourdi, le plus audacieux petit-maître qu'on eût jamais vu . . ." (129). MC's opinion of the count is summed up as follows: "Versac, tel qu'il était, m'avait toujours plu beaucoup. Je ne le voyais jamais sans l'étudier, et sans chercher à me rendre propres ces airs fastueux que j'admirais tant en lui" (130). MC refuses to believe Lursay when she rails against Versac, but MN provides correction: "Quelque vivacité que Madame de Lursay employât à me peindre Versac si désavantageusement, elle ne me persuada pas que ce portrait pût lui ressembler. Versac était pour moi le premier des hommes . . ." (139); "je ne voulus jamais croire que Versac eût pu me tromper" (141). The case of Senanges is different in that both narrator and hero seem to be in complete agreement about her character, the elapsed time having effected no change in Meilcour's opinion. There can be no doubt about the young man's judgment of Senanges: "Je me reprochai enfin de donner tant d'attention à quelqu'un qui se définissait au premier coup d'oeil. . . . Je voyais . . . ce que la nature la plus perverse, et l'art le plus condamnable, peuvent offrir de plus bas et de plus corrompu" (147). In MN's discussion of Senanges, there is no contrast, no corrective element provided: "Jamais elle n'avait su masquer ses vues, et l'on ne saurait dire ce qu'elle paraissait dans les cas où presque toutes les femmes de son espèce ont l'art de ne passer que pour galantes" (183). Absence of correction seems to confirm the younger Meilcour's perceptions by lending narrative authority to them. Senanges may be the only character whose behavior is so obvious that the naïve hero is able to make a valid judgment about her immediately.

Internal Focalization

In light of the narrator's guidance in the matter of these two characters, it is interesting to examine his attitude toward the two more sympathetic characters, Hortense de Théville and Madame de Lursay. Instead of shedding all possible light on these two women by portraying them with the knowledge he now possesses, the narrator abandons his temporal privilege and withholds vital information, thereby keeping the reader as confused as the hero.

Hortense presents the most clear-cut case of consonant self-narration, or of focalization by the hero instead of by the narrator. The mere fact that she is known to us for many pages only as "l'inconnue," and that we become aware of her identity only when the hero does, indicates clearly that our perspective is limited to that of the young man. Introducing her as "l'objet qui s'y offrit" (89) and "ma belle inconnue" (90), the narrator withholds her identity—information that he obviously possesses. This conventional form of paralipsis, used by all storytellers, is sustained through the narrator's silence and through his generous use of self-quoted and self-narrated monologue, associating the reader with the hero while the narrator effaces himself. Only when Meilcour visits Lursay and is introduced to Hortense is the reader made aware of her identity. What is unconventional, however, is that certain key questions about her are still unresolved, even at the end of this unfinished novel.

Hortense is first described at the opera: "Qu'on se figure tout ce que la beauté la plus régulière a de plus noble . . . à peine pourra-t-on se faire une idée de la personne que je voudrais dépeindre" (89–90). The present and future tenses could indicate the narrator's address to his reader, as in the opening pages of the novel. But here the instance of discourse does not seem to be that of the older narrator, because it provides no corroboration or correction of the hero's impressions, but rather conveys the latter's initial enthusiasm. The scene at the opera is punctuated with a present that lures the reader into the youthful infatuation: "Je ne sais quel mouvement singulier et subit m'agita à cette vue"; "je ne sais ce que mes yeux lui dirent" (90). In other words, the appearance of the present does not foreground the distance between hero and narrator; on the contrary, the present–past polarity disappears as consonant self-narration takes over:

> Elle n'avait pas en effet besoin de parure; en était-il de si brillante qu'elle ne l'eût effacée? était-il d'ornement si modeste qu'elle ne l'eût embelli? Sa physionomie était douce et réservée; le sentiment et l'esprit *paraissaient* briller dans ses yeux. Cette personne me *parut* extrêmement jeune. . . . (90)

Focalization is that of the hero, describing his vision and his thoughts at the moment of experience.

In the subsequent scenes in which Hortense appears, the signs of discourse disappear almost completely, as the present of the narrator is effaced. When Hortense is present, we identify with the hero, in the absence of any authoritative commentary from the narrator. Our knowledge of her opinion of others is no greater than that of MC, who is forced to interpret her facial expressions: "Elle regardait Versac avec une froideur singulière et une sorte de mépris qui ne laissèrent pas de me rassurer" (151).[9] As limited as the hero, we receive no guidance about Hortense's thoughts and feelings. She seems to be in love, but with whom? Is it Germeuil, as the young Meilcour suspects? His suspicions of Germeuil's relations with Hortense are neither denied nor confirmed by the narrator. Nor is the reader enlightened as to who might be Hortense's "inconnu." We wander with MC from thesis to antithesis and remain as ignorant as he. Sometimes his doubts are presented in the form of a mixture of self-quoted and self-narrated monologue:

> D'ailleurs, cet inconnu, selon ses discours, n'en était plus un pour elle; il fallait donc qu'elle l'eût revu? Pourquoi n'aurait-ce pas été

---

9. The importance of visual communication in the novel has been noted by Terrasse (1982) and by James F. Jones, Jr. (1974). Meilcour watches Hortense and Germeuil watching each other (Terrasse 1982, 27). James Jones (1974) observes that the entire plot of *Les Egarements* revolves around seeing and being seen (320).

> Germeuil? Savais-je depuis quand et comment il la connaissait? Hélas, me disais-je, que m'importe l'objet de sa passion, puisque je ne le suis point? (110)

Sometimes the doubts are based on Hortense's facial expression and attitude:

> Témoin de la tristesse d'Hortense, et de sa froideur pour moi, à quoi pouvais-je mieux les attribuer qu'à une passion secrète? Les premiers soupçons que j'avais portés sur Germeuil, se réveillèrent dans mon esprit; à force de m'y arrêter, ils s'accrurent. (164)

And sometimes, the uncertainties expressed by self-narrated monologue are supported by the visual perceptions of MC and by maxims that seem to emanate from MN:

> Un état aussi singulier que le sien, ne pouvait guère être attribué qu'à une passion secrète et malheureuse; mais s'il était vrai, comme ce jour même je l'avais cru, qu'elle aimât Germeuil, quelle pouvait être la cause de sa mélancolie? Quand je les avais quittés, aucun nuage ne *paraissait* devoir s'élever entre eux; son absence avait-elle pu faire naître un si violent chagrin? *On s'attriste quand on perd pour longtemps ce qu'on aime.* . . . Germeuil n'était donc pas l'objet de ses peines. (201)

In all these cases, MN provides no correction, no guidance. The reader follows MC back and forth in all his agitations.

But the narrator does not abdicate completely. His point of view is still present in his insistence on the subjective quality of the hero's impressions. The latter's beliefs are systematically mitigated by verbs that denote his mental operations and that maintain his distance from the narrator: "Malgré le peu de goût que je *supposais* à l'inconnue pour moi" (128); "cette inconnue que j'adorais, et à qui je *croyais* tant d'aversion pour moi" (142); "*J'imaginais* qu'elle pensait sans distraction à Germeuil, et que son coeur jouissait trop tranquillement d'une idée que je lui *croyais* si chère" (198), and so on. These verbs are indicators of subjectivity, attenuations that point to what the hero believed, without verification from the narrator.[10] Narratorial confirmation (e.g., "je savais," "je compris") is lacking. One might expect that these modal verbs create distance so that

10. Fort (1978) refers to these indicators as verbs of enunciation, used by the characters in Crébillon's novels to introduce a distance between themselves and their expressed thoughts (142). Here the narrator also uses them to maintain distance, but provides no authoritative commentary to dispel the ambiguity.

eventually the narrator will be able to correct the hero's erroneous perceptions, but such a correction never comes. At times MN does intervene, but only to comment rationally on the irrationality of the hero's conclusions about Hortense:

> C'était une chose assez simple, qu'elle fût réservée avec quelqu'un qu'elle connaissait aussi peu que moi; et, si je ne l'avais point aimée, je n'en aurais point pris d'alarmes. (172)

> De moment en moment elle parlait bas à Germeuil, se penchait familièrement vers lui; et ces choses qui, toutes simples qu'elles sont en elles-mêmes, ne me le paraissaient pas alors, achevaient de me désespérer. (177)

Once again, MN is dissonant toward MC, yet he provides no retrospective information about Hortense. Sometimes his attempt at rational explanation gives way to self-narrated monologue, focalized by MC:

> J'aurais pu, à la vérité, en allant voir Germeuil le lendemain, me tirer de cette inquiétude; *mais aussi comment lui exposer le sujet d'une curiosité si forte; quels motifs lui en donner?* Malgré tous les déguisements que j'aurais pu employer, *ne devais-je pas craindre qu'il n'en découvrît la source?* Et s'il était vrai, comme je le soupçonnais, qu'il aimât l'inconnue, *pourquoi l'avertir de se précautionner contre mes sentiments?* (92)

The focal shifts in this passage are typical of the episodes dealing with Hortense. External focalization by MN emphasizes his distance from MC's suspicions and beliefs, while the alternating internal focalization (in italics) allows us to empathize with the hero's experience. At other times the older narrator disappears while self-quoted monologue translates the young man's hesitations:

> Quoi! me disais-je, j'ai pu penser que c'était moi qui l'avais [Hortense] frappée! J'ai osé croire que cet inconnu si dangereux pour son coeur, n'était autre que moi! Quelle erreur! (144).

> Ciel! me dis-je, avec fureur, j'ai pu croire que je serais aimé; j'ai pu oublier que Germeuil seul pouvait lui plaire! (176)

In other words, MN is always a dissonant narrator when the object of focalization is MC; when the object is Hortense, he is unconventionally consonant.

Narrative silence leads to confusion, even in some critical readers who have attempted to resolve the mystery extratextually. Conroy's (1972) statement that Hortense's "inconnu" is none other than Meilcour himself (93) is pure supposition, textually unjustified. Etiemble (1961) states more cautiously that Meilcour supposes that Hortense is loved by Germeuil, whom she *supposedly loves* (xxiii). Gaubert (1975) affirms that the narrator is surely married to Hortense (44). Gaubert bases this judgment on Crébillon's preface, which alludes to Meilcour's later years with "une femme estimable" (68). Terrasse (1982) observes that Hortense is reading a novel about a lover who wrongly imagines he is not loved in return: "She tells Meilcour this story, which is probably their own" (27). Smith (1978) seems to be confused when he postulates that the narrator's refusal to pronounce final judgment on Hortense's relationship with Germeuil perpetuates "the ambiguity that prevents Meilcour from discerning *her true feelings*" (73). According to Smith, then, the narrator's silence prevents his younger self from realizing that Hortense loves him, as though they were two different characters on the same temporal plane. Dagen (1985) finds the key to the mystery in the following sentence, when MC sees Hortense in the Tuileries: "J'oubliai dans *ce moment, le plus cher de ma vie,* que je croyais qu'elle aimait un autre que moi; je m'oubliai moi-même" (105). For Dagen, this phrase provides a significant indication about subsequent events and the outcome of Meilcour's story: "The narrator attaches too much importance to this second meeting with Hortense for us not to see it as the announcement of a happiness that has come true at the time of the composition of his memoirs" (253, n. 39). In another passage, the narrator explains why Versac was unsuccessful in his attempt to make amorous advances toward Hortense: "il [Versac] ne pouvait pas croire qu'il pût manquer un coeur; mais, quand ce coeur [Hortense], qu'il voulait attaquer, n'eût pas alors été rempli de *la passion la plus vive,* il était vertueux" (151). According to Dagen, this sentence provides a bit of information that could be given only later in the novel, and it is very likely a question of Hortense's love for Meilcour (256, n. 67).

In fact, however, such information is not provided later in the novel, and we must agree with Boothroyd (1980) that we do not know who Hortense's "inconnu" is (239). Even on the rare occasion when MN provides his present thoughts about Hortense, the intervention tells us nothing authoritative about her feelings:

> Pour Mademoiselle de Théville, elle me regarda, à ce que je crus, avec une extreme froideur, et répondit à peine au compliment que je lui fis. *Il est vrai que j'ai pensé depuis* qu'il n'était pas impossible

qu'elle n'y eût rien compris; le trouble de mes sens avait passé jusqu'à mon esprit, et la confusion de mes idées m'empêchait d'en exprimer bien aucune. (143)

Dagen (1985) sees this statement as proof that the narrator has never ceased to be interested in Hortense (255, n. 58). Perhaps so, but it also seems to indicate that MN has *never* been able to understand Hortense's feelings, which hardly suggests that he subsequently came to know her better. The truth is that we simply do not know whom she loves nor how she feels about the hero. We cannot agree with Smith's contention that the restriction of the narrator's point of view to that of the protagonist was demanded by conventions of the memoir form (73). On the contrary, it is surely a temporal, paraliptic infraction of these conventions.[11] The result is that the reader remains in doubt, just as the hero himself flounders in the ambiguity of his complex and deceptive society.

Toward Nonfocalization

The case of Lursay is by far the most complicated. We see Meilcour's infatuation with this woman in the first section of the novel, but with the appearance of Hortense his opinion of Lursay begins to change. When he enumerates her vanities and affectations, the reader is bound to doubt as well, in the absence of correction by the narrative voice. The shift in attitude is complete with the advent of Versac, whose testimony renders Lursay even more suspect. Finally, after several minor reversals, Lursay tells Meilcour of her past, and the situation is again reversed in her favor. Meilcour is suddenly convinced that Versac has tricked him, while the reader receives no authoritative confirmation of the hero's judgment, no superior knowledge of Lursay's true character and history. Is she truly in love with Meilcour, or will he be just another in a succession of conquests? We simply follow the hero through his maze of opinion, from respect to hate and back again.[12] When the focalization is

11. Smith seems to have misread Stewart, to whom he refers to support this contention. Stewart (1969) is right to affirm that "the narrator cannot know the thought processes of other characters" (121), but that is not to say that the narrator's point of view is restricted to that of the protagonist. The two are, after all, not contemporaneous. If Hortense loved MC and later married him, it would be no break in convention for MN to tell us so.

12. Baril and Free (1980) have divided the novel into eight alternating segments, four dominated by emotional inclinations ("coeur") and four by rational considerations ("esprit"). In each segment the hero's ignorance begets doubt and jealousy, which triggers a shift in his attitude (26).

internal—and this is extremely rare when its object is Lursay—the young Meilcour must rely on his physical perceptions only: "A cette déclaration si précise de l'état de mon coeur, Madame de Lursay soupira, rougit, tourna languissamment les yeux sur moi, les y fixa quelque temps, les baissa sur son éventail, et se tut" (81). MC can only surmise the thoughts and motives of Lursay (as with those of Hortense), and no one confirms or denies that he is right in his suppositions: "Je *crus* voir, à son air froid qu'elle avait dans le fond envie que je partisse, et qu'elle destinait, *sans doute*, l'après-souper au marquis" (228–29). When the focalization is external, the narrator makes no explicit judgments about Lursay's character, although he seems to be largely sympathetic toward her. When he offers dissonant commentary, pointing to knowledge acquired later, it is not necessarily damaging to her character: "J'ai, depuis, senti toute l'adresse de Madame de Lursay, et le plaisir que lui donnait mon ignorance" (87). Indeed, the remark is more revealing of the narrator's amused attitude toward his younger self. His unwillingness to pass judgment on Lursay seems even at times to be based on his own present ignorance: "Depuis son veuvage et sa réforme, le public, qui, pour n'être pas toujours bien instruit n'en parle pas moins, lui avait donné des amants que *peut-être* elle n'avait pas eus" (86). It may be said that the narrator contributes indirectly to her defense, as it is he who advises the reader on Versac's lack of credibility. In the end, however, his refusal to pass judgment leaves the reader as "égaré" as the hero.

Unlike Hortense, however, Lursay is not at all presented only through the restricted perception of the hero. At the opposite end of the spectrum, and to complicate matters, the narrator gives a great deal of information about Lursay's thoughts and motivations that he could not possibly know, not even in the here-and-now of the speech situation:

> Pendant que je me faisais ces désagréables idées, Madame de Lursay se félicitait d'avoir assez pris sur elle pour me dissimuler combien elle était contente. (83)

> Je prononçai ces paroles avec une intrépidité dont la veille elle ne m'aurait pas soupçonné, et qui lui parut si peu dans mon caractère, qu'elle ne songea seulement pas à s'en choquer. (140)

Whereas MC remains confused about Lursay's feelings toward him, MN delves easily and endlessly into her thought-processes, providing insights in the manner of an omniscient narrator. These numerous psychological infractions of focalization have led to critical disagreement. Mylne (1981b) points to the innovation of this "omniscient penetration" of a narrator who goes beyond mere inference and enters the mind of other characters (132). Coulet (1967) explains this ability as the product of a narrator who has subsequently become so cunning that retrospectively, nothing that his earliest partners thought or felt escapes him (371). Stewart (1969) believes these passages were intended as "ironic hindsight, with no pretense at all of objectivity or, for that matter, of accuracy" (122, n. 12). Smith (1978, 78, n. 17) maintains, as do Brooks (1969, 33, n. 6) and Cherpack (1962, 83), that it is the narrator's worldly knowledge that permits him to reconstruct Lursay's past psychology. Such a reconstruction, says Dagen (1985), is based on signs that MC was unable to interpret, yet Dagen admits that Crébillon has mastered the technique of point of view (251, n. 22). Refusing omniscience altogether, Conroy (1972) states that Meilcour places individuals into categories that are susceptible to analysis from the outside (80).

Perhaps the disagreement stems from the variety of techniques used to represent consciousness in the novel. It is true that the narrator often reconstructs the thought-processes of others, which is possible in external focalization. In such cases he is usually careful to attenuate his suppositions in one of several ways:

1. With modal adverbs like "sans doute," "vraisemblablement," and "apparemment": "sans doute, elle se fit des idées plus gaies," "Elle avait apparemment compté plus tôt sur ma présence" (86).[13]
2. With verbs of appearance like "elle paraissait" and "il semblait"; these are rarely used to suppose Lursay's mental states, but when they occur they allow for the possibility, as with Hortense, of error and of dissonant correction: "elle paraissait plongée dans la rêverie la plus accablante" (123), "elle devait être indignée contre moi" (127).
3. With references to the present instance of discourse, such as "j'ai compris depuis": "Ce n'est pas, du moins j'ai eu lieu de le croire, qu'elle voulût retarder longtemps l'aveu de sa faiblesse. . . . Son coeur était alors tendre et délicat: selon ce que dans la suite j'en ai appris, il ne l'avait pas toujours été" (85).

In the latter case, the *passé composé* lends credence to the suppositions by converting them into knowledge learned subsequently. It is also true

---

13. Boothroyd views these "dubitative expressions" as characteristic of an open, indeterminate text, in which the narrator's authenticity cannot be verified (237).

that MN revels in generalizations about categories such as "les femmes dans cette situation" and "les personnes sensées": "elle jugea en personne sensée qu'il ne lui restait plus rien dans cet instant à espérer de moi" (127). Sometimes the reconstruction is supported by a maxim, given as a universally recognized truth:

> Elle crut qu'il lui était important, pour m'acquérir, et même me fixer, de me dissimuler le plus longtemps qu'il lui serait possible son amour pour moi. . . . Elle savait d'ailleurs, qu'*avec quelque ardeur que les hommes poursuivent la victoire, ils aiment toujours à l'acheter.* (75)

Occasionally, the supposition is freely admitted to be such. After a paragraph devoted to Lursay's thoughts, we read: "Elle était assez sage pour faire ces réflexions, et sans doute elle les fit" (230). The following passage, however, which is far more typical, makes it clear why we must agree with Mylne about the narrator's occasional omniscience:

> Sur le peu que je lui avais dit, elle avait cru ma passion décidée: cependant, je n'en parlais plus; quel parti prendre? Le plus décent était d'attendre que l'amour, qui ne peut longtemps se contraindre, surtout dans un coeur aussi neuf que l'était le mien, me forçât encore à rompre le silence; mais, ce n'était pas le plus sûr. Il ne lui vint pas dans l'esprit que j'eusse renoncé à elle: elle pensa seulement que, certain de n'être jamais aimé, je combattais un amour qui me rendait malheureux. (96)

Without a single attenuating "peut-être" or "sans doute," it is difficult to view this passage as anything but mind-reading. It contains two methods of representing psychological penetration that recur often throughout the novel. The first involves the use of unmitigated verbs denoting mental processes ("elle avait cru," "elle pensa," etc.). While the narrator explains his own past ignorance, he never explains how he knows now what Lursay thought then: "Elle jugeait," "Elle ne doutait pas," "elle craignait," etc. (178). The second method consists of representing Lursay's thoughts by means of a narrated monologue, a merging of discourse and historical utterance ("Quel parti prendre?" etc.). While narrated monologue is occasionally used to represent the hero's thoughts ("Quel parti me restait-il donc à prendre?" 72), it is more commonly a means of penetrating the mind of Lursay. Focalization is delegated to this character, who then becomes the subject of perception:

Son intention [Lursay] cependant n'était point de garder là-dessus le silence: l'insulte était trop vive. *L'avoir fait attendre, ar-river froidement sans m'excuser, sans paraître croire que j'en eusse besoin, n'avoir pas seulement remarqué qu'elle en était piquée, était-il de crimes dont je ne fusse coupable?* (113)

Ma froideur, car je ne me prêtai à rien, l'embarrassa; *des révérences, du respect, un air morne; quel prix, et de ce qu'elle avait fait pour moi, et des bontés qu'elle me préparait encore! Comment accorder aussi peu d'amour et d'empressement avec les transports que je lui avais montrés?* (167)

While the tense and person distinguish these thoughts from quoted monologue and link them to the narrative context, they are clearly outside the realm of the hero's knowledge. Intrusions of this kind give us still another perspective on Lursay, that of the omniscient, third-person narrator, or of the nonfocalized narrative.

But Crébillon goes still further than this. His narrator not only reads the mind of Lursay, but she reads the mind of young Meilcour as well, resulting in a kind of double mind-reading. Like the dissonant narrator, she too sees the naïveté of the hero, and it is the reader who becomes omniscient: "elle savait combien j'étais éloigné de la croire capable d'une faiblesse . . ." (74). Curiously, in most of the cases of double mind-reading, MN explains how Lursay arrived at her interpretation of MC's thoughts, showing how she interpreted a perceptible sign:

C'était me dire assez que je devais lui demander un rendez-vous. Elle attendit longtemps que je le fisse; mais *voyant* enfin que cela ne m'entrait pas dans l'esprit, elle eut la générosité de le prendre sur elle. (102)

Elle reconnut, *au ton de ma voix,* combien j'étais ému. (114)

Madame de Lursay . . . connut, *à la froideur de mes regards,* qu'elle ne faisait pas sur moi une aussi vive impression qu'elle aurait désiré. (229–30)

Perhaps this offers the key to the apparent focal infractions: if Lursay can read MC's thoughts by interpreting perceptible signs, then MN can surely do the same for Lursay. This kind of mind-reading is a device used by most storytellers. As Vitoux (1982) points out, it also happens that the interpreting character may reconstruct from perceived signs the thoughts and even the vision of others. What falls within the realm of his experience (what he has been told and what he has observed) permits him to deduce an interior reality. There is nothing here that breaks the rules, although the marks of extrapolation (of the type "he concluded from this that X was thinking . . .") are not always so obvious (363). It goes without saying that a narrator who moves in this direction will be faced with the temptation of paralepsis.

In any case, it seems useless to argue that these psychological insights are merely hypotheses reconstructed through reasoning and ulterior knowledge, as readers will generally view them as authentic information. These techniques of psychological penetration are well integrated into the historical utterance and are thereby given narratorial authority. As Kayser (1977) points out, even when the narrator is clearly a character in his own story, the reader will unconsciously grant his authority without questioning the sources of his knowledge (79). This is because MN and MC each hold a different kind of authority for the reader. As Lanser (1981) says, "the authority of intellection attaches most fully to the public voice [the narrator], while the authority of lived (fictional) experience is more fully embodied in the focalizing character" (142).

What Crébillon has achieved is a remarkable synthesis between first-person limitations and omniscient incursions. The latter have the merit of being unobtrusive because they alternate with the former. In the following passage MN admits his ignorance of Lursay's thoughts:

> J'avais connu qu'elle me faisait des reproches; nous étions seuls, et je n'étais pas tombé à ses genoux! Je n'avais pas fait de ce moment le plus heureux des miens! Je la laissais sortir enfin! Ignorais-je donc le prix d'une querelle? Je ne sais si elle fit ces réflexions, mais elle monta en carrosse d'un air qui m'assura qu'elle était infiniment mécontente. (170)

He has reconstructed her thoughts based on her conduct, yet the narrated monologue helps us to identify with Lursay before we are told that her thoughts have been reconstructed. In a reversed situation, MN begins by admitting ignorance of motives and then moves on to mind-reading:

> [M]ais, soit que ma façon de me comporter dans les rendez-vous lui eût déplu, soit qu'elle eût voulu me les faire désirer, elle avait décidé que je serais en proie à tous les importuns que mon destin pourrait amener chez elle ce jour-là. (136)

The narrator's occasional omniscience is frequently juxtaposed with his limited perspective, such as in the following famous scene:

> Je crois qu'elle voulut attendre, par méchanceté, que je rompisse le silence: enfin, je m'y déterminai. Vous faites donc des noeuds, Madame? lui demandai-je d'une voix tremblante. A cette intéressante et spirituelle question, Madame de Lursay me regarda avec étonnement. Quelque idée qu'elle se fût faite de ma timidité, et du peu d'usage que j'avais du monde, il lui parut inconcevable que je ne trouvasse que cela à lui dire. (122)

Here the dissonance between narrator and hero is quite clear, and the reader easily perceives the narrator's sarcasm toward his younger self. Toward Lursay, however, his attitude is ambiguous. First he does not know ("je crois qu'elle voulut") and then he knows too much ("il lui parut inconcevable"). The most important function of mind-reading is to maintain an ironic perspective on the hero's naïveté: the reader must be able to know, authoritatively, what the hero does not perceive.

When psychological insights are mingled with shifts between consonance and dissonance, the effect is interpretive chaos. How can we get a grip on Lursay's character when our information about her comes from all directions? During his first evening with her, the young Meilcour is puzzled by her behavior (84–85). At first we are presented with his perceptions ("elle semblait avoir oublié") and then with what appear to be her thoughts ("elle sentait qu'elle allait vieillir"), attenuated only by the "sans doute" of supposition on the narrator's part, who seems not to know. There follows a lengthy generalization about "des femmes dans cette situation," then another incursion into Lursay's mind ("il s'en fallait beaucoup qu'elle fût aussi effrayée qu'elle me l'avait dit"). Lursay is then described in an unrestricted, nonfocalized manner ("elle craignait," "elle était persuadée," "elle voulait"). The narrator provides reflections based on later knowledge ("selon ce que dans la suite j'en ai appris"), but his "peut-être" reveals a lack of certain knowledge or perhaps even an internal focalization by the unknowing hero. And so it goes. No authoritative guidance is provided, and confusion reigns.

Mylne (1981b) is quite right to point out that the narrator's mind-reading is not limited to Lursay (131). He seems equally aware of the thoughts and motives of others in his world:

> [Versac] ne douta donc pas un moment . . . qu'il ne séduisît promptement Mademoiselle de Théville. (150)

> Madame de Senanges qui . . . pensait plutôt au nombre de ses amants qu'au temps qu'ils avaient voulu demeurer dans ses chaînes, était très persuadée que ses charmes agissaient sur moi. (147)

> [Madame de Mongennes] jugeait aux façons froides que j'avais pour Madame de Senanges, que je ne l'aimais point, et trop sotte pour n'être pas excessivement vaine, elle ne doutait point que je ne lui cédasse aussitôt qu'elle le voudrait. (198)

We may accept certain judgments to be mere suppositions on his part: "Madame de Senanges . . . résolut de se comporter si bien, qu'on ne pût pas douter que je ne lui appartinsse" (185); "Versac, qui avait résolu de m'enlever à Madame de Lursay" (195). MN's occasional attempts to justify his knowledge of the thoughts of others appear awkward and contrived: "Ces réflexions, que *vraisemblablement* il [Versac] fit, le calmèrent" (151); "Ce n'est pas, elle [Senanges] me l'a avoué depuis, que j'eusse bien précisément tout ce qu'il fallait pour lui plaire" (146). At times he explains how he arrived at certain insights, yet one is at a loss to explain the following:

> [Senanges] se souvint en ce moment que Versac lui avait dit que Madame de Lursay avait des vues sur moi. . . . Elle imagina que, sans se compromettre, il lui serait aisé d'éclaircir ses doutes. (188)

> Madame de Senanges ne s'aperçut pas plus tôt des nouvelles idées de Madame de Mongennes, qu'elle en conçut des alarmes: elle jugea, et *je crois avec raison*, que si elle [Mongennes] ne voulait pas me plaire, elle voulait du moins qu'on pût penser qu'elle me plaisait" (186).

In the last example the narrator admits, in the present tense, that he is unsure about Mongennes's motivation, yet he seems knowledgeable about Senanges's judgment. Perhaps the most glaring case of paralepsis occurs when the narrator relates a conversation whispered between Versac and Lursay, one that the hero was not privileged to hear: "quel ange, quelle divinité est donc descendue chez vous, Madame? demanda-t-il tout bas à Madame de Lursay. . . . Madame de Lursay lui dit tout bas qui elle était" (148).

The desire to tell is in confrontation with the ability to perceive, bound by convention. The point of view of no single character, including the narrator, is capable of providing us with the information we need to know. As Siemek (1981) writes, there is no dominant perspective, but rather a complex game of correctives and confrontations, of reflections and counterreflections (215).[14] We must agree with Mylne (1981b) that "Crébillon is moving away from the point of view of the first-person narrator to that of the omniscient third person" (132). Nowhere in *Les Egarements* is the "bondage" of personal retrospective narration more evident than in the dinner-party episode *chez* Lursay. Each character at the table has a particular motivation that cannot be voiced in polite conversation: Senanges is seeking to seduce Meilcour, Lursay is trying to hide her previous affair with Pranzi from Meilcour, while Versac wants to please Hortense and to embarrass Lursay because he knows about the latter's past interest in Pranzi and her present interest in Meilcour. MC, who has eyes only for Hortense, is aware of none of this. The narrator's only solution is nonfocalized mind-reading: "En achevant ces paroles, on leva table; Versac commençant à douter de la réussite de ses projets, Madame de Senanges occupée à pousser les siens, et Madame de Lursay désespérée des façons malhonnêtes de Monsieur de Pranzi" (158). In order for the dinner-party scene to make sense to the reader, MN must penetrate the psychology of Lursay, Senanges, and Versac, all of whom know what MC does not. In order to say what they are simulating, he must be able to perceive what they are dissimulating. Only the consciousness of Hortense is never penetrated.[15]

Labrosse (1975) has grouped the characters of *Les Egarements* into several categories:

1. The nonsimulating characters: Madame de Meilcour and Madame de Théville.
2. Those who simulate constantly but about whom there is no mystery: Senanges and Mongennes.

14. Speaking of Crébillon's narrators in general, and using the terminology of Pouillon and Todorov, Siemek (1981) states that it is "vision from outside" (the narrator knows less than the characters) that dominates Crébillon's personal narratives. That may be what we would expect from a FPN, but it certainly does not apply to *Les Egarements*. As we have seen, there is a good dose of "vision from behind" involved (the narrator knows more than the characters). Neither can we agree with Siemek's contention that Crébillon's narrators see themselves from the outside, because it is not true of Meilcour (221–22).

15. Baril and Free (1980) mention the predominance of dialogue without retrospective commentary in scenes such as the dinner-party and Meilcour's promenade in the Tuileries with Senanges and Mongennes. These scenes are perceived by the gullible hero, but the reader has been conditioned by an atmosphere of distrust established by the narrator from the beginning (31). In fact, these dialogues are surrounded by MN's commentary, without which the reader would have little understanding of the characters' motivations.

3. Those with a double appearance: Meilcour, "naïve/experi-
enced"; Versac, "frivolous and conceited/shrewd and pro-
found"; Lursay, "sensitive/hypocritical"; and Hortense, "in
love/indifferent" (111).

It should now be clear that Labrosse's third category contains two subdi-
visions. Meilcour and Versac may have a double appearance, but there is
no mystery involved for the reader. Our dual perception of them is due
to a temporal difference, to the oscillation in point of view between MC
(*then*) and MN (*now*). With Lursay and Hortense, on the other hand,
both sets of perceptions come from MC (*then*), as his opinion shifts back
and forth. But even these two characters must be differentiated. Concerning Hortense, all perception comes from the hero. Concerning
Lursay, most of our knowledge comes from the narrator, who transgresses his focal limitations to provide us with a great deal of psychological insight. Yet this insight, in the final analysis, provides more information about the floundering hero than about Lursay herself, so that we
remain unsure of her true character. Surrounding both characters there
is indeed a mystery, which the narrator fails to solve.

The hero's confusion about the principal female characters is con-
veyed to the reader because (1) on Hortense, the narrator is completely
silent, and (2) on Lursay, he alternates between consonant and dissonant
narration, generalizations, suppositions, and omniscient penetration of
her thoughts. It is obvious that the narrator does not always reveal all
that he must know. The reader can see Hortense only through the perception of the hero. We do not know her thoughts but we are always
privy to his. Our interest is centered upon *her* but she remains a mystery.
While we can see certain aspects of Lursay's character that are unknown
to the hero, we cannot, in the end, really judge her any better than can
Meilcour. The narrator himself seems to change his opinion of her, depending on his younger self's perception at any one time. The hesitation
of this narrator seems particularly inconsistent next to passages in which
he gives more information than he should logically possess. We see
Lursay's thoughts as well as those of MC, but MN provides no guidance
about whether MC is right or wrong as he wavers between respect and
disdain. Our interest is centered upon *him* and upon his evolving attitude toward her. MN's inconsistency means that the reader, while being
somewhat better informed than the debutant MC, is still essentially
ignorant as regards the two romantic interests. The reader is no more
capable of making an informed choice than is MC. Since the essence of
the plot surrounds romantic interest, our blindness on this point must
increase our understanding of Meilcour's confusion about the women of

his society. At the same time, the narrator's comments and clarifications on certain points prevent the reader from sympathizing too much with the hero, who, as the narrator points out, is after all subject to the follies of his age and of his century.

2

LE PAYSAN PARVENU: TEMPORAL AMBIGUITY

Le Paysan parvenu (1734–35) is nearly an exact contemporary of *Les Egarements* (1736–38). Like Crébillon's novel, it was published in install-ments and left unfinished by the author. Its narrative situation is also the same, that of the classical memoir-novel, in which an older man writes about his youth for an unspecified narratee. What immediately distinguishes the two is the gregarious, "chatty" nature of Marivaux's narrator, who overlaps his retrospective narration with a heavy layer of discourse. In addition to telling the story of Jacob-character (JC), Jacob-narrator (JN) feels a need to chat with his narratee, making constant digressions about his present self, his present situation, and his present opinions about his world. Despite the ubiquitous presence of the speaker, however, it is often difficult to find a sharp line of demarcation between the spatiotemporal field of young Jacob and that of the older man who calls himself M. de la Vallée. Instead we shall see a fusion of the hero's focalization with the present instance of discourse. The narra-tor plays on the double temporality of story and narration as though they were contemporaneous.

JN's loquacious tendency is evident in the novel's opening pages, in which he seems to have trouble getting his story started. He begins by mentioning his humble origins and then digresses on the errors of being embarrassed about one's birth, ending this preamble with "Revenons à moi" (6). Then he talks about his memoirs, apologizes for his style, affirms the truth of his story, refuses to divulge his real name, and ends with "Commençons" (7). Next follows a brief background sketch of the family of his father's lord. When the narrator says "C'était là leur situa-tion, quand je vins au monde" (7), we expect the historical narration to begin, but instead he launches into a long development about his brother and nephews, which ends with "Laissons là mes neveux, qui m'ont un peu détourné de mon histoire" (9). Finally, after five pages we read: "L'année d'après le mariage de mon frère, j'arrivai donc à Paris" (9). His story begins, but it will certainly not go on uninterrupted by his frequent commentaries and digressions.

Narrator's Discourse

We shall begin by enumerating four functions of these abundant discursive elements, with a few examples of each. First, *narrative function.* Quite often—and much more often than Meilcour—JN makes explicit references to his act of storytelling. He reveals a consciousness of his narratorial freedom to arrange and choose the elements of his tale: "Je le peins ici, quoique cela ne soit pas fort nécessaire" (37); "Mais j'oubliais une chose, c'est le portrait de la jeune fille, et il est nécessaire que je le fasse" (87); "Par ce discours de Mme d'Alain que je rapporte . . ." (162). He refers constantly to what he has already said, a characteristic that lends an oral quality to his storytelling style: "la jolie blonde dont j'ai parlé" (21); "l'endroit qui m'était réservé, et dont j'ai déjà fait mention" (84); "Je retournai donc chez moi, perdu de vanité, comme je l'ai dit" (187). Since each installment of the novel was published separately at intervals of several months, this characteristic repetition is found at the beginning of several parts: "J'ai dit dans la première partie de ma vie . . ." (57); "J'ai dit dans la dernière partie que je me hâtai . . ." (221). JN feels free to skip over the less important details of his story, and this narratorial freedom extends even to the quoted speech of the characters, which he sometimes abridges:

> Je passe la suite de ces tristes événements; le détail en serait trop long. (39)

> Je laisse là le récit de tout ce qui se passa depuis la visite de Mlle Habert, pour en venir à l'instant où je comparus devant un magistrat. (154)

> Ce fut là le premier essai que je fis du commerce avec Mme Catherine, des discours de laquelle j'ai retranché une centaine de *Dieu soit béni!* et *que le ciel nous assiste!* qui servaient tantôt de refrain, tantôt de véhicule à ses discours. (50, Marivaux's italics)

Second, *emotive function*, that is, "those passages in narrative focusing on the narrator can be said to fulfill an emotive function" (Prince 1987, 26). While telling his story, JN occasionally draws attention to himself and to his present situation: "Quand j'y songe, je ris encore du prodigieux étonnement où ils restèrent tous deux en nous voyant" (160).

Third, *conative function*, that is, "those passages in narrative focusing on the narratee can be said to fulfill a conative function" (Prince 1987, 15). Emphasis on the narratee provides another element of oral style, one that is very frequent in *Le Paysan parvenu*. Unlike Meilcour, JN punctuates his narration with directives to the reader: "Imaginez-vous" (38), "notez" (43), "Jugez," "voyez" (161), "Souvenez-vous," "songez" (226), and so on. He attempts to draw the reader into his communicative act by asking questions and by imagining questions and comments from the reader: "Savez-vous qui était l'homme à qui probablement j'avais sauvé la vie?" (257); "Est-ce que vous aviez dessein de l'aimer? me direz-vous" (140); "Voici pourtant des airs, me direz-vous; point du tout" (250). Rosbottom (1977) suggests that Marivaux was striving to "remove the stubborn barrier that separates reader from writer, thereby establishing an intersubjectivity between the reader and the narrator" (251).

Fourth, the function of *maxims and shared truths*. The three functions that we have seen thus far call attention to the "I" of the speaker, the "you" of the reader, and the communicative act that is taking place between them. All three are almost totally absent from *Les Egarements*. Meilcour rarely calls attention to his storytelling process or to his present situation, and never addresses his narratee directly. The high frequency of these elements in *Le Paysan parvenu* contributes to our impression of Jacob's oral style and to our sense of familiarity with him. What is very characteristic of both novels is the narrator's sententiousness. Like Meilcour, JN uses maxims to reinforce his opinions by lending them the authority of universal truth: "Mais dans ce monde toutes les vertus sont déplacées, aussi bien que les vices" (38). He often takes personal responsibility for the maxims and backs them up with his own experience. Universal truth thus becomes subjective opinion: "j'ai remarqué que les gourmands perdent la moitié de leur temps à être en peine de ce qu'ils mangeront" (41); "Il y a pourtant des femmes silencieuses, mais je crois que ce n'est point par caractère qu'elles le sont" (78). Maxims tend to fuse the emotive and the conative functions of communication, by positing a truth that is supposedly shared by narrator and narratee. JN increases this fusion by means of the oblique "vous" that draws the reader into his shared truths: "En fait d'amour, tout engagé qu'on est déjà, la vanité de plaire ailleurs vous rend l'âme si infidèle, et vous donne en pareille occasion de si lâches complaisances!" (136). Sometimes the reader is drawn into JN's sententiousness by means of the first-person plural, which signifies the similarity of narrator and reader: "Il faut avouer que le diable est bien fin, mais aussi que nous sommes bien sots!" (53). Even when JN does not specifically refer to his narratee, he makes it clear that they share the same world. In his maxims he often points deictically to categories of people and feelings that the narratee is expected to recognize:

> Celui à qui elle s'adressa était un gros brutal, un de ces valets qui dans une maison ne tiennent jamais à rien qu'à leurs gages et qu'à leurs profits. (37)

> Je lui fis mon compliment avec cette émotion qu'on a quand on est un petit personnage, et qu'on vient demander une grâce à quelqu'un d'important. (203)

An important effect, then, of these various functions of discourse is the strengthening of the bonds between narrator and narratee and the foregrounding of the act of communication. Other discursive elements involve temporal problems, and we shall return to these later.

Double Register

Ever since Rousset (1962) coined the expression, there has been a great deal of critical discussion about the "double register" in *Le Paysan parvenu* as well as in *La Vie de Marianne*. According to Rousset, the two registers of narrator and character are never confused and always remain distinct.[1] For Stewart (1969), on the contrary, the two levels are not always kept distinct, while Coulet (1975) believes there is really no difference between the reflections of the past and those of the present.[2] Other

1. Rousset 1962, 52. Rousset continues to insist on the essential distinction between *alors* [then] and *à présent que j'écris* [at the present as I write] in *Narcisse romancier* (1973, 91). Laden (1983) writes that La Vallée succeeds in distancing himself from the peasant Jacob: the fusion between the two selves is not completed even in the last part of the novel, in which the narrator continues to objectify himself by referring to the protagonist in the third person (171–80). Elsewhere Laden (1987) points to the narrator's biting irony toward the peasant, who is often treated with the same ridicule as other characters (106–7). Démoris (1975) believes that the narrator's reflections and maxims are a measure of the distance he maintains toward the hero (410–11).

2. Stewart 1969, 103. Coulet (1975) writes that while JN might seem to be a disabused skeptic, detached from the illusions of his youth, the relation between the two registers is

critics have traced a progression from the double register at the beginning of the novel, through the evolution of Jacob to a final integration of
peasant and parvenu.[3] There is general agreement that the hero displays
a considerable talent in scrutinizing and analyzing other characters. The
disagreement concerns the attitude of the narrator toward his younger
self. Is he largely a dissonant narrator, like Meilcour, who regards his
younger self with ironic detachment, or does he display a tendency
toward consonance?

Certainly, there are moments of dissonance. Like most retrospective
narrators, JN finds occasions to distance himself from the ignorance,
awkwardness, and naïveté of JC. Dissonance, however, does not necessarily imply condemnation: "De sorte que je m'en retournai pénétré de
joie, bouffi de gloire, et plein de mes folles exagérations sur le mérite
de la dame. Il ne me vint pas un moment en pensée que mes sentiments fissent tort à ceux que je devais à Mlle Habert" (141). Despite the
scornful tone of the first sentence, there is a hint of justification in the
second. JC's ignorance is actually to his credit, for it exonerates him of
any wrongdoing toward Habert. In fact, it even makes him a more
sympathetic lover: "comme j'étais naturellement vif, que d'ailleurs ma
vivacité m'emportait, et que j'ignorais l'art des détours, qu'enfin je ne
mettais pas d'autres freins à mes pensées qu'un peu de retenue ma-
ladroite . . . je laissais échapper des tendresses étonnantes" (76). Here
JC is analyzed through external focalization, but there is no hint of
ironic detachment. Ignorance and clumsiness are excused in favor of
innocence and honesty. JN is not averse to revealing the occasional
duplicity of JC. When he first encounters Habert on the Pont-Neuf, JC
tells her his story:

> J'avais refusé d'épouser une belle fille que j'aimais, qui m'aimait
> et qui m'offrait ma fortune, et cela par un dégoût fier et pudique
> qui ne pouvait avoir frappé qu'une âme de bien et d'honneur.
> N'était-ce pas là un récit bien avantageux à lui [Habert] faire? Et je
> le fis de mon mieux, d'une manière naïve, et comme on dit la
> vérité. (44)

---

not that simple: JC is sometimes just as skeptical, whereas JN seriously subscribes to some
of JC's judgments (199–203; see also Coulet 1967, 1:348–49). Thomas (1973) agrees that the
narrator is not significantly different from the young man he has been, and that it is
difficult to establish an important distance between the two (364).

3. Ray 1976, 140–51; Bourgeacq 1975, 223–24. Ince (1968) takes his critique of Rousset
one step further, arguing that there is a third register, that of the author watching the
narrator watching the hero (122–24).

Self-narrated monologue, reflecting the speech of JC, merges with the analytical commentary of JN, who tells the reader how JC made the story reflect well upon himself. The present–past polarity is evident here, yet there is no trace of condemnation of JC's behavior. Revelation of duplicity can be accompanied by subtle justifications: "Je me ressouviens bien qu'en lui [Habert] parlant ainsi, je ne sentais rien en moi qui démentît mon discours. J'avoue pourtant que je tâchai d'avoir l'air et le ton touchant, le ton d'un homme qui pleure, et que je voulus orner un peu la vérité" (92). While JN admits that JC was affecting a certain tone and arranging his story to his advantage, the narrator also remembers that the hero felt no sense of falsehood in what he was saying. Even when JN is willing to admit that JC did wrong, he assures us that the young man had no consciousness of that wrong. A good example occurs early in the novel:

> Peut-être fis-je mal en prenant l'argent de Geneviève; ce n'était pas, je pense, en agir dans toutes les régles de l'honneur; car enfin, j'entretenais cette fille dans l'idée que je l'aimais et je la trompais. . . . D'ailleurs, cet argent qu'elle m'offrait n'était pas chrétien, je ne l'ignorais pas . . . mais je ne savais pas encore faire des réflexions si délicates, mes principes de probité étaient encore fort courts. (22–23)

Having evolved from a peasant to a man of quality, JN is highly conscious of social class, and it is on this subject that we might expect him to be the most dissonant. His attitude toward his rustic origins fluctuates. At times it is one of amused scorn:

> Pour moi, je n'avais plus de contenance, et en vrai benêt je saluais cet homme à chaque mot qu'il m'adressait. (226)

> Il fallait pourtant répondre, avec mon petit habit de soie et ma petite propreté bourgeoise, dont je ne faisais plus d'estime depuis que je voyais tant d'habits magnifiques autour de moi. (266)

At other times we can discern an element of shame about his background and an attempt to dissociate himself from the word "paysan":

> Ce discours, quoique fort simple, n'était plus d'un paysan, comme vous voyez. (210)

> Le fils d'un honnête homme qui demeure à la campagne, répondis-je. C'était dire vrai, et pourtant esquiver le mot de paysan qui me paraissait dur. (216)

It is difficult to speak of ironic detachment when the narrator seems to be just as embarrassed about the peasant as is the hero himself.[4]

JN can be dissonant, then, without condemning JC and while providing justifications for his behavior. He displays some good-natured humor toward his humble origins, but even there he is often defensive. Except for the hero's initial naïveté (which often seems to be exploited if not feigned), it is difficult to see any change in character between JC and JN. On the question of vanity, JN readily attributes it to JC, but he also acknowledges it as a present fault:

> Je retournai donc chez moi, perdu de vanité, comme je l'ai dit, mais d'une vanité qui me rendait gai, et non pas superbe et ridicule; mon amour-propre a toujours été sociable; je n'ai jamais été plus doux ni plus traitable que lorsque j'ai eu lieu de m'estimer et d'être vain; chacun a là-dessus son caractère, et c'était là le mien. (187)

This passage provides an example of the sameness of character, of the lack of change between *then* and *now*. About many things JC is just as knowledgeable as JN. He is particularly clever about the way in which he uses language: "je n'étais pas honteux des bêtises que je disais, pourvu qu'elles fussent plaisantes; car à travers l'épaisseur de mon ignorance, je voyais qu'elles ne nuisaient jamais à un homme qui n'était pas obligé d'en savoir davantage" (11).[5] Formal distinction between past and present sometimes hides the lack of change between JC and JN: "Jusqu'ici donc mes discours avaient toujours eu une petite tournure champêtre; mais il y avait plus d'un mois que je m'en corrigeais assez bien, quand je voulais y prendre garde, et je n'avais conservé cette tournure avec Mlle Habert que parce qu'elle me réussissait auprès d'elle . . . mais il est certain que je parlais meilleur français quand je voulais" (85). Here JN stresses his distance yet reveals that he is not so different from JC, who was equally aware of his ruses through the use of language.

Unlike Meilcour, who is always dissonant toward the ignorance and social awkwardness of his younger self, Jacob is most dissonant when he

---

4. Unlike *La Vie de Marianne*, says Thomas (1970), this novel does not involve the ironic detachment of an older writer looking back at his younger self. Thomas sees Jacob as detached even at the moment of experience (134–41), but this is clearly not true concerning his social status. For example, he is very self-conscious at Mme. Remy's house with the *chevalier* and at the Comédie with the Comte d'Orsan.

5. About this sentence Bourgeacq (1975) writes: "Once again, time is telescoped: the narrator lends to Jacob a lucidity that he can have acquired only later" (34). He also points out that Jacob seems to be more perspicacious than he should be about *dévotes*, about *directeurs de conscience*, etc. (83). On the other hand, says Bourgeacq, the narrator attributes to Jacob an innocence that the latter no longer possesses (47).

seeks to defend, to valorize, or to exonerate his earlier behavior. Since the presence of the narrating self is constantly foregrounded by an abundance of discursive elements, intrusive commentary, and direct address to the narratee, one might expect to find a focal dominance of the narrating self. Quite often, however, there is no clear division between the two selves. There is a fusion of the consciousness of the narrator with that of the hero, so that the observations provided by one are very similar if not identical to those offered by the other. From the standpoint of focalization, it is often very difficult to separate the two registers and distinguish between them. A number of passages suggest a fusion of the present speaker and the past perceiver. Let us compare the following examples, all of which are taken from Jacob's first day in the Habert household:

> [1] Mais, me disais-je, je ne cours aucun risque; il n'y aura qu'à déloger si je ne suis pas content. . . . D'ailleurs toute la maison me fait bonne mine . . . voilà déjà mes quatre repas de sûrs, et le coeur me dit que tout ira bien: courage! (51)

> [2] Ah! le bon pain! Je n'en ai jamais mangé de meilleur, de plus blanc, de plus ragoûtant; il faut bien des attentions pour faire un pain comme celui-là; il n'y avait qu'une main dévote qui pût l'avoir pétri; aussi était-il de la façon de Catherine. Oh! l'excellent repas que je fis! (49)

> [3] Malpeste, le succulent petit dîner! Voilà ce qu'on appelle du potage, sans parler d'un petit plat de rôt d'une finesse, d'une cuisson si parfaite. (51–52)

The first passage is self-quoted monologue, signaled by the inquit phrase "me disais-je" and clearly focalized by the experiencing self. In the second, since there is no inquit phrase, all discursive elements point to the narrating self and to the here-and-now of his communication. Yet the perception seems to be that of the young Jacob, savoring his meal. Except for the lack of quotational devices and the presence of past tenses, the second passage resembles self-quoted monologue. In the third passage, the past tenses disappear altogether and the unconjugated "voilà" contributes to the ambiguity, yet it is difficult to believe that JN can still be so excited about a meal he enjoyed long ago. In other words, the focalizer here is the experiencing self while the discourse belongs, curiously, to the narrating self.

Focalization can be delegated to the experiencing self to recapture an emotion felt at the moment of event: "Pour surcroît d'embarras, je regardais ce rouleau d'argent qui était sur la table, il me paraissait si rebondi! quel dommage de le perdre!" (28). Here the modal expression "il me paraissait" introduces the perception of the experiencing self. In many cases, however, the delegation is not so neat. The narrator's discourse is often contaminated by colloquial expressions and exclamations that reflect the hero's manner of perceiving and verbalizing his experience. Conversely, some passages that begin as self-narrated monologue, focalized by the hero, contain an element that can only be perceived by the narrator:

> Mon séjour à Paris m'avait un peu éclairci le teint; et, ma foi! quand je fus équipé, Jacob avait fort bonne façon. (14)

> Cette soie rouge me flatta; une doublure de soie, quel plaisir et quelle magnificence pour un paysan! (166)

The appellation "Jacob" in the first example and "paysan" in the second seem to be those of JN and are therefore inconsistent with self-narrated monologue. In the following passage there is an inconsistency resulting from the lack of transition between self-quoted monologue and the surrounding narrative:

> [1] Pourquoi m'en retourner? me disais-je quelquefois. Tout est plein ici de gens à leur aise, qui, aussi bien que moi, [2] n'avaient pour tout bien que la Providence. [3] Ma foi! restons encore quelques jours ici . . . à ce qu'il m'en coûte par repas, j'irai loin; [4] car j'étais sobre, et je l'étais sans peine. (40)

Here we have self-quoted monologue focalized by the hero, [1] and [3], followed by [4] a retrospective observation by the narrator. But [2] is problematic: for the sake of consistency, the verb should be in the present tense. In the imperfect tense, it suggests self-narrated rather than self-quoted monologue, but the former would require the imperfect tense throughout ("Tout était plein ici de gens"). The odd combination of present and imperfect tenses makes it difficult to separate the thoughts of JC from those of JN.

Much of the confusion between past and present results, then, from a lack of discrimination concerning self-quotation. Shifters and other discursive elements normally refer to the subject of the speech event (the narrator), but in signaled quotation they refer to the deictic field of its object (the hero). In the absence of quotational devices, the distinction between the deictic field of the enunciatory system and that of the referential system is blurred. Rather than maintaining the separation be-tween the temporal loci of hero and narrator, the discursive elements serve to confuse them. Not only is JN often a consonant narrator in that his judgments and opinions differ little from those of JC, but his meth-ods of self-quotation also serve to reduce the distance between narrator and hero by effacing the demarcation between them. That the two regis-ters tend to merge is due as much to stylistic blurring as to ideological agreement.[6]

Other Characters

There is really no sense of mystery surrounding any of the characters in the novel. JN treats many with irony, others with sympathy, but in either case he leaves little doubt about his present opinions of them. One of the ways in which he controls our response to the characters is through the use of epithets. Agathe is called "la malicieuse" and "la petite friponne" (107); Mme. d'Alain, the incorrigible gossip, is referred to as "la discrète d'Alain" (108) and as "notre officieuse tracassière" (167); Ferval is called "la nymphe de cinquante ans" (134). The characters are nonetheless allowed to speak for themselves. JN quotes them abundantly and shows a preference for direct over indirect discourse, yet he exerts a great deal of control over his report. Two observations need to be made about his treatment of reported speech. First, he does not reveal a great respect for the integrity of his report. We have already noted the liberty he takes in abridging the words of his characters. His disregard for precise quota-tion can be seen in the following speech of Habert:

> [C]ar je t'avoue, Jacob, que je ne veux point de Catherine; elle a l'esprit rude et difficile, elle serait toujours en commerce avec ma soeur, qui est naturellement curieuse, sans compter que toutes les dévotes le sont; elles se dédommagent des péchés qu'elles ne font pas par le plaisir de savoir les péchés des autres; c'est toujours autant de pris; et c'est moi qui fais cette réflexion-là, ce n'est pas Mlle Habert. (79)

6. In the words of Margolin (1984), the free indirect representation of thought and speech involves a "partial transfer of deictic center," a blending operation in which some elements relate to the deictic center of the speaker while others relate to that of the character (201). It introduces a certain indeterminacy without undermining the reliability of the speaker. This definition is particularly relevant to *Le Paysan parvenu*, in which the deictic field of many textual fragments cannot be easily identified.

JN's belated clarification is needed because the character's speech merges with his own discourse. He also indulges in false quotation, in which the report is obviously not a literal reproduction of the character's speech. Sometimes he reports typified speech, which conveys the impression that a similar speech has been heard several times. Such is the case during lunch with the Habert sisters: "Les oeufs me gonfleraient, dit la cadette; et puis *ma soeur* par-ci, *ma soeur* par-là" (49, Marivaux's italics). Although Jacob has witnessed this scene only once, the imperfect tense used to describe it and the typified speech convey a sense of iteration: "elles jetaient des regards indifférents sur ce bon vivre: Je n'ai point de goût aujourd'hui. Ni moi non plus. Je trouve tout fade. Et moi tout trop salé" (52). In his portrait of Ferval, JN reports her typical reaction upon hearing gossip: "Mais que me dites-vous là, ne vous trompez-vous point? cela est possible?" (143).

Typified speech is not always iterative, however. Sometimes JN uses it to pass over details of a singulative scene that seem unworthy of exact reporting. When JC returns home from prison, he is met by an inquisitive Mme. d'Alain who says: "Eh mais! dites-nous donc ceci, dites-nous donc cela" (162). The bargaining between Mme. d'Alain and Mme. de la Vallée over a robe for Jacob is reported as follows: "Et là-dessus: Je vous la laisse à tant, c'est marché donné. Non, c'est trop. Ce n'est pas assez. Bref, elles convinrent, et la robe de chambre me demeura" (166). Quite often false quotation is used to avoid mention of a specific person or place ("monsieur un tel," "en telle rue," "à telle auberge," "madame la marquise une telle"). On several occasions the false quotation is specifically attributed to the narrator's faulty memory: "Il y a dans un tel faubourg (je ne sais plus lequel c'était) une vieille femme" (177). It can be argued that false quotation and typified speech contribute to the narrator's conversational style and that they are more plausible than the convention of perfect recall.

In his initial presentation of one character, Mme. d'Alain, JN renders typified speech through FID. The portrait of Mme. d'Alain is combined with her first conversation with Habert and Jacob, which we need to quote in its entirety:

> [1] C'était la veuve d'un procureur qui lui avait laissé assez abondamment de quoi vivre, et qui vivait à proportion de son bien. Femme avenante au reste, à peu près de l'âge de Mlle Habert, aussi fraîche, et plus grasse qu'elle; un peu commère par le babil, mais commère d'un bon esprit, [2] qui vous prenait d'abord en amitié, qui vous ouvrait son coeur, vous contait ses affaires, vous demandait les vôtres, et puis revenait aux siennes,

et puis à vous. Vous parlait de sa fille, car elle en avait une; vous apprenait qu'elle avait dix-huit ans, vous racontait les accidents de son bas âge, ses maladies; tombait ensuite sur le chapitre de défunt son mari, en prenait l'histoire du temps qu'il était garçon, et puis venait à leurs amours, disait ce qu'ils avaient duré, passé de là à leur mariage, ensuite au récit de la vie qu'ils avaient menée ensemble; [3] c'était le meilleur homme du monde! très appliqué à son étude; aussi avait-il gagné du bien par sa sagesse et par son économie: un peu jaloux de son naturel, et aussi parce qu'il l'aimait beaucoup; sujet à la gravelle; Dieu sait ce qu'il avait souffert! les soins qu'elle avait eus de lui! Enfin, il était mort bien chrétiennement. (77)

The portrait begins rather conventionally in external focalization by the narrator [1], but several changes occur in [2]. The imperfect tense is no longer descriptive but iterative, suggesting habitualness. The verbs, most of which designate speech ("contait," "demandait," "parlait," "disait," etc.), express not her general situation but her specific actions during the conversation. The oblique pronoun "vous" occurs with nearly every verb, drawing the reader into the conversation on an equal footing with Habert and Jacob, who are the narratees of Mme. d'Alain. The rapid, paratactic sentence structure contributes to the impression of her "babil." Focalization is now internal, as we watch the character through the perception of JC. Finally in [3], we have a narrated monologue, marked by conversational exclamations without *verba dicendi*, sentence fragments, and lexical items that belong to the character. Mme. d'Alain herself is now the subject of perception, and we "hear" her speak. We might venture to say that no amount of psychological analysis by the narrator could create a more vivid impression of this woman's character.

A second observation concerning reported speech involves the generous use of asides or clarifications. JN reminds us of his presence many times by making parenthetical intrusions into the speech of the characters, in order to clarify a point that would not be obvious to the reader. These clarifications have several functions. First, they can serve to provide a referent for a name: "[a witness to the wedding is speaking] Est-ce que M. Doucin (parlant du prêtre) vous connaît?" (106); "Savez-vous, lui dit un de nos témoins, l'ami de l'hôtesse, ce que M. Doucin va dire à Mme d'Alain? (c'était le nom de notre hôtesse)" (107). Second, they can serve to provide a referent for a deictic expression: "[Habert] J'aime assez ce quartier-ci, me dit-elle (c'était du côté de Saint-Gervais" (76); "[Bono] Au reste, s'il ne vous donne pas un autre emploi (c'était à moi à qui il parlait, et de M. de Fécour) . . ." (212). Third, they can serve to validate or verify the speech of a character, including JC, from the perspective of hindsight: "[JC] Non, mademoiselle, lui dis-je alors, je ne crains rien (et cela était vrai)" (122); "[the prisoner] J'ai tué ma maîtresse, je l'ai vu expirer (et en effet, elle mourut quand on le ramena vers elle)" (155). Fourth and conversely, they can serve as a counterpoint to the speech of a character, to provide an insight from the narrator: "[Jacob's first master] Geneviève est une fille aimable, je protège ses parents, et ne l'ai même fait entrer chez moi que pour être plus à portée de lui rendre service, et de la bien placer. (Il mentait)" (25); "[Doucin to the Habert sisters] Nous parlons du jeune homme que vous avez retenu (cette jeunesse lui tenait au coeur)" (62). These last asides lead us to a significant problem shared by all personal narrators, the means of providing insight into the other characters.

JN's desire to report the speech of his characters leads him into one spatial infraction at the beginning of the novel: he quotes a conversation between the lady of the house and her chambermaid Toinette, which took place while JC was not present (21). Elsewhere he avoids this problem in the two famous eavesdropping scenes, which enable JC to witness the conversation between Doucin and the Habert sisters (60–66) and the one between Ferval and the *chevalier* (232–40). But he also provides a great deal of psychological insights into his characters, and we shall now turn to these.

What is especially noticeable about JN's psychological insights, particularly in comparison to those of Meilcour, is that very few are unjustified. Of these few cases, most are concerned with Geneviève and are thus concentrated at the beginning of the novel. JN resorts to the device of the lost letter to allow JC to know the details of Geneviève's relation to her master. JC's reading of this letter at some point (it is not situated in the chronology of events) may explain statements such as the following: "Geneviève avait fait à l'amour de son maître plus d'attention qu'elle ne me l'avait dit" (18). But it cannot justify the following examples of mind-reading:

> Dans la certitude où elle en était [of Jacob's love], et dans la peur qu'elle eut de me perdre . . . elle songea que les offres de monsieur . . . seraient des moyens d'accélérer notre mariage. Elle espéra que sa fortune . . . me tenterait à mon tour. (19)

> Volontiers, me dit-elle, charmée du goût que j'y prenais, et des conjectures favorables qu'elle en tirait pour le succès de ses vues. (22)

Later we read about Ferval: "Et ce qui est de plaisant, c'est que cette femme . . . ne savait pas qu'elle avait l'âme si méchante, le fond de son coeur lui échappait, son adresse la trompait, elle s'y attrapait elle-même, et parce qu'elle feignait d'être bonne, elle croyait l'être en effet" (143). These, however, are isolated examples. Most of the insights provided by JN are justified or justifiable in one way or another.

Sometimes JC's interpretation of another character's thoughts are only a reflection of his own, as in the following passage about Habert: "Pendant que nous avancions sans parler, ce qui venait, je crois, de ne savoir par où commencer pour entamer la conversation, j'aperçus un écriteau . . . et je saisis ce prétexte pour rompre un silence, dont, suivant toute apparence, nous étions tous deux embarrassés" (73). Like Meilcour, Jacob sometimes analyzes the thoughts of a character by placing him or her into a category: "M. le président baissait les yeux de l'air d'un homme qui veut rester grave, et qui retient une envie de rire" (127). Upon close inspection, numerous examples of the narrator's psychological penetration of others prove to be mere suppositions on his part. They may be identified as such by modal expressions such as "je crois," "sans doute," and "à ce qu'il me parut," and they are deduced from the keen observations of JC. When Jacob appears before the "tribunal," he carefully watches the *dévote* (Ferval) and the *présidente:* "Je n'avais pas négligé non plus de regarder la présidente, mais celle-là d'une manière humble et suppliante. J'avais dit des yeux à l'une: Il y a plaisir à vous voir, et elle m'avait cru; à l'autre: Protégez-moi, et elle me l'avait promis; car il me semble qu'elles m'avaient entendu toutes deux, et répondu ce que je vous dis là" (130). The reader is thus given insight into both women, yet by the narrator's own admission his account of their secret reactions is based only on the observations of the hero.

One of the narrator's most unusual techniques for revealing consciousness involves no focal transgression on his part. He often creates an imaginary monologue on the part of the character in order to reveal his or her thoughts. The imaginary nature of the speech is always freely admitted:

> [J]e suis persuadé qu'elle [Ferval] se disait: Je ne suis donc point de si mauvais goût, puisque tout le monde est de mon sentiment. (160)

> Asseyez-vous donc, me répéta-t-elle [Ferval] encore, du ton d'une personne qui vous dirait: Oubliez ce que je suis, et vivons sans façon. (172)

> Agathe avait le bras et la main passables, et je remarquais que la
> friponne jouait d'industrie pour les mettre en vue le plus qu'elle
> pouvait, comme si elle avait voulu me dire: Regardez, votre
> femme a-t-elle rien qui vaille cela? (247)

The narrator not only abridges and typifies the speech of others, but he
also invents their thoughts. These invented monologues are the imaginary creations of the narrator, and consequently he cannot be accused of
mind-reading. Technically, no change in focalization is involved, and yet
the intended effect is to give the reader the impression of gaining insight
into mental operations of the characters.

In sum, the narrator seems to be very conscious of his need to justify
his knowledge of other characters. After reporting the conversation between the Habert sisters he says: "Vous me direz: Comment avez-vous
su ces entretiens? C'était en ôtant la table, en rangeant dans la chambre
où elles étaient" (54). After tracing portraits of Agathe and Mme. de
Fécour, he feels the need to explain that they are the result of a long
experience, and he stresses the distinction between *then* and *now:*

> Ce ne fut pas sur-le-champ que je démêlai tout ce caractère que je
> développe ici, je ne le sentis qu'à force de voir Agathe. (88)

> Au reste, ce ne fut pas alors que je connus Mme de Fécour comme
> je la peins ici, car je n'eus pas dans ce temps une assez grande
> liaison avec elle, mais je la retrouvai quelques années après, et la
> vis assez pour la connaître. (181)

On the other hand, JN makes several remarks about justification of
knowledge and mind-reading that seem to be mocking in tone. After a
passage containing psychological incursions into Habert, Mme. d'Alain,
and Agathe, we read: "Je m'en aperçus à merveille; et cet art de lire dans
l'esprit des gens et de débrouiller leurs sentiments secrets est un don que
j'ai toujours eu et qui m'a quelquefois bien servi" (86). After a passage in
which the narrator gives possible explanations for the embarrassment of
Mme. d'Orville, we read: "Et ce sont là des remarques que tout le monde
peut faire, surtout dans les dispositions où j'étais" (210). Jacob admits to
being able to read minds and yet he protests that anyone can do as much
by keen observation. We might read these remarks as a self-conscious
parody of the problem inherent in memorialist conventions.[7]

---

7. We cannot agree with Mat (1977), however, that Marivaux rarely respects the limitations of his narrator, and certainly not with her statement that the intrusions into the

There are several occasions in which focalization is delegated, very briefly, to a character, whose thoughts are then revealed through narrated monologue. When Doucin, the *directeur de conscience* of the Habert sisters, realizes that he is losing his control over the younger sister, we read: "[1] L'ecclésiastique ne répondit rien à ce dévot et même tendre emportement qu'on marquait en sa faveur. [2] Ne conserver que l'aînée, c'était perdre beaucoup. [3] Il me sembla qu'il était extrêmement embarrassé" (66). In the three sentences of this passage, focalization shifts from [1] the narrator to [2] Doucin, whose thoughts are presented in FID, and then to [3] the eavesdropping hero. Wedged in between external and internal focalization, the narrated monologue is barely noticeable. Catherine's thoughts about the Habert sisters are revealed in a similar fashion: "dame Catherine n'avait jamais fait sa cour qu'à l'aînée . . . qui d'ailleurs avait toujours gouverné la maison. Mais la société des deux soeurs finissant, cela changeait la thèse, et il était bien plus doux de passer au service de la cadette dont elle aurait été la maîtresse" (81–82). If the second sentence is not recognized as FID, then it must be attributed focally to either narrator or hero, but clearly *someone* is perspicacious enough to read Catherine's mind. In the following passage it is the thoughts of Habert that are presented: "Toutes ces preuves de la discrétion de notre bonne hôtesse n'encourageaient point Mlle Habert: mais après lui avoir promis un secret, il était peut-être encore pis de le lui refuser que de le lui dire; ainsi il fallut parler" (100). All of the passages that we have examined could well be ascribed to a lucid narrator, and none can therefore be called a flagrant focal infraction. The next example is instructive in this regard. Jacob has just been released from prison, while Doucin and the elder Habert have just learned about his imprisonment from Mme. d'Alain. Upon returning home with the younger Habert, Jacob encounters his astounded sister-in-law and her confessor:

> [1] Jugez des espérances qu'ils en avaient tirées contre moi. [2] Un homme en prison, qu'a-t-il fait? Ce n'est pas nous qui avons part à cela; ce n'est pas le président non plus, qui a refusé de nous servir; il faut donc que ce soit pour quelque action étrangère à notre affaire. [1] Que sais-je s'ils n'allaient pas jusqu'à me soup-

---

consciousness of the hero reveal Marivaux's difficulty in respecting the restriction imposed by his own conventions (32). Whatever his transgressions toward others might be, the retrospective narrator always has access to the consciousness of his younger self. Nor can we agree with Coulet (1975), who states that justifications of the narrator's knowledge are rare in the novel (362).

çonner de quelque crime; ils me haïssaient assez tous deux pour avoir cette charitable opinion de moi. (161)

The beginning and the end of the quoted monologue are marked by the change of referents for the first- and third-person pronouns: in [1], "je" = Jacob and "ils" = Doucin and Habert, whereas in [2] "nous" = Doucin and Habert while "il" = Jacob. The narrator announces their speech and/ or thoughts before quoting them in unsignaled direct discourse, but then he admits not knowing what they might have thought. Passage [2] is thus easily identified as a supposition on his part. Narrated monologues, like imaginary quoted ones, may ultimately be attributable to the narrator and involve no real shift in focalization, yet they definitely give the impression of providing insight into the characters.

Sometimes the mind of another character is revealed by shifts in focalization between narrator and hero. Such is the case with Ferval, when she is surprised with Jacob by the *chevalier* at the house of Mme. Remy. JN sets up the scene with a cascade of directives to the reader ("Souvenez-vous," "songez," "n'oubliez pas"), reminding us that the *dévote* Ferval was in a terribly compromising situation and that the *chevalier* knew her well:

> [1] [E]t sur tous ces articles que je viens de dire, voyez la curieuse ré-vélation qu'on avait des moeurs de Mme de Ferval. [2] Le bel in-térieur de conscience à montrer, que de misères mises au jour, et quelles misères encore! [3] de celles qui déshonorent le plus une dé-vote, qui décident qu'elle est une hypocrite, une franche friponne. Car, qu'elle soit maligne, vindicative, orgueilleuse, médisante . . . tout cela ne jure point avec l'impérieuse austérité de son métier. [4] Mais se trouver convaincue d'être amoureuse, être surprise dans un rendez-vous gaillard, oh! tout est perdu; [5] voilà la dévote sifflée, il n'y a point de tournure à donner à cela. (227)

The focalization in [1] is clearly external, while [3] and [5] contain the narrator's sententious truths about *dévotes*. [2] and [4] are more ambigu-ous: they could represent the narrated monologue of the distraught Ferval; or the internal focalization of JC, who understood her emotion; or again the retrospective explanations of JN, on the same plane as [1], [3], and [5]. The narrator goes on to describe Ferval's embarrassed confu-sion and then turns his attention to JC:

> De mon côté, je ne savais que dire; ce nom de Jacob, qu'il m'avait appelé, me tenait en respect, j'avais toujours peur qu'il n'en

> recommençât l'apostrophe; et je ne songeais qu'à m'évader du
> mieux qu'il me serait possible; [1] car que faire là avec un rival
> pour qui on ne s'appelle que Jacob, et cela en présence d'une
> femme que cet excès de familiarité n'humiliait pas moins que moi?
> [2] Avoir un amant, c'était déjà une honte pour elle, et en avoir un
> de ce nom-là, c'en était deux; il ne pouvait pas être question entre
> elle et Jacob d'une affaire de coeur bien délicate. (227)

Whereas [1] concerns the mental agitations of Jacob, [2] reveals those of
Ferval. This entire passage could be an analysis by the narrator. On the
other hand, [1] could be internal focalization by a lucid JC, while [2]
could be focalized by either. In any case, we are left with no doubt about
the thoughts of Ferval during this scene. By contrast, we see none of
those of the *chevalier* except through his quoted speech in the following
pages.

As a narrator, Jacob holds a tight rein over the characters in his story.
He grants them focalization through quoted speech, but he controls our
response to that speech by arranging it and by interrupting it to provide
clarifications. While rarely transgressing his limitations concerning their
thoughts, he nonetheless makes avowed suppositions and even inven-
tions that give the impression of providing psychological insights. Finally, the fusion and confusion of the two registers of narrator and hero
obfuscate any overt incursion into the minds of the characters while
furnishing information about them that seems to come from observation
and reflection.

Tense and Temporal Ambiguity

We have seen that the narrator attempts to draw the reader into his act of
communication, and how he strives to reduce the distance between
himself and his younger incarnation. We shall now turn to his means of
drawing the reader into the fictional world of JC by obliterating the
distinctions between past, present, and future.

According to Benveniste (1966–74), historical narration (*histoire*) is the
objective recounting of events outside the person of a narrator. Its fundamental tense is the preterite, and its temporal period of reference is kept
separate from the moment of utterance by both tense and spatiotemporal indicators. Whereas discourse is characterized by involvement
of the speaker, preterite narration is detached from and anterior to the
here-and-now of narrator and reader. But even the preterite, as it dis-

tances the narrator from the hero, allows for an actualization of the latter's experience by the reader, for whom the events have yet to "take place" as he reads. The preterite is a sign indicating that events have taken place only for the narrator, not for the reader, whose experience is always simultaneous with that of the hero (except when the narrator affords us proleptic insights). In this sense, the hero and the reader share the same future, a future that has nothing to do with tense. Marivaux exploits this future in a most unusual way.

The narrator's use of the "historical" present tense does not really enhance this process of actualization, because it is not a tense of discourse but rather a substitute for the preterite.[8] Let us look at a passage from *Le Paysan parvenu* in which events are recounted in the present tense:

> Et là-dessus elle [Fécour] embrasse Mme de Ferval qui la re-mercie, qu'elle remercie, s'appuie sans façon sur mon bras, m'emmène, me fait monter dans son carrosse, m'y appelle tantôt monsieur, tantôt mon bel enfant, m'y parle comme si nous nous fussions connus depuis dix ans, toujours cette grosse gorge en avant, et nous arrivons chez elle. (185)

The narrative present is "a stylistic artifice" (Benveniste 1966–74, 1:245), a traditional device often used to accentuate an event and to produce a dramatic or emotive effect. Here and elsewhere in the novel, it seems to function as a means of synopsis, of passing quickly over the transition from one scene to another. Its intermittent use, providing a relief from the historical *passé simple,* may well be perceived as more vivid by some readers, but it clearly has nothing to do with the here-and-now of the speaker. It does not signal the coincidence of event and discourse, as the present tense normally does.

If the sporadic substitution of the historical present represents a rather banal attempt to convey a sense of involvement and immediacy, it is totally consistent with the conventions of historical narration that pre-

---

8. Hamburger ([1975] 1973) argues that it is only in first-person narration that the historical present retains its "past-ness" vis-à-vis the autobiographer, so that its historical character emerges clearly. The narrator "presentifies" the experience for the reader, yet the latter's consciousness of time is not altered (100). Casparis (1975) maintains that the historical present in first-person narration reflects the narrator's attitude toward the experience he relates, or the degree of narrative distance, which is a nontemporal quality (103). Margolin (1984) uses the historical present as an example of "displaced time and space deixis," in which the speaker places himself at the moment of event and refers to all other events in relation to that point, rather than in relation to the moment of speech (200).

vailed in the memoir-novel. On the other hand, Marivaux introduces certain elements of discourse into his narrative in a most unusual way. We shall look first at the use of person and then at that of tense. Both elements result in examples of narrative metalepsis, defined as the intrusion of narrator or narratee into the diegetic world of the characters (Genette 1972, 244). The novelist plays on the double temporality of story and narration, of historical utterance and discourse, as though they were contemporaneous.

As we have seen, the use of personal forms is a characteristic of discourse, which assumes a speaker and an other. The narrator uses second-person address, rather conventionally, to direct the reader's attention and to anticipate and represent the latter's response. More important, the second person sometimes forces the reader to assume the role of a character. Let us consider the following passages:

> Quand vous lui [Fécour] plaisiez, par exemple, cette gorge dont j'ai parlé, il semblait qu'elle vous la présentât, c'était moins pour tenter votre coeur que pour vous dire que vous touchiez le sien. (180)

> Oh! mariez-vous après trente ans d'une vie de cette force-là, trouvez-vous du soir au matin l'épouse d'un homme, c'est déjà beaucoup; j'ajoute aussi d'un homme que vous aimerez d'inclination, ce qui est encore plus, et vous serez pour lors une autre Mlle Habert. (163)

The "vous" of both passages is a substitute for "on," but not an entirely innocent one. Both represent attempts to convert the time and space of the reader into those of the characters—Jacob in the first and Habert in the second—and to bring them all into the same world. Coulet (1975) points out that the substitution of "vous" as the oblique form of the impersonal pronoun "on" makes the reader an accomplice in the plot (202, n. 64).

The reader can be included in the narrator's rather extensive use of the amplified first person, another sign of discourse ("you" + "I" = "we"). At times used to designate characters ("notre ecclésiastique," "nos trois hommes"), the first-person plural is more often found in the form of a command ("commençons," "revenons," "retournons"). These forms do not necessarily constitute a metaleptic intrusion but indicate discourse between narrator and reader. They imply an immediate relationship between speaker and receiver, as well as a necessary reference to the moment of utterance (Benveniste 1966–74, 2:84). The amplified first person, however, can also be exclusive of the second-person reader, including instead one or more of the characters ("I" + "he/she/they" = "we"). This becomes clear in the following passage: "Je ne vous dirai rien de *notre* entretien sur la route; arrivons à Paris, *nous* y entrâmes d'assez bonne heure" (217). The italicized forms refer to Jacob and his fellow travelers, while the imperative "arrivons" includes narrator and reader. All of them include the "I" of Jacob/M. de la Vallée. This indiscriminate mingling of inclusive and exclusive personal forms tends to blur the distinction between the diegetic world of the hero and the extradiegetic world of the reader. The narrator's liberal use of direct address to his reader, in both first and second persons, results in the confusion of the spatial and temporal planes of the *énonciation* with those of the *énoncé*.

The narrator is capable of keeping the planes separate, according to memoir-novel logic. At times he is careful to distinguish, by means of tense, between the hero's time and his own, as in the following examples:

> J'ai bien vu depuis des objets de ce genre-là qui m'ont toujours plu, mais jamais tant qu'ils me plurent alors. (172)

> Je ne fis pourtant pas alors cette réflexion; je la fais seulement à présent que j'écris. (262)

At other times, however, he seems to lose sight of this distinction and asks the reader to do one thing while the characters do another, as though the temporality of the story and that of the narration were one and the same:

> Mais laissons-les [Doucin and the elder Habert] dans leur confusion, et arrivons chez la bonne Mlle Habert. (161)

> [J]e sortis pour aller chez moi. Remarquez, chemin faisant, l'inconstance des choses de ce monde. (244)

These are classic examples of metalepsis, further enhancing the impression that hero, narrator, and reader inhabit the same time and space. Metalepsis also occurs, as we shall see, when the same verbal tense is applied to different temporal points of reference.

Tense is not indicative of time in the absolute sense but only in the relative sense. Verb forms do not locate an event in time but rather relate it to a specific point of reference. In other words, tense is used to designate a sequence of events with respect to a referential axis, the present instance of discourse.[9] A narrator who says "I," "you," "here," and "now" localizes his events as being contemporaneous with his discourse. All other references, anterior or posterior to this moment, can be situated and distanced from the speaker by means of verbal tense.

The most curious element of discourse in *Le Paysan parvenu* is an anomalous use of the future tense. Let us first distinguish between three types of future time represented in the novel. Future 1, an *appellative future*, refers forward to the moment of reading, or reception. The narrator points toward a future time that becomes the reader's present as he reads: "Le récit de mes aventures ne sera pas inutile" (6); "parmi les faits que j'ai à raconter, je crois qu'il y en aura de curieux" (6); "on trouvera peut-être les représentations . . . un peu longues" (27); "Je crois que ce détail n'ennuiera point" (46). This story, these facts and events, are part of the narrator's past, but they have yet to be discovered by the reader. Such statements refer to what Jacques Proust calls an imaginary future (47), a time not yet experienced but actualized with each reading. They are directed toward a second person, an "other," whether or not they actually contain second-person verb forms: "quelques personnes pourront me reconnaître" (7); "comme on le verra dans la suite" (12); "vous me direz" (54).

Future 2, an *expressive future*, refers to the narrator's own future, which becomes a present for him as he writes: "je les écrirai du mieux que je pourrai" (6); "je conterai toute ma vie" (9); "je ferai le portrait dans un moment" (125); "je n'en dirai pas de lui davantage" (125). These statements are in the future tense only because they represent the narrator's intentions. There is actually little or no difference between their temporal locus and the present moment of narration, which is unique and without progression: they refer to the spatiality of the text and to the temporality of the reader (Genette 1972, 234, n. 1). Indeed, both futures 1 and 2 are "anchored" on the narrator's instance of discourse. What distinguishes them, in the final analysis, is the personal pronoun: future 1 is addressed to the other ("vous verrez"), while future 2 refers back to the self ("je conterai"). Writing is necessarily anterior to reading.

Future 3, by contrast, the *referential future*, is anchored on the moment of event.[10] It refers forward to the hero's future (as yet unknown to him), but which becomes a present as he lives and as the reader reads. It is always a past for the narrator, who is telling his story from a retrospective

9. See Benveniste 1966–74, 2:74–75, and Casparis 1975, 103–4.
10. Morot-Sir (1982), from whom I borrow the term "anchor," describes the "extralinguistic anchor of reference" of a text as "the projection of language outside of the speech act [*énonciation*], and the formation of a field of reference [*énoncé*] 'disjoined' from the speech act" (121–22).

point of view. Future 3 constitutes the substance of prolepsis, or anticipation of posterior events. Indeed, it is the lapse of time between event and narration, between the moment of the hero's story and that of the narrator's discourse, that allows the latter to exploit the dramatic possibilities of the former's pseudofuture. According to the grammatical logic of memorialist convention, this pseudofuture can be expressed formally only in direct quotation, which allows for the intrusion of discourse into the narrative: "Voyons ce qu'ils deviendront, dis-je en moi-même . . . quel parti prendra-t-elle?" (241–42). Otherwise, the formal future is necessarily excluded from historical narration as it cannot refer to the moment of a past event. It is subjective, not objective. To designate an impending event in the story, a narrator might use what Benveniste (1966–74) calls the "prospective," a periphrastic substitute for the future ("nous allions continuer," 12; "il devait enfin lui fonder une pension," 18–19); or he may use indirect speech, in which historical utterance can merge with discourse through the conditional tense ("on vint me dire que deux personnes me demandaient en bas, qu'elles ne monteraient point," 149).

In order to express posteriority (future 3), it is common for futures 1 and 2 to coincide, the former referring to the temporality of reception and the latter to the spatiality of the text. The two are often joined by the classical formula of prolepsis, "nous verrons plus tard" or "plus loin." Marivaux, however, sometimes plays on the futurity of discovery shared by hero and reader and thus achieves the coincidence of all three future times. At such moments he eschews all formal substitutes in favor of the future tense, a proleptic future that refers to events that are temporally past for the narrator but spatially yet to be told, and thus are yet to happen for both the hero and the reader. Let us look at some isolated sentences of the text:

[1] Vous *verrez* dans les suites où cela nous *conduira.* (58)

[2] Quand ma compagne fut partie, je quittai ma robe de chambre (*laissez*-moi en parler pendant qu'elle me *réjouit*, cela ne *durera* pas; j'y *serai* bientôt accoutumé), je m'habillai. (250)

[3] Voilà tout ce que je *dirai* de lui [M. d'Orville] à cet égard. C'en est assez sur un homme que je n'ai guère vu, et dont la femme *sera* bientôt veuve. (255)

In the first example, the future tense is used to represent first the future of the reader and then that of the characters. The latter verb, however, is rendered ambiguous by the first-person pronoun, including in its referent both the characters ("I" + "they") and the reader ("I" + "you"). In the second example, the tenses of discourse refer first to the present time of the narrator and reader ("let me speak" *now*) and then to that of the hero ("it delights me" *then*), whereas the reference point of the future time is that of both the reader and the hero ("that will not last," for me *then* nor for you *now* as you read), as though the moment of event and that of speech were the same. The third example reveals still another ambiguous future: while the first verb refers to the future of the narrator, the second could refer to that of either the narrator or the hero, depending on whether or not Mme. d'Orville is a widow at the moment of utterance, which we do not know. As in the previous sentence, the adverb "bientôt" is deictic, but it is not clear to which instance of discourse it points. What is common to all three paradigms is that, paradoxically, the future experience of all three narrative existents is the same: the hero will live through what the narrator will tell, which the reader will read.[11]

Marivaux's use of this ambiguous future is not limited to isolated sentences. On one occasion the coincidence of futures 1 and 3 (of reader and hero) is achieved more concisely through the effacement of the narrator. The transitional scene in which Jacob and Mlle. Habert leave the latter's house and move into that of Mme. d'Alain (83–84) contains an excellent example of play on temporality. In our analysis of this scene, we shall represent the moment of speech as S, the reference period as R, and the event as E. E may be relative either to R or to S. In "absolute" time E is always viewed in relation to S, to the here-and-now of the speaker; in "relative" time E is viewed in relation to R, a different temporal setting that is established as the basis for a sequence of events. The sequence $R–E–S$ indicates posteriority, such as in the sentence "He promised me he would arrive the next day": R is the moment of the promise, and E, the posterior moment of arrival. Both are anterior to speech. The sequence $R–S–E$, as in the sentence "He promised me he would arrive tomorrow," indicates true futurity: the moment of speech is posterior to the promise, but anterior to the arrival. Futurity is deictic in that the speaker is looking forward from his or her present time of speech.[12]

The scene begins with an intrusion by the narrator, of the kind we have

11. The interference of several temporal planes has been noticed by several critics: Fabre 1979, 88, n. 9; Proust 1980, 44; and concerning the same phenomenon in *La Vie de Marianne*, Didier 1980, 161. In another article, Didier (1981) enumerates the functions of prolepsis in *Marianne* but does not distinguish between classical prolepsis and the ambiguous use of the future tense also found in that novel (103–4).

12. Our notational system is based on Fleischman 1982, 10–17.

come to expect in the memoir-novel format: "Il me tarde d'en venir à de plus grands événements; ainsi passons vite à notre nouvelle maison." We should note the first-person forms: "passons" means "you" and "I," reader and narrator, while "notre" refers to the house of the characters. Yet the reader, who is also about to move into the new house, seems to be included in both plural forms. Once the reader enters the diegetic world of the hero, preterite narration disappears. The shift from historical narration to discourse is signaled by the intrusion of the *passé composé*, "the autobiographical form par excellence" (Benveniste 1966–74, 1:244): "Le tapissier est venu le lendemain, nos meubles sont partis, nous avons dîné debout."[13] Since the deictic center of this tense is the moment of utterance rather than the moment of event, one gets the impression that the narrator's present has disappeared momentarily, that the hero's present is now the moment of speech, and that Jacob is recounting events of his recent past. The sequence here is R–E–S: the past tense locates the period of reference as anterior to speech, while the temporal adverb "le lendemain" indicates posteriority of the event. The verb of the following sentence clearly situates the reader in the present of the hero: "Catherine, convaincue enfin qu'elle ne nous suivra pas, nous a traités à l'avenant." This future indicates, not posteriority, not a pseudofuture usually expressed by means of periphrastic substitutes, but instead a true futurity anchored on the moment of the hero's utterance and looking forward from his present. It is as though the discourse were now emanating from JC, as though the narrator had disappeared momentarily. The sequence produced here is R–S–E.[14] In absolute time, however, these events are clearly in the narrator's past, and only spatially in his future as he writes. After a series of verbs in the *passé composé*, the formal present appears and refers to the present of young Jacob: "elle m'a voulu battre, moi qui *ressemble* à ce défunt Baptiste. . . ." The next sentence contains a variety of the tenses of discourse: "Mlle Habert *a écrit* un petit billet qu'elle *a laissé* sur la table pour sa soeur, et par lequel elle *l'avertit* que

13. Deloffre's (1967) position regarding the use of the *passé composé* in this passage is rather confusing. At first he says that the *passé composé* is impossible in retrospective narration (218); then he states that it is rare and appears only when the narrator wishes to resituate himself in a past moment (219); finally he maintains that as in Marivaux's comedies, the *passé composé* is used to narrate events that have occurred on the same day as their narration (400). It is clear that the day of these events is far removed from the narrator's present time. Moreover, Deloffre makes no mention of the future tense.

14. Proust (1980) describes this shift as a sudden jump of the past into the narrator's consciousness, as though the peasant momentarily effaces the older parvenu (47). Bourgeacq (1975) describes it as Jacob's appropriation of the narrator's psychological present (170). We could also say that focalization has been delegated to JC, who becomes the subject of perception.

dans sept ou huit jours elle *viendra* pour s'arranger avec elle, et régler quelques petits intérêts qu'elles *ont* à vider ensemble." The deictic indicator "dans sept ou huit jours" reinforces the hero's temporal locus: the sister has not yet come back to settle her affairs.[15]

This first paragraph constitutes a break from historical narration in a consistent way, in that the moment of event is established as the deictic center of all the tenses. The second paragraph contains, on the contrary, a confusion of time planes:

> Nous voilà à l'autre maison; et c'est d'ici qu'on va voir mes aventures devenir plus nobles et plus importantes; c'est ici où ma fortune commence: serviteur au nom de Jacob, il ne sera plus question que de monsieur de la Vallée; nom que j'ai porté pendant quelque temps . . . c'est sous cet autre nom qu'on me connaît dans le monde; c'est celui-ci qu'il n'est pas nécessaire que je dise et que je ne pris qu'après la mort de Mlle Habert.

The deictic "ici" refers all at once to the here-and-now of the narrator ("at this point in my story"), to that of the hero ("at this moment of my life"), and to that of the reader ("at this point in your reading"). The ambiguity is prolonged by a combination of the reader's future ("on va voir") with the future of the hero ("il ne sera plus question"), and of the narrator's present ("on me connaît") with his past ("je ne pris qu'après la mort de Mlle Habert"). The last example also contains a proleptic pseudofuture, a reference to a death that has not yet been witnessed by the hero or reader. This entire two-paragraph passage is both opened and closed by an imperative ("passons vite à notre nouvelle maison" and "passons à l'autre maison"). These examples of metalepsis also contribute to the impression that the narrator and reader are contemporaneous with the hero and can move with him to his new home.

In the scene of Jacob's wedding (162–63), the imperative form is again used to introduce discourse and to displace its temporal locus to that of the experiencing hero. The focal shift between the narrator and the hero can be seen by a transfer of deictic center within the same sentence:

> Mais tous ces menus récits m'*ennuient* moi-même; sautons-les, et supposons que le soir est venu, que nous avons soupé avec nos

15. Bronzwaer (1976) states that when a deictic time-adverb combines with a past tense (e.g., "Tomorrow I was going to be married"), there is not only a change in perspective from the narrator to the character, but the adverb also signals an "empathic involvement" of the narrator in the events he is describing (56). In our passage from Marivaux, however, the adverbial "dans sept ou huit jours" does not bear this burden alone.

témoins, qu'il *est* deux heures après minuit, et que nous *partons* pour l'église. Enfin pour le coup nous y sommes, la messe est dite, et nous voilà mariés en dépit de notre soeur aînée et du directeur son adhérent, qui n'*aura* plus ni café ni pains de sucre de Mme de la Vallée.

While the first verb in the present tense refers to the time of narration, the others signify the present moment of events. Once again we are confronted with an ambiguous future tense, one that could express the thought of either hero or narrator.

Another fusion and confusion of time planes occurs in the passage in which the narrator reflects on his love for Mme. de la Vallée (247–48). His discourse intrudes upon his story as he refers to his here-and-now by means of the present and future tenses: "C'est pour la dernière fois que je fais ces sortes de détails; et à l'égard d'Agathe, je pourrai en parler encore; mais de ma façon de vivre avec Mme de la Vallée, je n'en dirai plus mot." Then comes a temporal displacement:

> Nous voilà mariés; je sais tout ce que je lui dois; j'irai toujours au-devant de ce qui pourra lui faire plaisir; je suis dans la fleur de mon âge; elle est encore fraîche, malgré le sien. . . . Mme de la Vallée, toute tendre qu'elle est, n'est point jalouse; je n'ai point de compte importun à lui rendre de mes actions, qui jusqu'ici, comme vous voyez, n'ont déjà été que trop infidéles. . . . Suis-je absent, Mme de la Vallée souhaite ardemment mon retour, mais l'attend en paix; me revoit-elle? point de questions, la voilà charmée, pourvu que je l'aime, et je l'aimerai.

The spatial designator "voilà" serves, in this case, as a temporal shifter: it performs the antideictic operation of shifting our period of reference back to the there-and-then of the story. Immediately thereafter, the present and future tenses become anchored on the moment of event, the here-and-now of the experiencing hero. The passage seems to represent an unsignaled interior monologue, devoid of inquit phrases such as "me dis-je," and in which events of the past are recounted in the hero's present. This impression is reinforced by the fact that we know (and the narrator knows) that Mme. de la Vallée has since died. Clearly, she is no longer "fraîche," while the older narrator is no longer in the flower of his youth.[16] Nor can we consider this use of the present tense to be that of

16. The announced deaths of Mlle. Habert and M. d'Orville, neither of which is realized textually, make it difficult to understand the statement by Thomas (1973) that

the historical present, for it is used descriptively and iteratively to evoke persons and events that are long past for the narrator. When the latter says "je l'aimerai," he is once again reverting to a formal future to express futurity rather than posteriority–a futurity that can only belong to the hero. But the deictic "jusqu'ici" reintroduces confusion ("until this point" in my life/in my story/in your reading). It is followed by "comme vous voyez," another shifter that brings us forward to the discourse between narrator and narratee. The confusion is prolonged into the next paragraph:

> [Q]u'on suppose entre nous le ménage le plus doux et le plus tranquille; [1] tel sera le nôtre; et [2] je ne ferai plus mention d'elle que dans les choses où par hasard [3] elle se trouvera mêlée. Hélas! [4] bientôt ne sera-t-elle plus de rien dans tout ce qui me regarde; le moment qui doit me l'enlever n'est pas loin, et [5] je ne serai pas longtemps sans revenir à elle pour faire le récit de sa mort et celui de la douleur que j'en eus.

What is remarkable here is the use of the same tense, the future, to refer forward alternately from the moment of event, [1] and [3], the moment of narration, [2] and [5], and both moments at the same time [4]. Curiously, the same narrative voice that knows his married life *will be* happy and who refers to his wife in the present, also knows that she *will disappear* soon from his narration. The *passé simple* of the final verb, supported by the shifter "ce jour-là" of the following sentence, indicates a return to historical narration.

While the memoir-novel format is quite conducive to the intrusion of discursive elements into the historical narrative, Marivaux's use of these elements is certainly anomalous. Although there are some signs of dissonance, there is little condemnation forthcoming from the narrator. On the other hand, his discourse is not overtly rhetorical. More important than any calculated effort to justify or defend the hero is his attempt to collapse the temporal distance that separates them. The double register exists, but the two selves cannot be neatly compartmentalized. The text does not merely shift back and forth between external and internal focalization but presents a blending of the two, which leads to a fusion of time planes. In particular, we find a future tense that combines with certain deictic indicators and that refers not to historical times and places but to the present instance of discourse, thereby resituating the narrator

---

"throughout the novel, the storyteller does not refer to a single experience which the reader does not actually witness" (364).

and reader in the temporal locus of the hero. The same verbal tense is thus used for three different temporal points of reference: the moments of event, of narration, and of reception. The effect is to confuse the instance of discourse, to bring the hero and the reader into the same coextensive and contemporaneous world, and to efface the distance between them.

3

MANON LESCAUT: MANIPULATION AND RELIABILITY

Manon Lescaut differs from *Les Égarements* and *Le Paysan* in at least two ways. It is not, strictly speaking, a memoir-novel insofar as the principal narrator has not written a text about his life. Instead, the work forms a kind of addendum to Prévost's larger memoir-novel about the Marquis de Renoncour. The extradiegetic narrator of *Manon Lescaut* begins by telling of his two encounters with the Chevalier des Grieux, who then tells his own story orally, so that the greater part of the novel is an embedded or metadiegetic narrative.[1] A more important difference concerns Des Grieux's rhetorical purpose. Unlike Meilcour and Jacob, who seem to be telling a story for its own sake and with a certain amusement, Des Grieux–narrator (DGN) is intensely serious about the task at hand. He makes every effort to persuade his listeners that Des Grieux–character (DGC) deserves their sympathy and compassion. No longer in need of assistance from Renoncour, he nonetheless wants the respect of a man he considers to be his peer, and this need for self-justification distinguishes him from the other narrators we have examined. It is in part because his rhetorical manipulation is so palpable that critics have come to speak of his unreliability as a narrator.[2] In our analysis of Des

---

1. I agree with Stewart (1984) that there is no stylistic evidence in the text to indicate that it was narrated orally rather than in written form (161, n. 34). Des Grieux's references to his narratees do not confer an oral quality to the text. Indeed, *Le Paysan parvenu* seems in many ways more conversational than Prévost's novel.

2. Monty (1970) ascribes the unreliability to "a tendentious presentation of the facts" (49). For Sermain (1985b) it is the narrator's need to justify himself that gives evidence of

Grieux we shall isolate and consider separately three aspects of his persona: (1) elements of discourse that are anchored on the spatiotemporal situation of his storytelling, (2) DGN's retrospective presentation of DGC, or external focalization, and (3) DGC's vision at the moment of event, or internal focalization.

Narrator's Discourse

Like most narrators, Des Grieux interrupts his historical narration with references to his present speech situation. He describes himself in the present for the benefit of his narratees: he comes from a good family, he is good-natured, sensitive, faithful, and clever. He makes occasional comments that link his past experience to the present: "J'ai remarqué, dans toute ma vie" (124); "j'ai éprouvé, dans la suite" (183). Other than the final sentence of the novel, revealing his intention to return home to meet his brother, he refers to his future only once. During the studious period in his father's house Des Grieux wrote a commentary on the *Aeneid*, and the narrator says: "je le destine à voir le jour, et je me flatte que le public en sera satisfait" (38). DGN uses the achronic present to make statements about his world, to give geographic precisions about France and New Orleans, and to state general truths supposedly shared by his narratees. While some of these are neutral in tone, others have a rhetorical function in that they are designed to show the hero in a favorable light or to excuse his conduct:

> [J]e l'exhortais [Tiberge] à n'être pas plus scrupuleux qu'un grand nombre d'évêques et d'autres prêtres, qui savent accorder fort bien une maîtresse avec un bénéfice. (65)

his bad faith and sophistry: "the confession of Des Grieux consists entirely of a struggle against the speech of others" (397). Elsewhere Sermain (1985a) states that Des Grieux almost always announces his goal of persuasion, and by emphasizing premeditation he invites suspicion (44–45). Brady (1977) points to Des Grieux's lying, his deceit, and his vanity as posing problems of credibility, but also to the convention of perfect memory (48–52). This last criticism, however, could be leveled at every personal narrator. We must remember that we are dealing here with a *convention* and that readers tend not to question a narrator's powers of recall. Grahame Jones (1978) calls Des Grieux unreliable but states that the reader is induced to trust his vision (58), and Gossman (1968) agrees that most readers will not doubt the objective validity of his testimony (98).

> Comme il n'y avait rien, après tout, dans le gros de ma conduite, qui pût me déshonorer absolument, du moins en la mesurant sur celle des jeunes gens d'un certain monde, et qu'une maîtresse ne passe point pour une infamie dans le siècle où nous sommes, non plus qu'un peu d'adresse à s'attirer la fortune du jeu . . . (163)

> Je n'étais pas non plus de ces libertins outrés, qui font gloire d'ajouter l'irréligion à la dépravation des moeurs. (190)

These achronic statements belong to discourse but are inseparable from DGN's retrospective presentation of DGC. Compared to our other narrators, DGN is more sparing with this type of intrusion. He is far less sententious than Meilcour, and less generous with his present reflections than Jacob.[3]

A number of discursive elements call attention to DGN's storytelling process. Some of these have an emotive function in that they foreground the presence of Des Grieux as he narrates: "Le dirai-je à ma honte?" (64); "une retraite que j'ai horreur de nommer" (79); "Je dois confesser" (195). Many of these contain forms of direct address and remind us that DGN is relating his story to Renoncour and the young marquis. They may be proleptic references to later events in the story ("vous verrez"), or appeals to the imagination of the listeners ("figurez-vous"), or simply reminders of the storytelling situation ("Après ce que vous venez d'entendre," 201). It should be noted that the discursive pronoun "vous" has three separate referents. In the examples already cited, it is a plural form that designates the two listeners. In several cases toward the end of the story, "vous" is a singular and refers to Renoncour's role as an intradiegetic character: "l'état où vous m'avez vu à Pacy" (125), "Vous en fûtes témoin à Pacy" (182), and so on.[4] Finally, on one occasion the narrator interrupts his story to address God: "O Dieu! que mes voeux étaient vifs et sincères! et par quel rigoureux jugement aviez-vous résolu de ne les pas exaucer!" (199).

3. I owe this quantitative comparison in part to Frautschi (1972), whose study shows that Prévost's discreet use of the "present axis" in contrast with the preponderance of the "retrospective axis" differs radically from the more generous use of the present plane by Marivaux (104). From this *relative* discretion we should not conclude, as do Deloffre and Picard (1965), that Des Grieux almost always effaces himself as a narrator (cxvi, n. 1). On the contrary, interventions by the narrator are quite numerous. They are present, says Ehrard (1975), on an average of one page out of two (496).

4. Sermain (1985b) contends that while elements of direct address become more frequent at the end of the novel, the presence of the Marquis is by then so effaced that the reader can be assimilated into the "vous" (395). On the contrary, as the story reaches the episode at Pacy, "vous" assumes an intradiegetic referent and clearly designates Renoncour.

Des Grieux also reveals his present emotions to his listeners: he is still astonished at the boldness of his initial behavior toward Manon; he knows he should shed tears over his past treatment of Tiberge; he fears his past conduct has contributed to the death of his father, and so on. More important, he reveals that he is a most unhappy man: "Ce qui fait mon désespoir a pu faire ma félicité. Je me trouve le plus malheureux de tous les hommes" (25). He still, at the moment of speech, thinks fondly of Manon: "je trouve encore de la douceur dans un souvenir qui me représente sa tendresse et les agréments de son esprit" (119). The narration of her death is extremely painful and difficult to perform: "Pardonnez, si j'achève en peu de mots un récit qui me tue. Je vous raconte un malheur qui n'eut jamais d'exemple. Toute ma vie est destinée à le pleurer" (199).

At times Des Grieux must admit his failure as a narrator: at moments of intense emotion the hero's joy, his despair, the disorders of his soul cannot be expressed in words. Again we are crossing the theoretical line that separates discourse from retrospection. The chief reason why DGN cannot find words to express the emotions of DGC is that they are, he says, unique and exceptional. One of the functions of his discourse is to set up a dichotomy between noble sentiments (like his own) and vulgar ones, between unique experiences (his own) and common ones. The situations and emotions of DGC are such that they often cannot be explained or understood by others:

> Ce fut une de ces situations uniques auxquelles on n'a rien éprouvé qui soit semblable. On ne saurait les expliquer aux autres, parce qu'ils n'en ont pas l'idée. (69)

> Il y a peu de personnes qui connaissent la force de ces mouvements particuliers du coeur. Le commun des hommes n'est sensible qu'à cinq ou six passions. . . . Mais les personnes d'un caractère plus noble peuvent être remuées de mille façons différentes . . . et . . . elles ont un sentiment de cette grandeur qui les élève au-dessus du vulgaire. (81)

The dichotomy is set up in a way that conditions our response in favor of DGC: "Un barbare aurait été attendri des témoignages de ma douleur et de ma crainte" (30); "Où trouver un barbare qu'un repentir si vif et si tendre n'eût pas touché?" (47). In the words of Stewart (1984), these passages reflect an "insidious (and compelling) . . . rhetoric, which puts all the good sentiments on one side" (134). DGN imagines a spectator who witnesses the passion and the suffering of DGC and who is moved by them, as opposed to the "barbare" who is neither "honnête" nor "sensible." The reader, like the narratees, must choose between the vulgar masses and the noble elite.[5] Not only does the dichotomy stack the deck in favor of DGC, it is also intended to lead the reader to accept the narrator's position on the hostility of God and the overwhelming and fatal power of passion. Ideologically, DGN's discourse characterizes him as one who values love as the supreme happiness, who rejects Heaven and holds no doubt about love's power:

> Je suis persuadé qu'il n'y a point d'honnête homme au monde qui n'eût approuvé mes vues dans les circonstances où j'étais. . . . Mais se trouvera-t-il quelqu'un qui accuse mes plaintes d'injustice, si je gémis de la rigueur du Ciel à rejeter un dessein que je n'avais formé que pour lui plaire? Hélas! que dis-je, à le rejeter? Il l'a puni comme un crime. (191)

> S'il est vrai que les secours célestes sont à tous moments d'une force égale à celle des passions, qu'on m'explique donc par quel funeste ascendant on se trouve emporté tout d'un coup loin de son devoir, sans se trouver capable de la moindre résistance, et sans ressentir le moindre remords. (43)

This last passage contains an example of what Sermain (1985b) calls the "terrorist power of the indefinite": the impersonal pronoun "on" permits a personal case to become the model for all sensitive readers, and response becomes impossible (394).

Although the narrator likes to be seen as a victim of passion, it is quite clear that the supreme value in his present ideology is the pleasure of love: "Dieux! pourquoi nommer le monde un lieu de misères, puisqu'on y peut goûter de si charmantes délices?" (66). We shall return to this question of ideology shortly. For the moment, we can say that our analysis confirms the contention of several critics that it is not possible to speak of a religious conversion on the part of Des Grieux.[6] If conversion there had been, then signs of it could be seen in the discourse of DGN's present moment of speech. Instead, we see a narrator who valorizes sensual pleasure and who condemns Heaven as either helpless or hostile. He admits that after Manon's death "le Ciel . . . m'éclaira de ses lumières" (202), but this seems to mean only that it dissuaded him from

---

5. It seems safe to say that Des Grieux's intended effect on his narratees is equal to Prévost's intentions toward the reader. For the sake of simplicity, therefore, I will generally equate "narratee" and "reader."

6. Josephs (1986, 195); Stewart (1984, 153); Ehrard (1975, 500).

suicide and prompted his return to France. His only plans are to return home and to publish his commentary on Vergil. He feels doomed to spend the rest of his life mourning Manon, and he expresses little regret for anything else.[7]

External Focalization

Numerous critics have pointed out that it is often difficult to distinguish narrator from hero, both stylistically and morally, that there is no tension between *then* and *now,* and that Prévost is unwilling to maintain an ironic distance between the hero and the reader.[8] This general tendency toward consonance should not blind us, however, to many signs of the dissonant narrator that are present in the novel. Just as DGN often refers to his spatiotemporal situation as a speaker, he also presents DGC from an extradiegetic vantage point as though the latter were another character. As an external focalizer, he enjoys the privilege of hindsight.

In the early part of the text DGN, like most dissonant narrators, insists on the hero's innocence and lack of experience ("n'ayant point assez d'expérience pour imaginer," 21). Unlike the case of Meilcour, the emphasis on naïveté disappears rather quickly, as Des Grieux learns the ways of the world. We are not dealing here with a *roman d'apprentissage,* since the hero loses his innocence in the first few pages, and in another sense, he learns nothing at all despite repeated demonstrations. DGN does, nonetheless, have access to subsequent knowledge. His hindsight often shows up in concessive clauses that provide commentary on the actions of DGC:

7. Delesalle (1971) finds an incoherence in the question of the conversion: in the beginning of his narration DGN says he should have listened to Tiberge, whose cares have proven useless (therefore, no conversion); at the end, however, he says he told Tiberge that the latter's efforts had begun to produce virtue in his heart (735). What Delesalle has failed to notice is that DGN says he told Tiberge about his conversion "pour lui causer une joie à laquelle il ne s'attendait pas" [to cause him a joy that he did not expect] (204). This is perhaps another lie told to make his friend happy, just as DGC had earlier considered "feindre une nouvelle conversion" [feigning a new conversion] (57) in order to deceive his father. In any case, there are no traces of a conversion in his discourse.

8. Lips (1926, 149–50); G. Jones (1978, 57–58); Gossman (1968, 98); Monty (1970, 52). Nichols (1966) disagrees and sees a changed Des Grieux in the narrator, who is separated temporally *and* ideologically from the hero: "Abashed by the duplicity of his younger self, but too frank to conceal the extent of his depravity, the narrator can underline and deplore the unscrupulousness of the actor, but he cannot intervene" (152).

> J'avais le défaut d'être excessivement timide et facile à déconcerter; mais loin d'être arrêté alors par cette faiblesse, je m'avançai vers la maîtresse de mon coeur. (19)

> Ce dessein, tout extravagant qu'il était, nous parut assez bien arrangé. (132)

> Quoique je n'eusse pris cette précaution que par un excès d'inquiétude et de prévoyance, il se trouva qu'elle avait été absolument nécessaire. (174)

Another very frequent sign of dissonance may be seen in DGN's numerous proleptic comments. At the beginning of his narrative he uses prolepsis, as we might expect, to provoke an early interest in his story:

> J'avais marqué le temps de mon départ d'Amiens. Hélas! que ne le marquais-je un jour plus tôt! j'aurais porté chez mon père toute mon innocence. (19)

> Il est sûr que, du naturel tendre et constant dont je suis, j'étais heureux pour toute ma vie, si Manon m'eût été fidèle. (25)

Despite the clauses expressing conditions that are contrary to fact, we are informed early on that Des Grieux lost his innocence and that Manon was not faithful to him. The device continues to be used throughout the text. Before we are told of Manon's visit to Saint-Sulpice, DGN says that "un instant malheureux me fit retomber dans le précipice" (43); before we learn of the disastrous fire at Chaillot, he announces "un funeste accident" (52), and later speaks of "des malheurs qui ne tardèrent guère à m'arriver" (65). Quite a number of these proleptic remarks contain elements of the supernatural, which are designed to increase the sense of the tragic:

> Pendant ce temps-là, notre mauvais génie travaillait à nous perdre. Nous étions dans le délire du plaisir, et le glaive était suspendu sur nos têtes. (151)

> La Fortune ne me délivra d'un précipice que pour me faire tomber dans un autre. (75)

> [Manon] ignorait, et moi aussi, que c'était sur elle-même que devait tomber toute la colère du Ciel et la rage de nos ennemis. (194)

From the first encounter with Manon to the final one with Synnelet, DGN punctuates his narrative with references to fatality, fortune, and destiny.

At times DGN is careful to maintain his distance and to make a neat demarcation between *then* and *now:* "Pour moi, je sentis, dans ce moment, que j'aurais sacrifié pour Manon tous les évêchés du monde chrétien" (47); "J'aurais préféré la mort, dans ce moment, à l'état où je me crus prêt de tomber" (80). He is capable of describing some of the emotions and actions of DGC in a detached, dispassionate, and even analytic manner: "Effectivement, je n'étais pas assez revenu de mes transports pour me modérer à sa vue [G...M...]" (149); "Je commis une imprudence en lui confessant que je savais où était son fils; mais l'excès de ma colère me fit faire cette indiscrétion" (153). Here we see the narrator in his most dissonant posture, able to analyze his past conduct objectively. Nor does he shrink from admitting to the duplicity of DGC, who had the habit of arranging his version of the truth for his own advantage: "Je feignis de m'appliquer à l'étude. . . . Je dois le confesser à ma honte, je jouai, à Saint-Lazare, un personnage d'hypocrite" (83); "Je lui [the superior] représentai les choses, à la vérité, du côté le plus favorable pour nous" (86); "Je lui [Tiberge] ouvris mon coeur sans réserve, excepté sur le dessein de ma fuite" (90).

Hindsight enables the external focalizer to correct the mistaken beliefs and attitudes of the experiencing self, although he may choose to do so indirectly. DGN maintains a certain degree of distance from the feelings of DGC through modal verbs used in past tenses, which signify that the beliefs belong to *then* and not to *now:* "[Manon] avait pour moi des attentions si délicates, que je me crus trop parfaitement dédommagé de toutes mes peines" (49); "Je me croyais si heureux . . . qu'on n'aurait pu me faire comprendre que j'eusse à craindre quelque nouveau malheur" (124–25). It is noteworthy that these examples (and there are others) have to do with DGC's sense of security about Manon's love and his own happiness. If the modals do not always imply that his beliefs were misguided, they allow at least for the possibility of subsequent enlightenment and present disbelief. Just before Manon's visit to Saint-Sulpice, we read: "Je me croyais absolument délivré des faiblesses de l'amour" (43). In this sentence the modal is used because the belief was erroneous, and DGN proceeds to reveal that such was not the case. The alternative "J'étais absolument délivré" would indicate FID, focalized by the mistaken hero. The same cannot be said, however, about the following sentence, taken from the report of DGC's suspicions about Manon and the Italian prince: "Cependant je croyais voir, dans le fond de sa joie et de ses caresses, un air de vérité qui s'accordait avec les apparences" (121). Here DGN might well have said "je voyais" instead of "je croyais voir," since it turns out that the belief was correct. Yet the modal creates a distance from the narrator and shifts the emphasis to the experiencing self, so that the reader remains in doubt. Ultimately, the modals allow the narrator not to pronounce on these beliefs. If he makes no assertions, the reader—like the hero—will look to subsequent events for corroboration or correction.[9]

We have seen, then, that DGN uses all the formal devices of a dissonant narrator, yet he does not provide an ironic response to DGC. The principal explanation for this is that Des Grieux still shares, at the moment of speech, the ideology to which he ascribed at the moment of event. Even when the formal signs of the present–past polarity are evident, there is little or no detachment, no difference of philosophy between *then* and *now:*

> Donnez-moi un amant qui n'entre point aveuglément dans tous les caprices d'une maîtresse adorée, et je conviendrai que j'eus tort de céder si facilement. (129)

> Mais il aurait fallu que j'eusse perdu tous sentiments d'humanité pour m'endurcir contre tant de charmes. J'étais si éloigné d'avoir cette force barbare. (143)

Once again we see a dichotomy set up to condition our response in favor of DGC and his human weaknesses. We can easily distinguish the two consciousnesses, yet the "detached" narrator clearly shares the views of his younger self. We might call this a false dissonance in that there is an observable distance between narrator and character (i.e., we cannot speak of "fusion") and yet there is also an undeniable sameness between

---

9. Cohn (1978) lists the presence of modal verbs among the characteristics of dissonant self-narration because they stress "the cognitive deficiency of the past self" (148), a statement with which I concur. I do think it is important to note, however, that in a case in which the narrator uses modals but never calls attention to his hindsight, i.e. never corroborates or corrects the beliefs and impressions, then emphasis is shifted to the experiencing self as the reader follows him through the episode. This is not quite the fusion of consonance, but rather the silencing of the narrating self that is typical in what I call conventional paralipsis.

them. The sameness goes beyond ideology, and at times DGN even seems to share the excitement of DGC:

> Quel sort pour une créature toute charmante, qui eût occupé le premier trône du monde, si tous les hommes eussent eu mes yeux et mon coeur! (79)

> Dieux! de quels mouvements n'étais-je point agité! (141)

> J'aurais donné, pour être libre un moment . . . Juste Ciel! que n'aurais-je pas donné! (155)

We are approaching consonance here, a true fusion of two consciousnesses. Indeed, these passages could be read, even in context, as self-narrated monologue reflecting the internal focalization of DGC. There is no difference in emotion *then* and *now*. A comparison of the first passage quoted above to a later passage of DGC's direct discourse ("Quel sort pour une créature si charmante!" 157) suffices to reveal the similarity of sentiment, distinguishable only by the contextual graphics of quotation. With this ideology and emotional sameness in mind, we shall now turn to our third aspect.

Internal Focalization

It is not surprising that focalization is delegated to the experiencing self at the many moments of crisis in Des Grieux's story: betrayals by Manon, escape attempts, the report of terrible news, and so on. On the one hand, this focal shift permits conventional paralipsis, in which the narrating self remains silent so that the reader will discover events only as they unfold to the experiencing self. On the other, it allows the experiencing self to express his emotions at such moments, as quoted or narrated by the narrating self. Both possibilities may be seen in the episode of Manon's first betrayal. First we are alerted to impending disaster by the narrator, who warns that DGC had not the least suspicion of the cruel blow he was about to receive, and not the slightest distrust of Manon. DGC then learns, from a servant, about the visit of B... and he is thrown into consternation:

> [1] Il me paraissait si impossible que Manon m'eût trahi, que je craignais de lui faire injure en la soupçonnant. [2] Je l'adorais, cela

était sûr; je ne lui avais pas donné plus de preuves d'amour que je n'en avais reçu d'elle; pourquoi l'aurais-je accusée d'être moins sincère et moins constante que moi? Quelle raison aurait-elle eue de me tromper? Il n'y avait que trois heures qu'elle m'avait accablé de ses plus tendres caresses et qu'elle avait reçu les miennes avec transport; je ne connaissais pas mieux mon coeur que le sien. [3] Non, non, repris-je, il n'est pas possible que Manon me trahisse. (28)

Although he distances himself from the beliefs of DGC, the narrating self is barely visible in [1]. His retrospection merges unobtrusively with a passage of self-narrated monologue [2], conveying DGC's agitations over Manon's suspected infidelity. Our attention is fixed on the experiencing self and his uncertainties. His reassurance is related by self-quoted monologue in [3]. Although we have access to the precise thoughts of DGC, the distance between the two selves is reestablished by the inquit phrase, and consonance disappears. The passage continues as follows:

[1] Je rappelais aussi les petites acquisitions de Manon, qui me semblaient surpasser nos richesses présentes. Cela paraissait sentir les libéralités d'un nouvel amant. [2] Et cette confiance qu'elle m'avait marquée pour des ressources qui m'étaient inconnues! [1] J'avais peine à donner à tant d'énigmes un sens aussi favorable que mon coeur le souhaitait. [2] D'un autre côté, je ne l'avais presque pas perdue de vue depuis que nous étions à Paris. Occupations, promenades, divertissements, nous avions toujours été l'un à côté de l'autre; mon Dieu! un instant de séparation nous aurait trop affligés. Il fallait nous dire sans cesse que nous nous aimions; nous serions morts d'inquiétude sans cela. [1] Je ne pouvais donc m'imaginer presque un seul moment où Manon pût s'être occupée d'un autre que moi. (28–29)

DGN again uses modal verbs, shifting emphasis to DGC and merging his statements with self-narrated monologue. The analytical explanations [1], focalized externally, alternate here with the internal focalization of the more emotional DGC [2]. Not only does the narrator delegate focalization to DGC, but he also remains silent about his subsequent knowledge. There are no traces of his hindsight or of his tendency toward proleptic warnings. During the ensuing scene of the famous "interrupted supper," DGN distances himself from DGC through verbs denoting perceptual operations, thus in effect allowing the experiencing self to

focalize: "je crus apercevoir," "Je remarquai," "Je ne pouvais démêler . . . quoiqu'il me parût," "Je la regardai" (29). The reader is placed in
the same state of uncertainty and suspense as the hero, except that we
have been forewarned, earlier, that Manon was unfaithful. In this scene
the narrator withholds all his privileged information until Manon begins
to cry: "Enfin, je vis tomber des larmes de ses beaux yeux: perfides
larmes!" (30). The final exclamation, while its emotive tone resembles
that of the hero, can be focalized only by the narrator, who is certain
about Manon's betrayal.

The supper is interrupted by the "capture" of DGC by his brother.
During the journey home and the ensuing encounter with his father,
focalization continues to be largely internal, so that we follow the
hero's puzzlement about what has happened to him: "J'y trouvai
d'abord tant d'obscurité que je ne voyais pas de jour à la moindre
conjecture. J'étais trahi cruellement. Mais par qui? Tiberge fut le premier qui me vint à l'esprit. Traître! disais-je, c'est fait de ta vie si mes
soupçons se trouvent justes" (31). Here we see the same pattern, a
statement made by DGN followed by self-narrated monologue and
then self-quoted monologue. In all cases, however, the horizon of
knowledge is that of DGC. Signs of dissonance ("j'avais la crédulité de
m'imaginer," 31) are rare, and we do not learn the truth until DGC
hears it from his father. Emphasis on internal focalization occurs again,
but to a lesser degree, in the episode of the second betrayal with the
elder G...M..., and in that of the suspected betrayal with the Italian
prince. At such times the narrator prefers to abandon his hindsight in
favor of the emotional reactions of the hero.

Some passages are clearly recognized as FID because the emotions
contained therein are no longer shared by DGN. When, for example,
Manon pays a visit to Saint-Sulpice, we read: "J'allai au parloir sur-le-
champ. Dieux! quelle apparition surprenante! j'y trouvai Manon" (44).
Obviously, the narrator is no longer surprised by this visit. Similarly,
DGC's jealousy over Manon's dealings with the Italian prince is no
longer a problem for DGN: "Je ne pouvais faire un crime à Manon
d'être aimée. Il y avait beaucoup d'apparence qu'elle ignorait sa con-
quête; et quelle vie allais-je mener si j'étais capable d'ouvrir si facilement l'entrée de mon coeur à la jalousie?" (120). And when the
governor of New Orleans decides to give Manon in marriage to
Synnelet, self-narrated monologue renders DGC's desperate thoughts
about where to flee and how to move the people in his favor, whereas
DGN knows the outcome.

As we have seen, however, self-narrated monologue tends toward
consonance. It is often difficult to distinguish it from the exclamatory

comments of the narrator, especially when he seems still to share the same emotions. A good example occurs when DGC learns of the second betrayal, and in his bewilderment he begins to feel remorse: "je jetai les yeux . . . vers tous les lieux où j'avais vécu dans l'innocence. Par quel immense espace n'étais-je pas séparé de cet heureux état!" (72). Who is the focalizer of the exclamation? If this is FID, then it belongs to the remorseful hero, but does DGN still feel the same regret? Another ambiguous passage occurs as DGC plots his escape from Saint-Lazare: "[My plan] était bizarre et hardi; mais de quoi n'étais-je pas capable, avec les motifs qui m'animaient?" (95). Despite the formal similarity with FID, this question seems more likely to be that of the older narrator who looks back and comments upon his earlier desperation. If so, it can be more easily reconciled with the following passage, in which DGC, in an attempt to stop the deportation of Manon, thinks about murdering his enemies and then abandons the idea: "[l] La mort de nos ennemis eût été d'une faible utilité pour Manon, et elle m'eût exposé sans doute à me voir ôter tous les moyens de la secourir. [2] D'ailleurs, aurais-je eu recours à un lâche assassinat? [3] Quelle autre voie pouvais-je m'ouvrir à la vengeance?" (167). The first sentence [1] could represent the judgment of Des Grieux either *then* or *now*. The question [2] is problematic regardless of attribution, since at this point DGC has already committed one murder. The second question [3] is surely a case of internal focalization since the narrator knows what steps the young man took to liberate Manon. The difficulty critics have had in determining the narrator's attitude toward his younger self stems in part from this ambiguity of attribution.

That the two share the same attitudes and feelings is sometimes made clear by the merging of self-narrated monologue with the achronic statements of the narrator:

> [1] J'avais perdu, à la vérité, tout ce que le reste des hommes estime; mais j'étais maître du coeur de Manon, le seul bien que j'estimais. [2] Vivre en Europe, vivre en Amérique, que m'importait-il en quel endroit vivre, si j'étais sûr d'y être heureux en y vivant avec ma maîtresse? [3] Tout l'univers n'est-il pas la patrie de deux amants fidèles? (180)

The first sentence [1] is a case of external focalization. The narrator not only calls attention to the present–past polarity, but he also uses that polarity ("estime/estimais") to foreground the opposition between DGC and the rest of humanity. The question [2] is focalized internally by DGC and has characteristics of FID, while [3] is a rhetorical question posed by DGN in the atemporal present. Since the two questions express essentially the same sentiment, the distinction between past and present is blurred.

When DGC learns of Manon's third betrayal with the younger G...M...,
he decides to direct all his energies toward finding a solution:

> Je connaissais Manon; pourquoi m'affliger tant d'un malheur que j'avais dû prévoir? Pourquoi ne pas m'employer plutôt à chercher du remède? Il était encore temps. . . . Entreprendre de l'arracher avec violence des mains de G...M..., c'était un parti déses-péré. . . . Mais il me semblait que si j'eusse pu me procurer le moindre entretien avec elle, j'aurais gagné infailliblement quelque chose sur son coeur. J'en connaissais si bien tous les endroits sensibles! J'étais si sûr d'être aimé d'elle! (138)

This passage begins with the self-narrated thoughts of DGC. The internal focalization is interrupted, however, by the modal expression "il me semblait," which introduces distance between narrator and character and allows for some doubt on the part of the reader. The expression breaks up what would otherwise be a sustained passage in FID, with the final exclamation being attributed to DGC. As it stands, we are not sure whether the emotion of the last sentences is shared by DGN at the moment of his narration. When the young man confronts his lover and learns that her infidelity was indeed planned, we read: "Elle ne pouvait espérer que G...M... la laissât, toute la nuit, comme une vestale. C'était donc avec lui qu'elle comptait de la passer. Quel aveu pour un amant!" (147). FID reveals the young man's realization of Manon's intentions, while the emotion of shock is obviously shared by hero, narrator, and—it is doubtless intended—reader.

If we examine the passages of self-quoted monologue, those that reveal DGC's thoughts directly with no apparent intervention from the narrator, we can discern a certain evolution in the hero's attitudes. The earliest passages occur after the first betrayal and show the young man's efforts to convince himself that Manon is not at fault and that she loves him. Although he clings desperately to this conviction, he nonetheless refers to her as "l'ingrate Manon" (36). At the end of this episode, as he decides to enter Saint-Sulpice, his quoted thoughts point to his decision to lead a studious and Christian life. It is interesting that DGC draws a dichotomy between himself and the vulgar masses, but this time passion is on the other side: "Je mépriserai ce que le commun des hommes admire." Then he asks himself two questions: "Ne serai-je pas heureux? ajoutais-je; toutes mes prétentions ne seront-elles point remplies?" (40), to which the narrator replies that DGC had not forgotten Manon.

When DGC learns of the second betrayal, his thoughts run along totally different lines. In the first passage of self-quoted monologue he rails against the monstrous conduct of "l'ingrate" Manon and her "grossièreté de sentiments!" opposing them to his own "délicatesse" (70). This time Manon is on the side of the vulgar, whereas DGC insists upon his own sacrifice of fortune and family in order to satisfy her whims. This is the harshest criticism of Manon that we ever see, and it stands virtually undiluted by DGN, who introduces the monologue by affirming only his present inability to describe those past emotions adequately. The hero then begins to feel regret and remorse for his own conduct. In a second passage of self-quoted monologue, however, a new theme is introduced and a new target of blame is found: "Par quelle fatalité, disais-je, suis-je devenu si criminel? L'amour est une passion innocente; comment s'est-il changé, pour moi, en une source de misères et de désordres? Qui m'empêchait de vivre tranquille et vertueux avec Manon?" (72). While the answer to this last question may seem obvious to the reader, Manon is clearly not perceived to be the source of Des Grieux's problems. Nor is he himself to blame, despite his regret that he did not marry her. Instead, it is fate that has made him a criminal by depraving an innocent passion. This seems to be the point in the story at which DGC seizes on the idea of fatality, and later he will refer to "cette fatale tendresse" (90) while speaking with Tiberge, to "Fatale passion!" (162) with his father, and to "mon mauvais sort" (177) with one of the guards. DGN, we remember, has blamed fatality, destiny, and fortune from the beginning. When DGC first witnesses the convoy deporting Manon, his quoted thoughts are not addressed to God: "O fortune, m'écriai-je, fortune cruelle! accorde-moi ici, du moins, la mort ou la victoire" (175). Otherwise, his infrequent references to fatality and fortune are used only in direct address to other people. It is interesting to speculate that DGC found the concept useful in relating his misfortunes to others, so that DGN, in his narration to Renoncour, introduces it at the outset.[10]

10. My interpretation must be clarified with respect to that of Segal (1986), who states that "there is a marked change as the protagonist leaves France: terms suggesting pagan belief become rare and the invocation of or reference to God is increasingly frequent" and that "it is only after passing through le Havre that a sense of religious belief begins to revive in Des Grieux" (195, 196). Segal's statements suggest that the narrator is a converted man. It is true that DGC calls upon Heaven quite often between the deportation and the death of Manon. The narrator, on the other hand, continues to speak of DGC as "asservi fatalement à une passion" [fatally enslaved to a passion] (191) and of "le sort, qui voulait hâter ma ruine" [fate, which sought to hasten my ruin] (195). More important, the references to God and Heaven that can be attributed to the narrator reveal clearly that he regards them as hostile and vindictive (194, 199, 200, 202).

On the other hand, self-quoted monologue reveals that the hero holds more faith in divine providence than does the older narrator. In a long mental justification for cheating the rich, DGC feels that Providence has arranged these things wisely (53–54). When he learns of Manon's internment at the Hôpital, he cries out to God and to the justice of Heaven (85).[11] He asks Heaven to save his life long enough for him to rescue her (101). When arrested by the elder G...M..., his attitude toward Heaven is one of submission with despair (156). After the break with his father, he cries out that Heaven is his only hope (173). He receives favors from Heaven and he is duly thankful. By contrast, DGN speaks rarely of Heaven except to decry its anger and its severe punishments. The single time he addresses God directly, it is to complain of the latter's harsh judgment, and Ehrard (1975) is quite right to point out that the narrator's language hardly creates an impression of Christian resignation (500).[12]

To compare Des Grieux *then* and *now* ideologically, we can say that DGC seems to show a Christian faith until the death of Manon, whereas DGN impugns the weakness and hostility of Heaven. Even after the second betrayal, DGC is willing to blame Manon and to contrast her unfavorably with his own goodness, but from then on he seems more accepting of her nature and turns his energies toward removing all obstacles to his passion. He finds the concept of fatality to be an effective tool in his verbal justifications to others, which perhaps explains why DGN

11. Although Stewart (1984) points out the slippery nature of Des Grieux's "perverse theology" (154), I think we are safe in assuming that "le Ciel," in the eighteenth century and today, has a specifically Christian referent. Moreover, we find "O Dieu!" [O God!] and "justice du Ciel!" [justice of Heaven!] in the same sentence (85).

12. In his otherwise excellent analysis, Ehrard (1975) states that the language of fatality is used almost as frequently by the hero as by the narrator, although with the hero it is concentrated in the last part of the novel, as one might expect. I find this to be not quite the case. My objection is that Ehrard seems to believe that the lexical items used in indirect discourse always belong to the quoted speaker. While I agree with Sternberg (1982) that the inset, though paraphrased, can still reflect the reportee's point of view, the opposite is surely true as well, i.e. the words used to paraphrase the report may well be those of the reporter, hence the perspectival ambiguity. Ehrard has a problem with the sentence "J'en fus touché, jusqu'au point de déplorer l'aveuglement d'un amour fatal, qui me faisait violer tous les devoirs" [I was touched by this, to the point of deploring the blinding of a fatal love, which made me violate all my duties] (61). He suggests that the word "aveuglement" belongs to the hero, whereas he considers "fatal" to be an addition by the narrator (502). I find no problem here. It is completely consistent with Ehrard's thesis (and mine) that DGN is using a word in his summary that would not yet have occurred to DGC. If all references to fatality occurring in indirect discourse are attributed to the narrator, then we find a great disproportion: DGC refers very seldom to "fatalité" and "fortune" and much more frequently to "le Ciel."

uses it so heavily in his own. Love becomes the supreme virtue, and those who fail to understand fall into the wrong side of the dichotomy. DGN uses the formal devices of dissonance to foreground an initial naïveté, to foretell the accidents and vicissitudes of fate (for which he is not responsible), and to explain feelings that no longer affect him (such as DGC's anger at G...M... or his flirtation with suicide). There is hindsight only when emotions are gone and events are past. In moments of crisis, however, he creates suspense and provokes interest in the unfolding events by shifting focalization to DGC. This tendency toward consonance is compounded by the fact that many of DGC's beliefs and emotions are shared by DGN and are sometimes indistinguishable from his own. It suits his rhetorical purpose that there be no double standard by which DCG can be judged.

Other Characters

Much has been written about characterization in *Manon Lescaut*. Josephs (1968) writes that the characters are rigorously divided into good and bad, according to the quality of their sensibility and to their willingness to help the hero (192). According to Deloffre and Picard (1965), Des Grieux lives in an essentialist world, in which people are judged for what they *are* and not for what they *do* (cx). This is not entirely true, however, and Monty (1979) is quite right to point out that some characters are defined by their deeds, from which certain qualities can be deduced: "If the reader is encouraged to believe that Manon and Des Grieux's outward appearance is a true reflection of their soul, he is also taught that others can not be known on that basis alone" (154). Monty goes on to show that two patterns of characterization are possible. In the first case, the narrator introduces a character in terms of observed qualities and then relates past history as confirmation. In our terms, this essentialist view stems from external focalization. In the second case, no portrait of the character is given by the narrator. Instead we follow a report of each action as seen by the hero, whose opinion may vary considerably. Such an existentialist view results from internal focalization. Our task will be to study the ways in which the narrator uses the focal possibilities at his disposal to present the characters and to further his rhetorical enterprise.

We may begin by considering the ability of DGN to abide by the spatial and psychological limitations of the retrospective narrator. Spatially, most of the events described by DGN are proximal ones, that is, DGC was present as they occurred and was able to witness them personally. When he is separated from Manon after the first betrayal, our attention is focused on *his* life and not on hers, just as we should expect. By eavesdropping he is able to report on the supper shared by Manon, Lescaut, and the elder G...M... ("J'étais à la porte, où je prêtais l'oreille," 76). When DGC is interned at Saint-Lazare after the second betrayal, we learn before he does that Manon was taken to the Hôpital, as DGN explains: "Je n'appris ce triste détail que longtemps après" (80). Although he at first remains outside of Manon's prison cell, he overhears her conversation with T... (103). It is just after the third betrayal that the narrator encounters his most difficult spatial problems. While the lovers romp in the bedroom of young G...M..., DGN shifts his attention to the elder G...M..., who is alerted by a lackey and who undertakes to locate his son (151). After the arrest of the lovers, the elder G...M... leaves them in the bedroom to interrogate the servants, and we are told of his conversation with the faithful Marcel who is intimidated into betraying his master (154). DGC could not, of course, have witnessed these scenes. The subsequent incarceration of DGC in the Châtelet further necessitates a narration of distal events. There is a conversation between Des Grieux's father and Tiberge (159) and another between the father and the elder G...M... (164). In the latter case DGN inserts a rather lame justification: "Je n'ai jamais su les particularités de leur conversation, mais il ne m'a été que trop facile d'en juger par ses mortels effets," whereupon he proceeds to report the visit of the two fathers to the lieutenant-general of police and the transfer of Manon to the Hôpital (165). A final spatial transposition occurs near the end of the novel, as DGN relates the "resurrection" of Synnelet while DGC has fled with Manon. Again, we learn of this event before the hero does.[13] Do these spatial shifts represent focal infractions? Do they stem from external focalization based on subsequent knowledge, or are they simply non-focalized, nonrestricted? The only answer to these questions lies in the likelihood of DGN's having learned of these events at some point prior to his narration of them. Some, like the revival of Synnelet, are easily ascribed to external focalization. Others are more problematic in that they contain psychological as well as spatial insights. How, for example, can DGN know that Synnelet was so inflamed by Manon's beauty that "il se consumait en secret pour elle" (192)? A similar difficulty arises when he reports the elder G...M...'s conversation with his son's lackey:

---

13. Delesalle (1971) finds an incoherence in the fact that DGC believes he has killed Synnelet and so the reader is obliged to believe it also (735). For us, this is simply an example of internal focalization and conventional paralipsis. We are told the truth by the narrator before the hero learns it, but DGN is under no obligation to tell us right away.

> Il voulut savoir d'abord du laquais tout ce que son fils avait fait l'après-midi, s'il s'était querellé avec quelqu'un, s'il avait pris part au démêlé d'un autre, s'il s'était trouvé dans quelque maison suspecte. Celui-ci, qui *croyait* son maître dans le dernier danger et qui *s'imaginait* ne devoir plus rien ménager pour lui procurer du secours, découvrit tout ce qu'il savait de son amour pour Manon et la dépense qu'il avait faite pour elle. . . . C'en fut assez pour faire *soupçonner* au vieillard que l'affaire de son fils était une querelle d'amour. (151–52)

Despite the fact that the old man's questions and the lackey's answers are summarized and not quoted by the narrator, it seems unlikely that either character would have reported this conversation to him in such detail at a later time. Moreover, DGN reveals here that he has some insight into the thoughts of both characters—a clear case of nonfocalization.

Psychologically, Des Grieux often maintains the expected distance from the minds of other characters that is logical in first-person narration. Ignorance of the mental operations of others is usually shared by hero and narrator. On one occasion he admits to his narratees that he is still uncertain about Manon's motivations for coming to Saint-Sulpice: "mais un reste de curiosité, ou peut-être quelque repentir de m'avoir trahi (je n'ai jamais pu démêler lequel de ces deux sentiments) . . ." (43). More often his ignorance is signaled by modal expressions ("peut-être," "sans doute," "apparemment") that allow a narrator to insinuate what he cannot normally affirm:

> [Tiberge] savait que j'étais à Saint-Lazare, et peut-être n'avait-il pas été fâché de cette disgrâce qu'il croyait capable de me ramener au devoir. (90)

> [J]e la [Manon] vis trembler, apparemment par un effet de sa crainte. (141)

> [My father] s'imaginait bien, sans doute, que tant de préparations ne s'étaient pas faites sans un dessein d'importance. (171)

Alongside these precautions, however, we see numerous cases of undiluted and unrestricted incursions into the thoughts of others. Using verbs such as "il s'aperçut," "il crut," "ils doutèrent," and "ils s'imaginèrent," DGN gives us momentary insight into the minds of his father, Tiberge, his servants, the superior, and the archers. In doing so, he reveals thoughts that are at best suppositions on his part. In some cases the psychological infraction also involves a shift in focalization from the narrator to the character:

> Mon père était surpris de me voir toujours si fortement touché. Il me connaissait des principes d'honneur, et ne pouvant douter que sa trahison ne me la fît mépriser, il s'imagina que ma constance venait moins de cette passion en particulier que d'un penchant général pour les femmes. (36–37)

Here the father becomes the focalizer, the perceiving subject who incorrectly interprets the cause of his son's emotion. DGC, in turn, becomes the object, perceived as a man of honor and fidelity. The father is thus allowed to contribute to the composite portrait of DGC. Others are invited to contribute as well:

> Ma tristesse parut si excessive au supérieur, qu'en appréhendant les suites, il crut devoir me traiter avec beaucoup de douceur et d'indulgence. (82)

> Je lui [T...] marquai quelque chose de ces sentiments, d'une manière qui le persuada aussi que je n'étais pas d'un mauvais naturel. (101)

DGN turns other characters into spectators by delegating focalization to them, thereby offering multiple perspectives on the hero. We perceive DGC as they do, and they never fail to add something flattering to his portrait.[14]

An external focalizer can always condition our view of a character without in any way overstepping the bounds of his focal limitations. Armed with the knowledge of hindsight, he can trace an essentialist portrait at the outset, or merely designate the character by a tendentious appellation, which relieves us of the burden of uncertainty. DGN uses epithets rather generously. Tiberge not only benefits from a favorable introductory portrait, but he is later referred to as "ce fidèle ami" (90) and as "un ami si généreux et si constant" (204). Lescaut receives an unfavorable portrait: "C'était un homme brutal et sans principes d'honneur. Il entra dans notre chambre en jurant horriblement, et . . . il l'accabla [Manon] d'injures et de reproches" (51). When Lescaut proves

---

14. Brady (1973) writes that by means of this "hypothetically transferred point of view" (105–6), the narrator is able to picture himself as an Other seen by other characters, even nameless ones ("nos hôtes," "tous les assistants" [our hosts, all those in attendance]).

to be a useful confederate, however, the portrait must be modified: we are told later that "Lescaut . . . ne manquait pas d'esprit et de prudence. . . . Son conseil était sage" (97–98). The elder G...M... is called "ce vieux libertin" before we have a chance to see him (75), "le barbare" when he comes to Saint-Lazare (85), and "ce vieux tigre" when he surprises the lovers in his son's bed (156). DGN leaves no doubt about his opinion of the archers accompanying the convoy: "Cinq hommes hardis et résolus suffisaient pour donner l'épouvante à ces misérables, qui ne sont point capables de se défendre honorablement lorsqu'ils peuvent éviter le péril du combat par une lâcheté" (174). The ship's captain is set apart from the vulgar masses because he recognizes that the lovers are not common either: "Il eut la bonté de nous regarder d'un autre oeil que le commun de nos misérables associés" (183).

In some cases DGN allows for some doubt as to his opinion of a character until the latter has demonstrated kindness and understanding toward the hero. The initial portrait of T..., for example, is based briefly on the observations of DGC: "J'augurai bien de sa physionomie et de ses civilités." The uncertainty does not last long, however. T... quickly proves to be sympathetic, and internal focalization yields to external:

> Il parut fort sensible à cette marque d'ouverture et de candeur. Sa réponse fut celle d'un homme qui a du monde et des sentiments; ce que le monde ne donne pas toujours et qu'il fait perdre souvent. (100)

> Nous nous embrassâmes avec tendresse, et nous devînmes amis, sans autre raison que la bonté de nos coeurs et une simple disposition qui porte un homme tendre et généreux à aimer un autre homme qui lui ressemble. (101)

The portrait of T... does no harm to that of DGC. If T... is judged by his deeds, the superior of Saint-Lazare is judged by his words. He, too, is presented through internal focalization without benefit of hindsight, and at first we do not know what kind of character he will be. Unlike T..., the superior himself is allowed to focalize through his own quoted speech, and we should not be surprised about what he is quoted as saying to DGC: "Vous êtes d'un naturel si doux et si aimable, me dit-il un jour, que je ne puis comprendre les désordres dont on vous accuse" (82). To G...M..., who has just been attacked by the young man, the superior says: "ce n'est point avec une personne de la naissance de M. le Chevalier que nous en usons de cette manière. Il est si doux, d'ailleurs, et si honnête, que j'ai peine à comprendre qu'il se soit porté à cet excès sans de fortes raisons" (85). One good turn deserves another. While the superior contributes to the favorable portrait of DGC, the portrait of the superior is completed by DGN, who refers to him as "le bon Père" (86) and "bon supérieur" (89).

Monty (1979) points out that when DGN presents characters as friends or foes, the judgment is usually valid until the end (157). As we have seen, however, he does not always pronounce on a character right away but instead lets the portrait be drawn existentially. A good example may be seen in the governor of New Orleans. The governor is first introduced through the vision of the experiencing self ("Je lui trouvai beaucoup de politesse," 186) and in the direct discourse of DGC ("Le Gouverneur est un homme civil," 187). These sentiments are confirmed when the governor gives DGC a job ("Il eut la bonté," 189) and when he offers to pay for his wedding ("il eut la générosité," 192). In these cases the narrating self seems to agree, or should we say that there are no signs of disagreement. When the governor decides to give Manon to his nephew Synnelet, he is transformed into "ce barbare" and "cet opiniâtre vieillard, qui se serait damné mille fois pour son neveu" (194). No dissonant comment, no proleptic warning has prepared us for this kind of setback. The horizon of knowledge and the perception of the man's character throughout this episode are those of the experiencing self.

Manon is the character whose presentation is the most biased and tendentious, and yet she remains, in the minds of many readers, the most enigmatic of the novel.[15] Given the fact that she is the most important person in Des Grieux's life and the center of his story, we may well wonder why we are offered so little insight into her character. She is seldom allowed even to speak, although such minor characters as the hotel owner, the guards, and the anonymous murderer of Lescaut are quoted directly. In a masterly article, Fort (1985) has shown how Des Grieux manipulates the reader's impressions of Manon Lescaut through the ways in which he reports her speech. Only when the narrator removes himself and allows Manon to speak for herself do we get a direct and seemingly unbiased glimpse of her character. In fact, this rarely happens. Fort demonstrates that Manon's words are most often summarized by the narrator or presented in indirect discourse. Summarized speech (Genette's "narrated discourse") eliminates Manon as a speaking identity by shifting the focus from her words to the effect they have on the hero. Indirect discourse, although more direct than summarized

15. According to Gossman (1982), Manon "appears to have escaped from the controlling frame of [Des Grieux's] narrative and to have acquired an autonomous existence in the imagination of the novel's readers," where she is "constantly reborn and reinvented" (36).

speech, is nonetheless only an illusion of a quotation and is often contaminated by the narrator's evaluation of it (as an example, Fort quotes the sentence "Elle me répéta, en pleurant à chaudes larmes, qu'elle ne prétendait point justifier sa perfidie," 44–45, in which "perfidie" seems to be his word, not hers). Even when Manon is quoted directly, the narrator provides a context that modifies the meaning of her words. The three scenes in which she is quoted at some length (at Saint-Sulpice and at the houses of the elder and younger G...M...) all deal with her response to the hero's accusations of betrayal. Her declarations of love and commitment to him are never spontaneous. According to Fort, then, the mystery surrounding Manon is a deliberate creation: "Revealingly, the double register which helps Des Grieux exculpate himself in the reader's opinion throughout the novel helps him project from the start an ambiguous image of Manon, one whose innocence is constantly endangered by the slightest touch of his informed retrospective judgment" (180).[16]

This conclusion is borne out by other aspects of focalization that do not deal with speech. In his introduction of Manon, DGN combines the knowledge of hindsight with the first impressions of the experiencing hero. He uses modal expressions to create a distance between the two and to give us insight into DGC's views of Manon: "Elle me parut si charmante" (19); "elle reçut mes politesses sans paraître embarrassée" (19–20); "sans paraître déconcertée le moins du monde" (21); "[Manon] parut fort satisfaite de cet effet de ses charmes" (22). To DGC, then, Manon *appears* charming, flirtatious, and anything but shy. At the same time, DGN intervenes to provide a great deal of information about her background that DGC could not have known. He mingles the knowledge of hindsight about her past with unrestricted insight into her mind, to create a portrait that does not evoke innocence and modesty:

> [E]lle était bien plus expérimentée que moi. C'était malgré elle qu'on l'envoyait au couvent, pour arrêter sans doute son penchant au plaisir, qui s'était déjà déclaré et qui a causé, dans la suite, tous ses malheurs et les miens.[17] (20)

16. My brief summary hardly does justice to this excellent article, which deserves a complete reading.

17. Fort (1985) reads the phrase "C'était malgré elle . . . couvent" as FID, the ambiguity of which makes it difficult to say whether or not it is a reflection of the point of view of Manon (178). It may be an example of the kind of FID that Lips (1926) calls "inexpressive" (150), used by Prévost to make his characters speak. As examples Lips cites the valet's report of the Italian prince ("L'étranger avait reparu au bois de Boulogne . . . il lui avait parlé de son amour" [The foreigner had reappeared in the Boulogne park . . . he had

> Élle voulut savoir qui j'étais, et cette connaissance augmenta son
> affection, parce qu'étant d'une naissance commune, elle se trouva
> flattée d'avoir fait la conquête d'un amant tel que moi. (22)

While DGN tells us much about Manon, he says nothing about her true
feelings for DGC. This silence, together with the modals marking the
hero's perception, create a mystery around Manon that the narrator
could easily have dispelled. Indeed the narrator, so eager to reveal her
mind in these opening pages, maintains a strict observance of his focal
limitations toward her throughout the rest of the novel. Moreover, when
he comments on her love for DGC, he does so in a way that shifts the
emphasis to the latter's *belief* in that love: "Quelque passionné que je
fusse pour Manon, elle sut me persuader qu'elle ne l'était pas moins
pour moi" (24). Only near the close of the novel does DGN make another incursion into Manon's mind: "Elle jugeait, par mon trouble, de la
grandeur du péril, et, tremblant pour moi plus que pour elle-même,
cette tendre fille n'osait pas même ouvrir la bouche pour m'exprimer ses
craintes" (194). This does so little to elucidate her feelings that the narrator is compelled to insist upon her selflessness. He *shows* us so little of
Manon's thought-processes that he is constantly obliged to *tell* us about
them: "Manon parut effrayée à la vue d'une si triste demeure. C'était
pour moi qu'elle s'affligeait, beaucoup plus que pour elle-même" (187).
But is DGN's vision of Manon radically different from that of DGC?
Certainly, the double register is easily identified in any negative epithet.
We have no trouble in ascribing "mon ingrate et parjure maîtresse" and
"la perfide Manon" (135) to the betrayed, disillusioned experiencing self,
yet "cette amante incomparable" (198) proves more difficult. Indeed,
more often than not, the two selves share the same opinion of Manon.
Let us compare the following passages:

> Je connaissais Manon; je n'avais déjà que trop éprouvé que,
> quelque fidèle et quelque attachée qu'elle me fût dans la bonne
> fortune, il ne fallait pas compter sur elle dans la misère. Elle
> aimait trop l'abondance et les plaisirs pour me les sacrifier: Je la
> perdrai, m'écriai-je. (53)

---

spoken to her about his love], 120) and Manon's letter about young G...M... ("G...M...
l'avait reçue. . . . Il l'avait comblée de présents" [G...M... had received her. . . . He had
showered her with gifts], 134). In these cases the narrator is merely summarizing the *speech*
of others without using the inquit phrases of indirection that usually burden his style. I
have found no examples of narrated monologue representing the *thoughts* of any character
in the novel other than DGC.

J'ai toujours été persuadé qu'elle était sincère; quelle raison aurait-elle eue de se contrefaire jusqu'à ce point? Mais elle était encore plus volage . . . lorsque, ayant devant les yeux des femmes qui vivaient dans l'abondance, elle se trouvait dans la pauvreté et dans le besoin. (110)

The first, introducing a self-quoted monologue, seems to be focalized internally. The second, clearly a case of external focalization because of discursive elements ("J'ai toujours été"), reveals exactly the same sentiments, the same lucid judgment of Manon. Now let us compare two passages that suggest a dissonant view of her:

Ne vous ai-je pas promis, me dit-elle, que je trouverais des ressources? Je l'aimais avec trop de *simplicité* pour m'alarmer facilement. (27)

Elle pèche sans malice, disais-je en moi-même; elle est légère et imprudente, mais elle est droite et sincère. Ajoutez que l'amour suffisait seul pour me fermer les yeux sur *toutes ses fautes*. (148)

In the first, Manon's direct discourse (the very first time she is quoted directly in the novel) is followed by DGN's dissonant comment. In the second, the self-quoted monologue of DGC is contradicted by DGN. These rare examples of dissonance have more to do with the hero, however, than with Manon. They reveal more about his delusions than about DGN's present opinion of Manon. To elaborate on Fort's findings, then, we can say that when DGN is dissonant, he subtly reveals the delusions of DGC and emphasizes not Manon's love but the hero's belief in that love. He remains silent about her feelings for DGC and perpetuates the mystery so that attention is centered upon the hero. Both narrator and hero appear to be lucid, however, about her true nature.

If Des Grieux refuses to give much expression to the point of view of the object of his passion, he does not deny such expression to its two principal opponents, his friend Tiberge and his own father. Our response to Tiberge is conditioned from the outset. He is immediately introduced by the narrating self, who tells us that Tiberge was a mature and sensible young man who loved him tenderly. The narrator uses the subsequent knowledge of hindsight to give proof of the nobility of Tiberge's character and to predispose us toward him: "Il avait mille bonnes qualités. Vous le connaîtrez par les meilleures dans la suite de mon histoire, et surtout, par un zèle et une générosité en amitié qui surpassent les plus célèbres exemples de l'antiquité" (18). In the first

quoted conversation of his story, the direct discourse of Tiberge alternates with the indirect discourse of DGC, so that it is the point of view of
Tiberge that predominates:

> Je suis sûr, me dit-il sans déguisement, que vous méditez quelque
> dessein que vous me voulez cacher; je le vois à votre air. Je lui
> répondis assez brusquement que je n'étais pas obligé de lui
> rendre compte de tous mes desseins. Non, reprit-il, mais vous
> m'avez toujours traité en ami, et cette qualité suppose un peu de
> confiance et d'ouverture. (23)

It should be clear already that the case of Tiberge is far different from
that of Manon. Not only does the narrator present Tiberge's words
directly, but he also tells us they are "sans déguisement." The words
reveal an honest and loyal friend, whereas the indirectly reported
speech of DGC shows the latter in a less favorable light. Even the
narrator's indirect report of Tiberge's speech allows the friend's point
of view to be expressed semantically, if not syntactically: "Il me dit . . .
que, si je ne renonçais pas ensuite à *cette misérable résolution,* il avertirait
des personnes qui pourraient l'arrêter à coup sûr" (23). Finally, when
Des Grieux quotes himself directly, the quoted words reveal his own
duplicity as he hides from Tiberge his planned abduction of Manon: he
asks Tiberge to meet him at nine o'clock whereas he plans to leave at
dawn.[18]

Des Grieux's next conversation with Tiberge takes place when the
former is a prisoner in his father's house. Although the narrator is in
control as he reports Tiberge's words, the summarized speech allows a
clear expression of the latter's condemnation of his friend's behavior: "Il
plaignit *l'égarement* où j'étais tombé. Il me félicita de *ma guérison,* qu'il
croyait avancée; enfin il m'exhorta à profiter de *cette erreur de jeunesse*
pour ouvrir les yeux sur *la vanité des plaisirs*" (38). The lexical choices are
surely those of Tiberge. When quoted directly, Tiberge states that he,
too, once had a penchant for pleasure, which he was able to overcome
through divine grace and the use of his own reason. He also praises Des
Grieux: "Je connais l'excellence de votre coeur et de votre esprit; il n'y a
rien de bon dont vous ne puissiez vous rendre capable" (39). The implica-
tion is that the two young men are similar, with the exception that DGC
has not received any heavenly help against his passions. It is this visit

---

18. Blanchard (1973) has stated that Des Grieux spares us the words of the characters by
reporting their speech indirectly (753). Sermain (1985b) notes, however, that even in indirect discourse Des Grieux often characterizes the speech of others (385).

that inspires in DGC a decision to give up worldly pleasure and the faithless Manon, and to become, like Tiberge, a cleric.

Until this point, the moral position of Tiberge has been dominant and has even convinced DGC, especially in view of Manon's infidelity. Their third meeting, however, takes place after the reconciliation of the lovers, and DGC is in need of financial aid. Indirect discourse is used to report their initial conversation on the subject of friendship. DGC's appeal to Tiberge's compassion for his own pain is related through direct discourse. His own point of view is maintained, however, even through summarized speech:

> Je la [his passion] lui représentai comme un de ces coups particu-
> liers du destin qui s'attache à la ruine d'un misérable, et dont il est
> aussi impossible à la vertu de se défendre qu'il l'a été à la sagesse
> de les prévoir. . . . [E]nfin, j'attendris tellement le bon Tiberge,
> que je le vis aussi affligé par la compassion que je l'étais par le
> sentiment de mes peines. (59)

Tiberge's response is reported directly and reveals his desire to help his friend and to bring him back to "la vertu, que je sais que vous aimez, et dont il n'y a que la violence de vos passions qui vous écarte" (60). Regardless of the means used to report the speech of the two friends, the dominant moral position is shifting from condemnation of DGC's behavior to compassion for a helpless victim of love.

In the long central conversation between the two friends at Saint-Lazare, the direct discourse of DGC alternates with the indirect discourse of Tiberge, and this time the impact of the latter's arguments is weakened. Whereas Tiberge's moralizing is summarized, DGC says "Laissez-moi raisonner à mon tour" (90), and we read his own words in a lengthy direct quotation. This formal differentiation, however, is not the only element that lends more weight to the hero's arguments than to those of his friend. Whereas Tiberge's concerns are consistent and familiar, DGC expounds a doctrine that is startling and new. He exalts the tangible pleasures of the flesh as the sure road to happiness and contrasts them with the uncertain promise of celestial rewards, using a logic that is difficult to refute. Tiberge, indeed, is almost swayed himself: "Il convint qu'il y avait quelque chose de raisonnable dans mes pensées," and "Il comprit qu'il y avait plus de faiblesse que de malignité dans mes désordres" (93). Until now Tiberge has shown compassion for his friend's weakness, but here he also admits, reluctantly, that DGC's conduct can be defended rationally. Neither seems to notice that this long speech, defending the hero's voluntary pursuit of happiness, undermines his newfound excuse, "cette fatale tendresse" of which he claims to be the helpless victim. From this point forward, Tiberge ceases to be an effective opponent of his friend's love for Manon. He will reappear periodically in the novel, but he no longer represents a serious moral opposition.

Unlike Tiberge, Des Grieux's father does not benefit from the same careful introduction. There are no preliminary assurances of the man's noble character and kindly nature, and no proleptic regrets about the narrator's mistreatment of him. Instead, his portrait is developed existentially, and we must infer his qualities from his words and deeds. Whereas Tiberge exhibits compassion toward his friend's errors and weaknesses, the father reacts with humor and sarcasm toward his son's stupidity and blindness. As with Tiberge, his point of view comes across clearly in the narrator's indirect report of his speech:

> Il se contenta de me faire quelques reproches généraux sur *la faute que j'avais commise*. . . . [I]l me dit . . . qu'il espérait que *cette petite aventure* me rendrait plus sage. (32)

> Il me demanda d'abord si j'avais toujours eu *la simplicité de croire* que je fusse aimé de ma maîtresse. . . . Il ajouta mille railleries de cette force, sur ce qu'il appelait *ma sottise et ma crédulité*. (33)

His direct discourse is hardly more sympathetic: "Tu es une jolie dupe" (33), he laughs, and later scolds more sternly, "Vous êtes un enfant" (37). While direct discourse reveals the disparity between father and son, the narrating self seems to agree with the father: [1] "Il continuait toujours de m'apporter les raisons qui pouvaient me ramener au bon sens et m'inspirer du mépris pour l'infidèle Manon. [2] Il est certain que je ne l'estimais plus; [3] comment aurais-je estimé la plus volage et la plus perfide de toutes les créatures?" (36). The first sentence [1] contains semantic elements of the father's point of view, [2] reveals that the narrating self concurs, while the question posed in FID [3] seems to be focalized by the experiencing self, the despairing young man. A dissonant narrator could easily create a bond here between the father and the reader, both of whom would scoff at the hero's naïveté. DGN does indeed make a case for the father's viewpoint: "Je reconnaissais trop clairement qu'il avait raison. C'était un mouvement involontaire qui me faisait prendre ainsi le parti de *mon infidèle*" (37). Yet he also points to the hero's filial respect and obedience. Moreover, the father's lack of sensitivity creates a certain affective distance between him and the reader. Showing little sympathy for the young man's anguish, the father is set up as a heartless obstacle to his happiness.

Much later in the novel, when Des Grieux's father visits him in prison, his harsh attack on his son is reported directly: "Asseyez-vous, monsieur, me dit-il gravement, asseyez-vous." He speaks of the "scandale de votre libertinage et de vos friponneries" (161) and despairs over "les désordres d'un fils vicieux qui a perdu tous sentiments d'honneur" (162). A grudging admission of guilt on the part of the narrator is followed by the suggestion that the father is overreacting: "Quoique je fusse obligé de reconnaître que je méritais une partie de *ces outrages*, il me parut néanmoins que c'était les porter à l'excès" (162). In a long, quoted passage Des Grieux insists on his filial piety, again blames the fatality of passion, and begs his father for pity. The strategy is effective, for the father switches to the familiar "tu": "Viens, mon pauvre chevalier, me dit-il, viens m'embrasser; tu me fais pitié" (163). The narrator then intervenes to say that there is, after all, nothing so dishonorable about having a mistress or cheating at the gaming-table. DGC enumerates, in direct discourse, several examples of such conduct among the nobility. The narrator then tells his narratees that he could have also provided examples to justify his conduct toward the elder and younger G...M..., but out of honor he chose instead to blame this conduct on his own weakness.

The final meeting of father and son completes the transformation of the father into an unfeeling tyrant. DGC's passionate pleas on behalf of Manon are related through direct discourse. Direct discourse also translates the father's bitterness and anger, as he tells his son he would rather see him dead than dishonored. The narrator speaks of the father's "ton sec et dur" and of his "coeur . . . inflexible" (172). DGC, also in direct discourse, appeals to his father's own tender love for Des Grieux's mother, and asks a loaded question: "Peut-on être barbare, après avoir une fois éprouvé ce que c'est que la tendresse et la douleur?" (172). The hero is seen as a victim of persecution and the reader is asked to identify with his pain. Father and son are never more polarized than in their final words to one another, and each point of view is quoted directly: "Va, cours à ta perte. Adieu, fils ingrat et rebelle. Adieu, lui dis-je dans mon transport, adieu, père barbare et dénaturé" (172).

As we have seen, both characters—Tiberge and Des Grieux's father— are often quoted directly, and even indirect discourse allows for a partial presentation of their points of view. Unlike Manon, each is granted a large measure of focal autonomy. This does not mean, however, that focalization is not used as a device of manipulation. Tiberge's moral position is subtly undermined as the focal dominance shifts from the friend to the hero. By contrast, Des Grieux's father is an important focalizer in every scene in which he appears, and even the final confrontation is reported directly. While the father's attitude moves from good-natured sarcasm to bitter anger, the devoted son continues to plead for sensitivity and paternal compassion. The growing polarization of the two is foregrounded through the alternating focalization. The reader is left to decide, but once again the choice is biased and the response is conditioned.

Does all of this add up to unreliability on the part of the narrator? Booth (1983) states that when a novelist chooses to deliver his facts as though from the mind of one of his characters (and the personal narrator must be qualified as such), then the convention of absolute reliability has been destroyed (174–75). In this sense, all personal narrators are unreliable: they are mortal characters and therefore fallible (Glowinski 1977, 104), they may be trying to deceive us (Brady 1977, 52), and they are more likely to exhibit a certain bias in order to elicit our sympathy (Stanzel [1979] 1984, 150–51; Démoris 1975, 400). We are aware that all the "facts" are filtered through the consciousness of the personal narrator, but he is the only one on whom the reader can rely.[19]

Prince (1987), following Booth and Chatman, gives two definitions of an unreliable narrator: "A narrator whose norms and behavior are not in accordance with the implied author's norms" and "a narrator the reliability of whose account is undermined by various features of that account" (101). The first definition falls, in my opinion, outside the realm of structural narratology in that it depends upon each reader's construct of the implied author and his values. According to the second definition, I would say that Des Grieux is not an unreliable narrator. We may question his ideology and his interpretation of events, but we have no reason to question his report of the facts or even his self-portrait, since we have no alternative basis for comparison.[20] In this I concur with Stewart (1984): "The reader really has no choice but to 'believe' Des Grieux. The alternative is to react subjectively to his account, independently of the text . . . which . . . offers no substitute for the data supplied" (135). Des Grieux is, of course, a skilled manipulator, and every critical reader is

19. Scholes and Kellogg (1966) point out that the ancients considered personal narration to be less reliable than impersonal or "third-person" narration: a document had a better chance of appearing factual if it did not seem too personal (243). It is interesting that eighteenth-century fiction, on the contrary, strove for an appearance of historicity through personal narration.

20. Prince (1982) notes elsewhere that "a reliable narrator is not necessarily one that I—as a reader—always agree with: after all, however honest and trustworthy he may be portrayed as, I may find his values repugnant and his conclusions stupid" (12).

aware of the "slant" that the narrator casts upon the hero, upon Manon and the other characters in his story. If this tendentiousness is a sufficient criterion for classifying Des Grieux as an unreliable narrator, then the same must be said of the "supernarrator" who records the entire text and who predisposes us favorably toward the young lovers. Renoncour describes Manon's noble appearance as one that inspires respect and pity, and even the chief of the guards says "il me semble qu'elle vaut un peu mieux que ses compagnes" (12). The marquis also recognizes the noble birth and education of Des Grieux as well as the shameful venality of the guards. He quotes an archer, an old woman witnessing the deportation, the chief guard, and Des Grieux but fails to give us even an echo of the words of Manon. Finally, he characterizes the scene at Pacy as "[une] des plus extraordinaires et des plus touchantes" (14). Based on his introduction, there is every reason to believe that Renoncour will accept Des Grieux's report wholesale and without question. He is the perfect narratee whose reception of the tale will fulfill the narrator's intentions. In short, he provides no conflicting evidence upon which we could judge the narrator's reliability.[21] Moreover, Des Grieux is quite open about even his most sordid behavior. He divulges his duplicity and deceptions candidly, even though he ultimately tries to justify them and to exonerate himself. His rhetorical purpose is only too obvious, but it has proven effective on generations of readers. Focalization, as we have seen, is a major component in his arsenal of manipulative weapons.

21. Brady (1977) admits that the credibility of Des Grieux is somewhat increased by the presence of this "super-narrator" (50). Josephs (1968) states that the total acceptance of Des Grieux's narrative by Renoncour makes the latter morally indistinguishable from the hero (191).

4

LA RELIGIEUSE:
DENIAL OF COGNITIVE
PRIVILEGE

Both in form and in narrative technique, *La Religieuse* is certainly an anomaly in eighteenth-century French fiction. Diderot's heroine uses the epistolary form to record her memoirs, a technique that turns the text into a compromise between the epistolary novel and the memoir-novel. Despite its single narrative voice, it resembles a dialogue more than the usual monologue of the memoir-novel. The narrator's purpose in writing is directed toward a specific extralinguistic situation: she finds herself in dire straits and is requesting urgent assistance from the marquis, to whom her text is addressed. Her future depends upon the perlocutionary force of this text, that is, its ability to provoke a positive reaction from her potential benefactor. While Suzanne is clearly the center of interest, the presentation of her story is largely organized around her narratee and her discourse is insistently addressed to him, as in a dialogue. The text constantly refers to this speech event and to the time of Suzanne's enunciatory process. The reader is reminded, by the presence of discursive elements on nearly every page, that the narrator is "conversing" with her narratee. We shall consider each of these elements separately.

Narrative situation.   The conversation is set up in an unorthodox manner. In the opening paragraph of the novel (81–82), the here-and-now of the narrator's speech event is established by the tenses of discourse: "La réponse de M. le marquis de C***, s'il m'en *fait* une, me *fournira* les premières lignes de ce récit. Avant que de lui écrire, j'*ai voulu* le connaître. C'*est* un homme du monde." We learn that the narrator is a woman ("je ne m'étais point compromise"), although we will not know her name until she is addressed by a character in her story, several pages later. As she writes, she is waiting for a response from another character, an unnamed marquis to whom she has already written. The very existence of her text, however, is problematic. The deictic ("ce récit") seems to indicate the text we are reading, one that she is now writing at the moment of the narrative instance, and one whose first lines have, presumably and paradoxically, yet to be written. As Sherman (1985) says, the novel's first sentence "attains a logic if one sees it as a note for the eventual framing of a *livre à venir*" [a book to come] (63).[1] "This" text does not yet exist in its final form. There will be another, completed text to come later, after the marquis has replied. But the narrative realizes that this man may want to know who she is: "et c'est ce motif qui me résout à vaincre mon amour-propre et ma répugnance, en entreprenant ces Mémoires où je peins une partie de mes malheurs." Now the text begins to resemble a preface, introducing these memoirs that will be sent to the marquis in the form of a second letter, once again not the completed text that will eventually begin with the latter's response. A letter, however, needs no explanatory preface; and a preface presupposes that what is to follow has already been written ("où je peins une partie de mes malheurs"). The narrator goes on to speak of finishing her memoirs at a later date (which presupposes that they have been begun) and of "l'abrégé qui les termine" (which suggests they have been finished, albeit in the form of a résumé). Already, in this opening paragraph, the deictic field is blurred: is the narrator speaking (to an unknown narratee) before she produces her "récit"—the one yet to be written—or is she referring to the present text, these "Mémoires" that have already been written and that we are about to read? Her temporal relation to her own text is unclear.

In the following paragraph (82–85) the narrator begins to narrate her story in the past, by describing her relationship with her family. As though loath to yielding to historical narration, Suzanne continues to use discursive language: "Il s'en manque bien que j'en puisse faire cet éloge" [of her father]; "dès mes plus jeunes ans j'ai désiré de leur ressembler" [her sisters]; "O combien j'ai pleuré de fois." The presence

---

1. Stewart (1987) agrees that both the first paragraph and the postscript should be read as notes by Suzanne to herself "regarding the manner in which the uncompleted manuscript . . . is to be finally assembled" (84). Mylne (1981a) believes that the first paragraph creates problems due to Diderot's revisions and additions, and that it may be better to ignore it (24).

of these discursive elements, this conversational language that punctuates her narrative, results in the foregrounding of Suzanne-narrator (SN) with respect to Suzanne-character (SC). The conversation soon becomes explicit: "vous l'avouerai-je, Monsieur?" and further on, "que risquerais-je à vous les confier? Vous brûlerez cet écrit, et je vous promets de brûler vos réponses." The unspecified narratee is revealed at this point to be "Monsieur," addressed directly in the second person, another sign of discourse. This man is apparently a potential correspondent, as Suzanne expects written responses from him. This fact might establish the identity of her narratee as the aforementioned marquis, even though the vocative "Monsieur le marquis" will not be used until nearly a hundred pages later.[2] If so, then "cet écrit" is not the same as "ce récit" of the first paragraph, in which the marquis was introduced and described as a third person, outside the discourse. The opening paragraph appears to be, in retrospect, set off from the discourse of Suzanne with the marquis, which forms the body of her text. It constitutes a flagrant break with epistolary tradition yet resolves the problem of exposition. It provides a kind of frame, a rather unconventional way of presenting the narrative after it has been written.

In an attempt to impose coherence on this text, let us postulate, in addition to SC (the character) and SN (the original narrator of "cet écrit"), the existence of a third Suzanne, a retrospective Suzanne-editor (SE), who admits in her postscript to having reread at her leisure what was hastily written by SN (288). Let us suppose that SE writes the opening paragraph as an introduction for her forthcoming "récit," the completed text that she intends to send to the marquis and to which we have no access. We shall return later to this concept of SE, which for the moment will be a working hypothesis.[3]

---

2. Curiously, by the time this identity is firmly established, Suzanne seems to have received a response from the marquis: "Monsieur le marquis, je vois d'ici tout le mal que je vous cause, mais *vous avez voulu savoir* si je méritais un peu la compassion que j'attends de vous" [I see from here all the pain I am causing you, but *you wanted to know* if I was deserving of the compassion that I await from you] (171). Since she makes his identity more explicit in the second half of the novel, it is not clear what Pedersen (1978) means when he writes of a progressive "supplanting of the epistolary addressee by a narratee, more neutral and less explicit" (222).

3. This hypothesis of an editing Suzanne corresponds to Diderot's subsequent revisions of his text, which have often been cited as the cause of its incoherences. See May (1975, 10), Dieckmann (1975, 17, n. 7), and Mylne (1982, 167). On the other hand, these same critics have suggested that the incoherences might have been partly intentional. Mylne, for example, is no longer convinced, as she once was, that the inconsistencies are due to Diderot's inability to handle the retrospective vision of the memoir form (172). In a masterly article Hayes (1986) contends that the contradictions are essential in that they

Discourse is prominent throughout the novel. Let us examine the major functions of these discursive elements.

Establishment of the I–you relationship.   Elements of discourse enable Suzanne to establish and strengthen her relationship with her narratee, which is crucial to her narrative enterprise. Aside from numerous vocatives, her narrative contains many forms that are typical of conversation: imperatives ("Imaginez, Monsieur" 91; "Mais fermons vite les yeux là-dessus" 114; "car songez bien, Monsieur" 168); questions ("Une question, Monsieur, que j'aurais à vous faire" 134; "Mais qu'est-ce que cela signifie?" 148; "Voulez-vous que je vous donne . . . ?" 209); and exclamations ("O têtes folles de religieuses!" 148; "Combien ces journées me parurent longues!" 205). Such forms imbue the text with the oral qualities that epistolary narratives strive to emulate. Equally conversational is Suzanne's assumption that her narratee can anticipate and imagine events, especially when they cast aspersion on nuns and convents: "Vous vous doutez bien tout ce qu'elle put ajouter du monde et du cloître" (91); "Je vous laisse à penser le murmure qui s'éleva dans la communauté" (157); "Croirez-vous bien qu'on m'ôta mon bréviaire et qu'on me défendit de prier Dieu? Vous pensez bien que je n'obéis pas" (165). She assumes that his response will be, like her own, one of outrage and indignation. At one point she not only imagines the narratee's responses but also represents them textually:

> Lorsque toutes nos soeurs furent retirées . . .——Eh bien, que fites-vous?——Vous ne devinez pas? . . . Non, vous êtes trop honnête pour cela. Je descendis sur la pointe du pied et je vins me placer doucement à la porte du parloir et écouter ce qui se disait là. . . . Cela est fort mal, direz-vous. . . . Oh pour cela, oui, cela est fort mal; je me le dis à moi-même. (273)

It is evident that the intrusion of discursive language into the narrative foregrounds the temporal locus of the "I" and "you" of communication. Whereas on occasion Suzanne highlights differences between the con-

---

remind us of the textuality of the experience at hand: the reader must constantly return to what was read previously, and successive revelations continue to undermine what has gone before (234). For Champagne (1981), Suzanne's slips are due to her dual nature, a psychological complexity that causes her to write in "serial discourse" instead of in a logical sequence (342–44). Interpretive trends are clearly moving away from the notion of a careless author.

vent and society ("ces scandaleux applaudissements que l'on donne à vos comédiens" 144), more often direct address is used to stress the fact that narrator and narratee share the same world: "Vous savez, Monsieur, que le Jeudi l'on transporte le St. Sacrement" (144). The marquis shares the same deictic field as Suzanne, not only as a reader of her text in the here-and-now, but also as a participant, as a character in the there-and-then of her historical narration. Suzanne associates him with her story and integrates him into it: "Une foule de personnes . . . sollicitèrent pour moi. Vous fûtes de ce nombre, et peut-être l'histoire de mon procès vous est-elle mieux connue qu'à moi" (167); "J'excusais donc l'avocat Manouri . . . et vous-même, Monsieur le marquis" (202). It is noteworthy that Suzanne knew the marquis, or at least knew of him, before she began to compose her text. The discursive relationship with her narratee is maintained so that Suzanne can better provoke a positive reaction from him. She asks him to judge her actions: "Je pris un parti dont vous jugerez, Monsieur, comme il vous plaira" (96); "Mais vous, Monsieur, qui connaissez jusqu'à ce moment tout ce qui s'est passé, qu'en pensez-vous?" (115); "des actions que vous appellerez ou imprudence ou fermeté selon le coup d'oeil sous lequel vous les considérerez" (129). Finally, and most important, she reminds him of her appeal for help, of his capacity to determine her future: "Voilà l'époque de mon bonheur ou de mon malheur, selon, Monsieur, la manière dont vous en userez avec moi" (92); "ce pressentiment, Monsieur, se vérifiera si vous m'abandonnez" (112); "Monsieur, que je ne sache pas où aller ni que devenir, cela dépend de vous" (116).

Reference to the narrative process.   Like any narrator, Suzanne can (and often does) point to the text she is writing and to her own storytelling process. The deictics "voici" and "ici" are commonly used means of simultaneously presenting a temporal moment in the story and a spatial locus in the text: "Le voici pourtant arrivé ce moment" (93); "Voici le moment le plus terrible de ma vie" (168); "c'est comme vous l'avez pu voir jusqu'ici" (206). And like any narrator, Suzanne can draw attention away from the moment of event, using other discursive formulae to move backward and forward in her story. A move backward can serve as a reminder ("Je vous ai dit que j'avais le même directeur que ma mère" 103) or as an analeptic filling-in of overlooked events ("J'oubliais de vous dire que je vis mon père et ma mère" 89). Proleptic sentences used to create suspense ("mais vous allez apprendre à quel prix" 167) are not common in Suzanne's narrative. As we shall see, she chooses to create suspense through other techniques. When she refers forward from the moment of event, it is more often to mark an ellipsis: "Je ne vous ferai pas le détail de mon noviciat" (91); "je passe rapidement sur ces deux années" (118). SN refers to her written text each time SC recounts her story, in her legal brief ("c'était en abrégé, tout ce que je viens de vous écrire" 135) and in her oral report to the superior of Sainte-Eutrope ("Je commençai donc mon récit à peu près comme je viens de vous l'écrire" 231). Her modesty as a narrator can be seen in her often-avowed inability to express certain past emotions in writing, even when they are her own: "Je ne saurais vous peindre ma douleur" (201); "Je ne saurais vous dire l'effet qu'il produisit sur elle" (231). What is important to note here is that each of these various references to the narrative process constitutes an intrusion of discourse into the historical narration and a foregrounding of the I–you relationship.

Attestation of veracity.   In order to move the marquis to action on her behalf, Suzanne must convince him of the truth of her narrative. The mere fact that she is a participant in her story serves to guarantee its veracity to a certain extent, but in addition her discourse fulfills a testimonial function. Many of the narrator's statements attest to the truth of their content: "je vous assure qu'une fille plus fine que moi y aurait été trompée" (89); "car il est sûr, Monsieur, que sur cent religieuses qui meurent avant cinquante ans, il y en a cent tout juste de damnées" (92); "Je ne dis rien qui ne soit vrai" (280). Suzanne anticipates disbelief on the part of her narratee(s): "Je vous entends vous, Monsieur le marquis et la plupart de ceux qui liront ces mémoires. . . . Cela n'est pas vraisemblable, diront-ils, dites-vous; et j'en conviens; mais cela est vrai" (178). She alludes to the possibility of other readers, all of whom will have the same reaction of disbelief that she anticipates from the marquis. She forestalls this disbelief by insisting on the unusual (if not incredible) behavior encountered in monastic life: "Je vais vous dire une chose qui vous paraîtra fort étrange peut-être et qui n'en est pas moins vraie" (132).

Admission of ignorance.   Related to Suzanne's concern for veracity and her attention to the narrative process is her readiness to attenuate the certainty of what she recounts. Even more striking, quantitatively, than her attestations of truth are her admissions of what she does not know with certainty (the expressions "je ne sais," "je ne saurais," and "que sais-je?" occur more than fifty times throughout the novel). Some of these attenuations are quite mundane, referring to small details that the narrator cannot remember: "C'était, je crois, le jour de l'Ascension" (162); "C'était le mardi, autant qu'il m'en souvient" (205). Very often, however, Suzanne maintains an impression of objectivity by denying certainty about what other characters were doing and thinking: "Je ne sais ce qui se passait dans l'âme des assistants" (100); "Je ne sais ce qu'elle pensait" (234); "je ne sais ce qu'elle lui avait répondu" (253). At times SN is still uncertain about the mind of SC ("Je ne sais ce qui se passa dans mon âme" 101) and obviously knows nothing of what happened when SC was unconscious ("Je ne sais combien je restai dans cet état" 170). Limitations are placed on what the autodiegetic narrator can know about the consciousness of other characters, and Suzanne seems to respect these limitations by her admission of ignorance. Ignorance, as we shall see, plays a major thematic role in the novel. Here we shall limit our observations to the fact that the narrator is especially and persistently ignorant regarding two series of events. First of all, she is ignorant of what happens to her during the various ceremonies in which she takes vows: "Le jour fut pris, mes habits faits, le moment de la cérémonie arrivé sans que j'aperçoive *aujourd'hui* le moindre intervalle entre ces choses" (89; the deictic points to SN, who still lacks knowledge about SC's decision to become a novice); "je ne me souviens ni de m'être déshabillée, ni d'être sortie de ma cellule. . . . J'ai appris ces choses depuis" (99; SN does not remember what happened to SC the night before she refused to pronounce her vows); "On disposa de moi pendant toute cette matinée qui a été nulle dans ma vie, car je n'en ai jamais connu la durée; je ne sais ni ce que j'ai fait, ni ce que j'ai dit. On m'a sans doute interrogée, j'ai sans doute répondu, j'ai prononcé des voeux, mais je n'en ai nulle mémoire" (123–24; the same phenomenon occurs on the day of her final profession at Sainte-Marie). A second pattern of ignorance can be observed in SN's account of SC's relationship with the lesbian superior of Sainte-Eutrope. So unable is SN to explain the behavior of SC and that of her superior that her discourse during this episode constitutes a litany of denials: "je ne sais si ce fut de plaisir ou de peine" (227); "je ne sais ce qui se passait en moi" (228); "je ne sais comment cela se fit" (229); "je ne sais ce que nous dîmes encore" (237).

Self-description.   The abundance of quoted dialogue in the text provides a certain kind of self-portrait through which Suzanne can reveal her own character. In addition, she uses the present tense to describe herself, not the way she was *then*, at the moment of event, but the way she still is *now*, at the moment of utterance. The composite self-portrait is most attractive: "J'ai du courage" (131); "mon esprit va vite"

(135); "mon âme s'allume facilement, s'exalte, se touche" (147); "J'ai la figure intéressante . . . j'ai un son de voix qui touche" (174); "j'ai le caractère porté à l'indulgence, je puis tout pardonner aux hommes" (202); "j'aime à louer" (217); "je suis naturellement compatissante" (263). She announces from the outset that she has written her story "avec la naïveté d'un enfant de mon âge et la franchise de mon caractère" (82). At times Suzanne appears to be a bit more modest and attenuates the flattery of her self-descriptions by projecting them onto another character: "je ne sais s'il me convient de vous dire qu'elle m'aima tendrement et que je ne fus pas des dernières entre ses favorites. Je sais que c'est un grand éloge que je me donne" (117); "En vérité, je serais bien belle, si je méritais la plus petite partie des éloges qu'elle me donnait" (222). Suzanne knows that her self-portrait is quite flattering. In the postscript to her narrative she expresses the fear that she may appear to be trying to seduce the marquis by portraying herself "beaucoup plus aimable que je ne le suis" (288). It is obviously important for her purpose that she present herself in the most attractive fashion. By her own admission, this concern affects her narration:

> Je prévois, Monsieur le marquis, que vous allez prendre mauvaise opinion de moi. . . . Disons donc que j'ai un tour d'esprit bien singulier; lorsque les choses peuvent *exciter votre estime ou accroître votre commisération*, j'écris bien ou mal, mais avec une vitesse et une facilité incroyables. . . . [I]l me semble que vous êtes présent, que je vous vois et que vous m'écoutez. Si je suis forcée au contraire de me montrer à vos yeux sous un aspect défavorable, je pense avec difficulté, l'expression se refuse, la plume va mal . . . et je ne continue que parce que je me flatte secrètement que vous ne lirez pas ces endroits. (273)

To write unflattering things about herself is to ignore her precarious situation and to weaken the perlocutionary force of her text. She can bring herself to do so only by pretending she has no narratee, by suspending momentarily the I–you relationship upon which so much depends.[4]

Commentary.   Suzanne is an intrusive narrator who uses the present tense to provide achronic commentary on her world. Only rarely are

---

4. Undank (1986) states that Suzanne "borrows other people's eyes, and the eyes of those who surround her are vital for her narration and therefore vital for the reader" (154). Knight (1985) studies Suzanne's speculation on how others see her, particularly men: "It is the potential clairvoyance of the Marquis de Croismare that Suzanne fears the most" (25).

these comments expressed in the form of a modalized, subjective opinion: "Le monde a ses précipices, mais je n'imagine pas qu'on y arrive par une pente aussi facile" (91). Far more often they take the form of an objective statement, an aphoristic comment on society or human nature: "A force de s'occuper d'une chose on en sent la justice et même l'on en croit la possibilité" (135). As one would expect, the overwhelming subject of Suzanne's commentary is monastic life. Sometimes her remarks are merely explanations, for the benefit of her narratee, of the truths that prevail in the convent: "Il n'est permis en couvent ni d'écrire ni de recevoir des lettres sans la permission de la supérieure" (189); "nous portons nos voeux d'une maison dans une autre" (210); "C'est une grande affaire pour une maison de religieuses que le choix d'un confesseur" (252). Such explanatory remarks are necessary for a proper understanding of her story. A great many other comments, however, are more ideological in nature and contain acerbic criticism of monastic life. The quantitative preponderance of these critical statements is striking. They are often disguised as objective aphorisms through use of the achronic present tense: "L'acharnement à tourmenter et à perdre se lasse dans le monde, il ne se lasse point dans les cloîtres" (134); "Il y a dans les communautés des têtes faibles, c'est même le grand nombre" (163). The achronic present is often combined with the impersonal "vous," lending a conversational tone to the supposedly objective statements: "Ces femmes se vengent bien de l'ennui que vous leur portez; car il ne faut pas croire qu'elles s'amusent du rôle hypocrite qu'elles jouent et des sottises qu'elles sont forcées de vous répéter" (92). The narrator's lexical choices play a large role in her critical commentary: she refers to religious writings as "le nombreux fatras" (91), to a religious ceremony as "une momerie" (159), to her superior at Longchamp as "l'hypocrite" (155); she speaks of "des pieuses fadaises dont on remplit ces premiers moments" (115) and of "les méchantes créatures que des femmes recluses . . . qui croient servir Dieu en vous désespérant!" (168).

As the last few examples suggest, Suzanne's commentary is not always achronic. The discourse of SN sometimes intrudes into the diegetic world of her narrative to comment upon characters or events—a kind of intrusion that is quite common in autobiographical novels. Just after she has been urged to take the veil, Suzanne has a conversation with the superior of Sainte-Marie:

> "J'étais dans un désordre qui ne se peut expliquer. Elle me dit: Et qu'avez-vous, ma chère enfant? [1] (Elle savait mieux que moi ce que j'avais.) Comme vous voilà!" [Suzanne continues to speak of the superior.] Elle parut avoir pitié de moi. . . . [E]lle me promit

> de prier, de remontrer, de solliciter. [2] O Monsieur, combien ces
> supérieures de couvent sont artificieuses! vous n'en avez point
> d'idée. Elle écrivit en effet. Elle n'ignorait pas les réponses qu'on
> lui ferait . . . [3] et ce n'est qu'après bien du temps que j'ai appris
> à douter de sa bonne foi. (87)

The first intrusion [1], signaled by parentheses, allows the narrating self
to interrupt the quoted speech of another character. The focalizer of this
parenthetical remark is probably SN, especially since it occurs early in
SC's experience with convents. There can be no doubt, however, that
the focalization of the second intrusion [2], signaled by a vocative that
interrupts the historical narration, is that of the narrating self. The final
intrusion [3], signaled by the present and *passé composé*, makes it clear
that the sarcasm belongs to the later, ideological thought of SN, who has
learned to distrust her superior. Consequently, a sentence like "Elle
n'ignorait pas les réponses," while appearing less objective (and even
paraleptic) on the surface than "Elle parut avoir pitié de moi," must be
interpreted as a mere supposition on the part of the narrator, who is
commenting directly and indirectly on the behavior of this character.
Intrusive commentary is thus used as a kind of self-defense, to correct
what may be a false impression created by other characters. In another
passage SN interrupts the indirectly reported speech of a nun, a speech
that SC was not even present to hear: "Une autre ajouta . . . que je
foulais le Christ aux pieds et que je ne portais plus mon rosaire (qu'on
m'avait volé); que je proférais des blasphèmes que je n'ose vous répéter"
(165–66). Here SN intervenes twice in her own defense, first by correcting the information provided indirectly by a character, and then by refusing to repeat the blasphemies that SC is supposed to have said. The
second intrusion is predicated on the dual referentiality of the first-
person pronoun, "*je* proférais" being diegetic whereas "*je* n'ose" is discursive. Commentary of this type emphasizes the narrator's knowledge
of hindsight. It is used to direct the opinion of her narratee, to persuade,
and to highlight an ideology.

Relation of past to present.   It is important to Suzanne's narrative enterprise that she emphasize the continuity of experience, that she
not allow the events of her story to slip too far back into the historical
past. Temporal distance of this kind might induce an affective distance
on the part of her narratee. The relation of past to present is the function
of the *passé composé*, the tense that creates a living connection between
the past event and its evocation in the present. It is a subjective tense of

discourse, one that expresses an accomplishment that still has an enduring result in the present of enunciation. When Suzanne says "Je n'ai jamais rien vu de si hideux" (92), she still, at the moment of narrative instance, has not seen anything so hideous. When she speaks of Moni as "cette femme rare qui a laissé après elle des regrets qui ne finiront point" (126), she means that those regrets still exist, and the value of the first verb as a perfect is underscored by the future tense of the second. Use of the *passé composé* in cases such as these is common in classical narration. In discourse, however (and this was true as early as the seventeenth century), the *passé composé* can have the value of a preterite as well as that of a perfect, because it has assumed the function of the *passé simple.* This functional equivalence can be seen in the following passage: "Et pourquoi Dieu ne m'a-t-il pas prise dans ce moment? j'allais à lui sans inquiétude. C'est un si grand bonheur, et qui est-ce qui peut se le promettre deux fois?" (196). The verb in Suzanne's question clearly functions as a preterite, since it is linked to a specific moment, but it is expressed in the *passé composé* because it is also clearly an element of discourse. This bifunctionality of the *passé composé* will have consequences for the problem of focalization, as we shall see.

Our analysis has shown so far that Suzanne is a ubiquitous, self-conscious narrator whose discourse dominates her historical narration. She constantly draws attention to her narratee and to her narrative process. While she strives to guarantee the truth of her story, she is also careful to confess her ignorance of certain facts. In the process, she describes herself in a most flattering way and provides commentary on her story which is most critical of monasticism. In an effort to relate her past to the present of her narratee, she shows a certain predilection for the *passé composé*, a tense that can function either as a perfect or a preterite, yet a tense that definitely belongs to the realm of discourse and thus points toward her current discursive situation with the marquis. We must now turn to the ways in which Suzanne uses focalization to further her narrative goals.

Spatial and psychological transgressions.   As we have seen, when a narrating subject is also the object of her narration, convention requires that certain limitations be imposed. The narrating self has the vantage point of seeing the whole picture temporally, but her field of perception is limited both spatially (for physical perceptions that as a character she was not in a position to have) and psychologically (for the mental perceptions of other characters). In other words, the objects of her focalization must be proximal and physically perceivable, according to memoir-novel logic. If she wishes to provide information that transgresses these limitations, she must logically account for her sources. Spatially, the focalization in this novel is almost always fixed on the proximity of SC and follows the latter throughout most of the historical narration. There are, however, several occurrences of spatial transgressions in the text, most of which are brief. SN relates the deliberation of the nuns at Longchamp and their vote for exorcism, even quoting their speech indirectly, while SC was presumably not present to hear this (165). SN states that Manouri and others were assembled at Sainte-Eutrope before the arrival of SC (206); and SN mentions that the superior of Sainte-Eutrope watched SC for hours without the latter's noticing her (261). In the longest of these passages, the distal object is Moni:

> Je dormais, et cependant cette sainte femme allait dans les corridors, frappait à chaque porte, éveillait les religieuses et les faisait descendre sans bruit dans l'église. [Moni invites them to pray with her, and we read her quoted prayer.] Le lendemain elle entra de bonne heure dans ma cellule. Je ne l'entendis point, je n'étais pas encore éveillée. Elle s'assit à côté de mon lit . . . et c'est ainsi qu'elle m'apparut lorsque j'ouvris les yeux. (120–21)

The passage seems to be nonfocalized insofar as the reader witnesses an event not perceived by the sleeping SC. Who is the subject of perception here? Given that there is no formal evidence of a shift in focalization, we must attribute this presentation to SN herself, who after all is not limited *now* to the spatial location of SC *then*. The function of these spatial infractions is clearly to enable the reader to witness an event that SN deems important but that SC did not perceive.

The objects of focalization can be psychological as well as spatial. Psychological infractions occur when the narrator makes incursions into the minds of other characters and reveals thoughts that SC could not have known. At times the incursion is so brief that it is hardly noticeable, and indeed may be attributed to a supposition on the part of the narrator ("l'on *affecta* de croire le contraire" 90). On one occasion, SN provides us with information that SC could not have known for both spatial and psychological reasons: "Nous [Suzanne and Thérèse] en étions là, lorsque la supérieure entra. Elle avait passé à ma cellule, elle ne m'y avait point trouvée; elle avait parcouru presque toute la maison, inutilement; il ne lui vint pas en pensée que j'étais chez Ste. Thérèse" (220). On another occasion SN seems to read the minds of both Hébert and the nuns at Longchamp:

[C]ar songez bien, Monsieur, que j'ignorais absolument sous quelles couleurs on m'avait peinte aux yeux de cet ecclésiastique, et qu'il venait avec la curiosité de voir une fille possédée ou qui le contrefaisait. On crut qu'il n'y avait qu'une forte terreur qui pût me montrer dans cet état, et voici comment on s'y prit pour me la donner. (168–69)

Here it is clear that SN is admitting to something that SC did not know, and then proceeds to explain it. Perhaps this points to subsequent knowledge.

Psychological infractions such as these raise more serious questions of plausibility than their spatial counterparts: SN may not be limited to the thoughts of SC in the there-and-then, but as a represented human being she cannot be omniscient, and a reader may well demand some justification for her knowledge. On the other hand, it is quite possible for SN to recount events that SC did not know at the time but about which SN has learned subsequently. The quoted prayer of Moni and even the indirect speech of the nuns' deliberation might stretch credibility a bit, but surely no more so than the long quoted dialogues that SN reports verbatim. Similarly, it is possible that the narrator's mind-reading of other characters is merely supposition on her part. Her retrospective stance, indeed, favors such possibilities, so that a less rigorous narratee might not ask for documentation.

As it turns out, however, Suzanne seems to be conscious of the need to justify her information in some cases. There are several passages in the novel in which SN appears at first to be committing infractions but which are later justified, or at least partially explained. She details the progress of her legal litigation and concludes that "ce fut là ce qui accéléra *apparemment* le visite du grand vicaire" (167). The spatial transgression is at least partially justified by the adverb of supposition. She enumerates, analeptically, all the services Ursule has rendered, but not until she has learned about them: "J'ignorais tout cela" (137). She reports all the searches ordered by the superior Sainte-Christine in order to find her *mémoire*, and explains: "je vis une partie de ces recherches, je soupçonnai le reste" (137). Her knowledge of certain events at Sainte-Eutrope that took place while she was sleeping is justified gradually:

La nuit suivante, lorsque tout le monde dormait et que la maison était dans le silence, elle [the superior] se leva. . . . Elle s'arrêta; en s'appuyant le front *apparemment* contre ma porte. . . . Pendant que je dormais on entra . . . on tenait une petite bougie dont la lumière m'éclairait le visage, et celle qui la portait me regardait

> dormir, ce fut du moins ce que *j'en jugeai* à son attitude lorsque j'ouvris les yeux. (237–38)

Finally, the superior tells her the whole story, confirming everything Suzanne has supposed.

So it seems that despite the logic of convention, the narrator has a great deal of focal freedom, even when her objects are spatially distal and psychologically inaccessible. While in some cases she takes pains to document her sources of information, in most cases she does not, any more than she justifies her knowledge of events that we do not see, such as the death of her attorney. These infractions, however, do not necessarily pose a serious threat to the credibility of the narrator, whose retrospective stance allows for hypothetical explanations of them. As Genette (1972) points out, we must reserve the term *paralepsis* for those cases in which the narrator tells us something she could never have known.

Representation of speech and thoughts.   Unlike Des Grieux, Suzanne shows a predilection for quoting the speech of other characters directly, thereby ceding focalization to them.[5] We should note that the text does not always distinguish graphically between quoted speech and narration, or between the discourse of SN and her self-quoted monologues. Speech and thoughts are often not signaled by quotation marks or inquit formulae. As a result, their propositional content is sometimes the only clue as to their status.[6] In the following very brief example of quoted speech mingled with narration, the change in verb tense is the only signal: "Elle examina les couvertures . . . elles sont bonnes. Elle prit le traversin" (212). In another example the attributive phrase comes after the unsignaled quotation: "O Monsieur, quelle nuit que celle qui précéda! Je ne me couchai point, j'étais assise sur mon lit. J'appelais Dieu à mon secours, j'élevais mes mains au Ciel. . . . O Dieu! que vais-je devenir? . . . En prononçant ces mots, il me prit une défaillance générale" (98–99). The proximity of the two vocatives makes the latter seem at first like another discursive element rather than self-quoted speech, espe-

---

5. Mylne (1981a) has stated that about one-third of the novel consists of direct speech. Although this is a higher proportion than for most fiction of the period, Crébillon and Marivaux use dialogue even more liberally (61).

6. I am essentially ignoring the use of punctuation here as it is often the result of an editorial decision, according to Varloot (1975) in his preface to this edition (78). There are some contradictions between the usage of Diderot and that of his copyist Girbal to distinguish between speech and the narrative. Use of ellipses is not systematic enough to constitute a signal.

cially since SN is pleading for help from her narratee. In both of these examples and in the following one, the narrator seems to be concerned with economy of expression, deleting the usual phrases of attribution: "Elle me demanda comment je me portais, que l'office avait été bien long aujourd'hui; que j'avais un peu toussé, que je lui paraissais indisposée" (94). This is indirect discourse striving to be free; like indirect discourse in tense and person, it resembles direct discourse in deixis ("aujourd'hui") and nearly so in subordination (the subordinating verb "demanda" can apply only to the first of the four clauses). This economy of expression even extends on one occasion into dialogue. SN relates the conversation SC had with Moni on the morning of SC's profession:

> [1] [E]lle me demanda seulement si je m'étais couchée de bonne heure. [2] Je lui répondis, à l'heure que vous m'avez ordonnée. [3]——Si j'avais reposé. [4]——Profondément. [5]——Je m'y attendais . . . [6] Comment je me trouvais. [7]——Fort bien. Et vous chère Mère? [8]——Hélas! me dit-elle. (121)

In this remarkable passage, which prefigures some of the dialogic techniques of *Jacques le fataliste,* we have [1] an attributed indirect question, [2] an attributed direct answer, [3] then all signs of narration disappear with a free indirect question, [4] a free direct answer, [5] a free direct response, then [6] another free indirect question, [7] a free direct answer, and finally [8] an attributed direct answer. This hybrid technique, midway between indirect discourse and the direct speech of dialogue, foregrounds the presence of Suzanne, both as SC whose words are quoted directly, and as SN who narrates the responses of Moni. It also points to the lack of graphic distinctions among various kinds of represented speech in the text. In the following passage, introducing the superior of Sainte-Eutrope, the identity of verb tense makes the distinction even less apparent:

> [U]ne religieuse alors manque-t-elle à la moindre chose, elle la fait venir dans sa cellule, la traite avec dureté, lui ordonne de se déshabiller et de se donner vingt coups de discipline; la religieuse obéit. . . . [L]a supérieure devenue compatissante lui arrache l'instrument de pénitence, se met à pleurer; *qu'elle est bien malheureuse d'avoir à punir!* lui baise le front, les yeux, la bouche, les épaules, la caresse, la loue; *mais qu'elle a la peau blanche et douce! le bel embonpoint! le beau cou! le beau chignon!* Soeur Ste. Augustine, mais tu es folle d'être honteuse. . . . Elle la baise encore. . . . On

> est très mal avec ces femmes-là, on ne sait jamais ce qui leur plaira
> ou déplaira. (209)

SN passes without perceptible transition from the iterative present to the reported speech of the superior (in italics), returns to the iterative present, then again to reported speech, then to unsignaled quoted speech (which turns the iterative into a pseudo-iterative), then back to the pseudo-iterative present before returning to her own discourse with her narratee. The superior's speech is reported in another hybrid form, one that retains the third person of narrated monologue and the present tense of quoted monologue. Since the entire passage is written in the present tense, all forms of speech seem to blend together and only the propositional content can distinguish one form from another. The result provides a most interesting technique for introducing a character, moving gradually from the iterative to the singulative and from the oblique to the direct.

The most famous and most commented-upon pages illustrating the uncertainty of attribution constitute the long rhetorical passage at the center of the novel, which contains its ideological thrust (181–84). The narrator describes Manouri's *mémoire* and defends him to her narratee, explaining SC's reasons for placing restrictions on him. With "Quand on donne des bornes si étroites à ses défenses," there begins a series of long sentences condemning the judicial process. This appears at first to be achronic commentary, but it is still anchored deictically on the narrator by first-person pronouns ("on s'occupe à nous décourager et à nous résigner toutes à notre sort"). The quotation marks that open the sentence "Il me semble pourtant que dans un Etat bien gouverné" signal a quoted monologue, apparently distinguishing this "me" from the first person of SN. The focalization has shifted, but to whom is still unclear. Two pages later, after a long series of rhetorical questions condemning monasticism, we read: "On ne sait pas l'histoire de ces asiles, disait ensuite M. Manouri dans son plaidoyer, on ne la sait pas." This sentence closes the quotation and indicates a return to the narrative context. Its attributive phrase comes as a bit of a surprise, revealing as it does that all this commentary has been focalized by the attorney.[7] SN thus allows the most virulent antimonastic attack of her entire text to be presented from the point of view of a sympathetic character.

Aside from the many dialogues in which SN quotes the words of other

---

7. The quotation marks before "Il me semble" were a later addition to the manuscript. Some modern editors choose to ignore them, thereby removing the signal of quoted monologue and the shift in focalization. The attributive phrase at the end is then even more incongruous.

characters, she also embeds their speech into her historical narration through narrated monologues. Always unsignaled by definition, narrated monologue presents a speech or thought in the character's language while retaining the tense and person of narration. Indeed, the embedded speech can sometimes take on the appearance of a narrated fact, as in the following example in which the superior of Sainte-Marie is trying to persuade Suzanne to take the veil: [1] "Elle joignit à ces propos insidieux tant de caresses, tant de protestations d'amitié, tant de faussetés douces; [2] je savais où j'étais, je ne savais où l'on me mènerait, [3] et je me laissai persuader" (88). The focalizer of [1] is clearly SN, and its vocabulary is part of her rhetoric. The past tenses and the identical personal pronouns in [2] and [3] make the entire statement appear to be historical narration ("je savais . . . je ne savais . . . je me laissai persuader"). But only section [3] is a narrative fact. Section [2] represents a speech or a thought and does not belong to SN, who has briefly yielded the focalization. It can be read as self-narrated past thoughts, focalized by SC. It can also be read as an example of the "propos insidieux," as the embedded speech of the superior, especially since their neutrality contrasts sharply with the sarcasm of SN in [1]. The ambiguous focalization thus affords ironic insight into the kind of reasoning that could fool an innocent girl, and at the same time represents her thoughts leading to persuasion.

Narrated monologue is an effective device for foregrounding irony. Suzanne casts the subjective speech of her fellow nuns into the grammar of objective narration, in order to better display their hypocrisy. In the following passage SC has just announced her decision to make profession:

> Voilà la joie répandue dans toute la maison. . . . "Dieu avait parlé à mon coeur; personne n'était plus faite pour l'état de perfection que moi. Il était impossible que cela ne fût pas, on s'y était toujours attendu. On ne remplit pas ses devoirs avec taut d'édification et de constance quand on n'y est pas vraiment destinée. La mère des novices n'avait jamais vu dans aucune de ses élèves de vocation mieux caractérisée; elle était toute surprise du travers que j'avais pris, mais elle avait toujours bien dit à notre mère supérieure qu'il fallait tenir bon et que cela passerait." (96–97)

The quotation marks (a later addition) represent an attempt to signal the shift in focalization, yet this is clearly not a quotation but rather narrated speech. Even without the punctuation, the semantic content would be sufficient evidence that these words do not represent the opinion of either SC or SN. The irony is only too obvious. Sometimes there are lexical clues as well as semantic ones: "Il ne se passe pas une histoire fâcheuse dans le monde qu'on ne vous en parle; on arrange les vraies; on en fait de fausses; et puis ce sont des louanges sans fin et des actions de grâce à Dieu *qui nous met à couvert de ces humiliantes aventures*" (91–92). Here the italicized section is actually quoted speech, blending not with the historical past but with the iterative present of the narrator's discourse. In addition to the semantic clues, there is the word "humiliantes," which cannot reflect the view of SN, who has just said the stories were contrived and false, and she seems to exclude herself from the "nous." The nuns' hypocrisy is thus amplified through the use of their own idiom.

In addition to representing speech, the narrator uses narrated monologue, very sparingly, to convey the thoughts of other characters, particularly the thoughts of "on," the other nuns, the composite enemy:[8] "l'on apporta encore bien de l'embarras et de la violence à une chose qui n'en exigeait que parce qu'on y avait pourvu; il fallait que ce prêtre me vît obsédée, possédée ou folle" (174). Rather than explaining the nuns' behavior, SN delegates the focalization to them, and their thoughts betray their own cruelty. Yet this technique raises once again the problem of the source of these insights. The problem is even more complicated in the following passage: "Tout cela fut remarqué, et l'on en conclut que le papier que j'avais demandé avait été employé autrement que je ne l'avais dit. Mais s'il n'avait pas servi à ma confession, comme il était évident, quel usage en avais-je fait? Sans savoir qu'on prendrait ces inquiétudes, je sentis . . ." (136). SN wants her reader to know what was going on behind SC's back, and the narrated monologue of "on" (presumably the superior) serves to heighten the suspense. The last sentence reveals a dissonant narrator but does not explain how she knows now. The perceived objects are not only psychological, they are also distal, since SC was obviously not present. Even if the "on" is read as a plural and the narrated monologue as speech, the distal problem remains.

To represent the speech of her sisters, Suzanne uses a hybrid method that moves from oblique to direct presentation. Narrated monologue serves as a transition from the narrative context to reported speech:

> [C]et acte que je leur [her sisters] proposais, fait tandis que j'étais encore engagée en religion, devenait invalide, et il était trop incertain pour elles que je le ratifiasse quand je serais libre. [1] Et

8. By Mylne's (1981a) count, Suzanne uses the pronoun "on" to designate her family or the treacherous nuns over seven hundred times (28).

puis leur convenait-il d'accepter mes propositions? [2] Laisseront-elles une soeur sans asile et sans fortune? Jouiront-elles de son bien? Que dira-t-on dans le monde? [3] Si elle vient nous demander du pain, la refuserons-nous? S'il lui prend en fantaisie de se marier, qui sait la sorte d'homme qu'elle épousera? Et si elle a des enfants? . . . Il faut contrarier de toute notre force cette dangereuse tentative. [4] Voilà ce qu'elles se dirent et ce qu'elles firent. (151)

The narrated monologue of the first question [1] yields to an unusual form [2], midway between narrated and quoted speech. Like the narrated form, it retains third-person reference to the sisters, while its future tense, like the quoted monologue that follows, is deictically anchored on the moment of event. In the unsignaled quoted speech [3], the pronoun references are of course reversed. The final attributive sentence [4] returns to the person and tense of historical narration. Here we see a transfer of deictic center, from that of the I–you relationship of SN and the narratee to that of the characters, who focalize the entire speech and whose direct discourse eventually dominates that of the narrator. The transfer is effected gradually, first through tense and then through person. The narrating agent gives up all authority and allows her reader to perceive the sisters' reasoning directly, a reasoning that is sure to condemn their selfishness and avarice.[9] SN is of course unable to present this conversation as a witnessed event in the context of her narrative. By backgrounding her own presence, she sidesteps the distal problem involved. As we have seen, she willingly delegates focalization to others, particularly when their speech and even their thoughts are likely to evoke censure.

Representation of her own past thoughts.　　Theoretically, the experiencing self is the one character whose consciousness is accessible to the narrating self without restriction. When Suzanne presents her own past thoughts indirectly, the experiencing self becomes the focalizer: "Je m'aperçus qu'il [a suitor] me distinguait et qu'elle [her sister] ne serait incessamment que le prétexte de ses assiduités" (84); "je crus qu'on penserait à moi et que je ne tarderais pas à sortir du couvent" (86). The focal shifts here are made explicit by the verbs of

---

9. In the original manuscript, this entire passage was written as quoted monologue and later changed by the author to reflect a progression in presentation. I shall occasionally refer in the notes to the original version of certain passages, using the symbol OV, and shall discuss these later in the chapter.

physical and mental perception. One might expect a narrator as intrusive as SN to be largely a dissonant one, distinguishing carefully between past and present thoughts. We have indeed seen instances in which she intrudes into her historical narration and even into the speech of other characters to correct impressions and guide the opinion of her narratee. In point of fact, however, SN manifests a tendency toward consonance regarding SC, so that the polarity between past and present is not always observed.

Self-quotation of past thoughts is rare in this text. When it occurs, it is unsignaled: "On veut que je sois religieuse, peut-être est-ce aussi la volonté de Dieu, eh bien, je le serai; puisqu'il faut que je sois malheureuse, qu'importe où je le sois?" (111–12). With no introductory or concluding phrase of attribution, this interior monologue has the formal appearance of the discourse of SN although it is obviously the thought of SC. Again the referential distinction is blurred because the discursive tenses are here anchored in both deictic fields. Rather than emphasizing her temporal distance, SN is identifying with SC, to whom she delegates the focalization.

Self-narrated monologue is far more common and provides another means of identification with past thoughts. It can reveal the mental agitations involved in making a major decision, such as Suzanne's plan to have her vows rescinded: "J'y rêvai d'abord légèrement; seule, abandonnée, sans appui, comment réussir dans un projet si difficile, même avec tous les secours qui me manquaient?" (134); "De quoi s'agissait-il? De dresser un mémoire et de le donner à consulter; l'un et l'autre n'étaient pas sans danger" (135). On another occasion, the focalization is ceded to the experiencing self in order to reveal why the latter decided to enter a convent, but this time the narrating self cannot keep silent:

> Je n'avais point de père, le scrupule m'avait ôté ma mère; des précautions prises pour que je ne pusse prétendre aux droits de ma naissance légale; une captivité domestique fort dure; nulle espérance, nulle ressource. Peut-être que si l'on se fût expliqué plus tôt avec moi . . . il se serait trouvé quelqu'un à qui mon caractère, mon esprit, ma figure et mes talents auraient paru une dot suffisante. La chose n'était pas encore impossible, mais l'éclat que j'avais fait en couvent la rendait plus difficile. *On ne conçoit guère comment une fille de dix-sept à dix-huit ans a pu se porter à cette extrémité sans une fermeté peu commune. Les hommes louent beaucoup cette qualité, mais il me semble qu'ils s'en passent volontiers dans celles dont ils se proposent de faire leurs épouses.* C'était pourtant une ressource à tenter avant que de songer à un autre parti. (107–8)

This narrated monologue is interrupted by SN, who regains her temporal distance and cognitive privilege to make an aphoristic observation about the plight of women. The focalization is handed back and forth between SC and SN, as past thoughts are mingled with present ones. Again we see how narrated monologue takes on the appearance of narrative fact. This possibility of Suzanne's being able to find an indulgent young man is "in fact" not possible except for the experiencing self and for the reader who does not know the outcome.

SC's ignorance about the outcome of the Sainte-Eutrope episode provides the basis for irony, the vehicle of which is self-narrated monologue. Since she does not understand the jealousy of Thérèse, she is puzzled by the latter's embarrassment: "Soeur Thérèse baissait les yeux, rougissait et bégayait; cependant que j'eusse les doigts jolis ou non, que la supérieure eût tort ou raison de l'observer, qu'est-ce que cela faisait à cette soeur?" (217). Similarly, SC does not understand the comportment of the superior: "Oh qu'elle était mal!" (240); "Que je la plaignais!" (242). Nor does she see the need to avoid the latter's caresses: "mais le moyen de se refuser à des choses qui font grand plaisir à une autre dont on dépend entièrement, et auxquelles on n'entend soi-même aucun mal?" (251). In the passages containing narrated speech of other characters, discussed above, the focalization is ceded for ironic effect, an effect predicated on the superior knowledge of narrator and narratee, who reconstruct the true meaning. Here, however, irony arises from the contrast between what is not understood by SC and what the reader probably suspects. Whether or not this is conscious irony on the part of SN toward her younger self depends upon SN's understanding of the situation at Sainte-Eutrope. We shall see the implications of this problem shortly.

Consonant self-narration.   While self-narrated monologue allows the narrator to identify momentarily with her earlier self, consonance may be achieved by other means as well. Any narrative technique that effects the disappearance of the narrator's temporal distance and that foregrounds the deictic field of the experiencing self may be seen as a move toward consonant self-narration. One rather traditional technique that effaces narrative distance is the use of the historical present. It is not common in *La Religieuse*, except in the "abrégé" where it becomes the dominant tense and suggests an unfinished and hastily written text. When used in the body of the novel, it signifies either rapid movement or a dramatic and suspenseful moment: "je descends; on m'ouvre les portes, après avoir visité ce que j'emportais, je monte dans un carosse et

me voilà partie" (206); "lorsque tout à coup on frappa deux coups vio-
lents à la porte. Effrayée, je me jette sur-le-champ hors du lit d'un côté,
et la supérieure de l'autre; nous écoutons, et nous entendons quelqu'un"
(241). While the historical present is designed to bring events closer to
the world of the reader, it is in fact, as its name suggests, narrative and
not discursive. A succession of verbs in the historical present is perceived, in the final analysis, as a succession of past events. Yet its similarity to the present of the narrator's discourse does seem to bring event
and speech act closer together, as in the following example: "je restai au
milieu du troupeau auquel on venait de m'associer. Mes compagnes
m'ont entourée, elles m'embrassent et se disent: Mais voyez donc, ma
soeur" (89).[10] The shift forward, as it were, from *passé simple* to *passé
composé* to present, seems to move toward the present of SN, yet the
scene is focalized by SC experiencing, not remembering.

The bifunctionality of the *passé composé* is another element that contributes to consonance, or at least to an ambiguity of temporal reference.
When read as a preterite, it designates the historical past; when read as a
perfect, it relates the past to the present of SN. There are numerous
passages in the text in which the particular value of this tense is difficult
to assign. Let us examine several examples (translations follow):

> [1] (Speaking of the contagious aspect of Moni's mysticism):
> Quelques-unes m'*ont dit* qu'elles sentaient naître en elles le
> besoin d'être consolées comme celui d'un très grand plaisir, et
> je crois qu'il ne m'*a manqué* qu'un peu plus d'habitude pour en
> venir là. (119)

> [2] [L]e changement de l'habit religieux en habit du monde est la
> seule chose dont je me ressouvienne; depuis cet instant j'*ai été*
> ce qu'on appelle physiquement aliénée. Il *a fallu* des mois
> entiers pour me tirer de cet état. (124)

> [3] [J]'avais peine à obtenir de l'eau, j'*ai* plusieurs fois *été* obligée
> d'en aller chercher moi-même au puits, à ce puits dont je vous
> *ai parlé*. (161)

The value assigned to these verbs is a matter of reception. The distinction may be seen more clearly in English translation. They could be

---

10. OV: "Toutes mes compagnes s'assemblèrent autour de moi. Elles m'embrassèrent et
on me disait . . ." [All my companions assembled around me. They kissed me and said to
me . . .].

interpreted as the preterites of conversation, especially since no enduring result can be seen with regard to SN, and since they are contaminated by other elements of discourse alongside of which the *passé composé* often has the value of a preterite. In this case we read:

[1] Some of the other nuns *told* me that they felt the need to be consoled growing in them like the need of a very great pleasure, and I believe I *lacked* only a little more practice to arrive at that point.

[2] The change from monastic habit to worldly clothing is the only thing I remember; from that moment on I *was* what is called physically alienated. It *took* entire months to pull me out of that state.

[3] I had trouble obtaining water, I *was* obliged several times to go get some myself from that well I *have told* you about.

This interpretation calls attention to SN, to her temporal detachment from these events. Only the last verb of [3] retains the value of a perfect because it is clearly discursive. On the other hand, and from a classical and literary point of view, these verbs could all be interpreted as perfects, since they coexist with preterites in the narrative context. They would therefore draw attention to events that have resulted in the present state, as there is no historical detachment, and they would be focalized by the experiencing self. If so, then we read:

[1] Some of them *have told* me . . . and I believe that I *have lacked* only a little more practice . . .

[2] . . . from that moment on I *have been* what is called physically alienated. It *has taken* entire months . . .

[3] . . . I *have been* obliged several times . . . from that well I have told you about.

In other words, we live these events along with SC, who is temporally very close to them. We have the impression that she has written these episodes shortly after having experienced them. Imbs (1960) tells us that in literary language, events recounted in the *passé composé* belong to a space of time that is identical or contiguous to that in which the speaker places himself, so that the past remains mentally attached to the present

(103–4). It is very strange to find sentences such as "Quelques soeurs m'ont craché au visage" (162) and "je me suis blessée cent fois, je ne sais comment je ne me suis pas tuée" (168) in the midst of historical narration, uncontaminated by other elements of discourse. Why use the *passé composé* in such cases, unless to confuse the temporal locus of SC with that of SN?[11]

Even when discursive elements are present, one cannot be sure of remaining within the here-and-now of narrator and narratee. The deictic field of the narrating self is often confused with that of the experiencing self. Just after her interrogation by Hébert at Longchamp, SN suspends her narrative to address the marquis: "Plus j'y réfléchis, plus je me persuade que ce qui m'arrive[12] n'était point encore arrivé, et n'arriverait peut-être jamais" (179). This passage is an excellent example of the temporal indeterminacy that pervades the text. The discursive elements emphasize SN, and the present–past polarity should therefore be obvious, which would suggest dissonance. The present tense of the first three verbs is anchored on the here-and-now of the narrative instance. But "ce qui m'arrive" clearly situates Suzanne back at Longchamp ("what is happening to me" *now*) and reveals a focalization by the experiencing self. The reader identifies with the deictic fields of both SN and SC, both of which provide an anchor for the present tense. Reflections of the past seem to be recorded in the present, yet the pluperfect and conditional of the last two verbs should be, according to the anchorage of the first three, expressed in the *passé composé* and future. The fact that they are not, that these tenses are anchored on the moment of event, makes the entire sentence unreadable: that is, the reader cannot identify it with either deictic field. The text constantly blurs the distinction between the here-and-now of discourse and the there-and-then of experience. In the scene introducing the superior of Sainte-Eutrope (207–10), already mentioned above, it is equally difficult to situate the focalization in a particular temporal perspective. At the moment when SC arrives at

---

11. And why change what was originally written in the *passé simple?* We cannot know, of course, whether or not Diderot's use of the tense was a conscious and deliberate one. Cohen (1973) states that while the *passé composé* was becoming a preterite in spoken language and assuming the function of the *passé simple* as early as the late seventeenth century, this change is not shown in the usage of eighteenth-century writers (255). François (1966) points out that Diderot uses the *passé simple* even in dialogue and in reference to a recent moment (which would support a reading of the *passé composé* as a perfect), but he also states that observance of the rules was quite arbitrary (1783). In any case, our hypothesis depends not upon the author's intention but upon reception. We have already noted the special use of this tense by Marivaux to situate the reader at the moment of event.

12. OV: "ce qui m'est arrivé" [what has happened to me].

her third convent, we read: "Cette supérieure s'appelle madame***. Je ne saurais me refuser à l'envie de vous la peindre avant que d'aller plus loin." There follows a lengthy description of the superior in the present tense, narrated from the perspective of one who obviously does not yet know that this character has died. Yet the discursive elements point to SN, who does indeed know. Moreover, the iterative nature of this paragraph ("Il y avait des jours où tout était confondu") and the pluperfect verb form that ends it ("Voilà celle à qui j'avais fait le voeu solennel d'obéissance") indicate clearly that it is not focalized by a new arrival at Sainte-Eutrope but rather by one who has experienced daily life there. The result is focal and temporal ambiguity.

One final technique that leans toward consonance is the use of temporal and spatial deictics. The following passage is a good illustration: "Les favorites du règne antérieur ne sont jamais les favorites du règne qui suit. Je fus indifférente, pour ne rien dire de pis, à la supérieure actuelle,[13] par la raison que sa précédente m'avait chérie" (129). While the first sentence is an explanatory comment of SN, the temporal deictic "actuelle" in the second points to the moment of event, to the *now* of SC. The following example shows a similar use of a spatial deictic: "Je vis qu'après l'éclat que j'avais fait il était impossible que je restasse ici longtemps, et que peut-être on n'oserait pas me remettre en couvent" (101). The deictic adverb "ici" shifts the perspective to SC in her first convent, while the modal adverb "peut-être" reveals her uncertainty about the future. These elements tend to obscure the referential duality between the "je" of the speech act and the "je" of the narrated event, thereby reducing the distance between SN and SC. Since the deictics are proximal rather than distal, the reader is led to identify with the moment of event. As we shall see, this temporal indeterminacy can be exploited.

Disappearance of cognitive privilege.   When the narrating self cedes the focalization to the experiencing self and abolishes the temporal distance that separates them, she must also hide some of her knowledge acquired subsequently to the moment of event. At this moment, the heroine is unaware of what the future holds for her. Paralipsis, the suppression of information by the narrating self, serves to place the reader in the same position of ignorance. What is most curious about *La Religieuse*, however, is that the narrating self often appears to be hardly more knowledgeable than the experiencing self, as though there were virtually no temporal distance between event and narration. Many critics

13. OV: "la supérieure en règne" [the reigning superior].

have noted the narrator's odd combination of retrospective distance from events and her temporal proximity to them, the former being typical of a memoir-novel and the latter more characteristic of an epistolary novel.[14] This phenomenon is responsible for three well-known examples of chronological confusion which we shall examine in detail. They involve Suzanne's knowledge, or lack of it, concerning (1) her illegitimate birth, (2) the death of Ursule, and (3) homosexuality.

(1) Early in the novel, Suzanne admits to the marquis that she suspects her own illegitimacy, which her confessor will reveal to her some twenty pages later:

> Souvent je me suis demandé d'où venait cette bizarrerie dans un père, une mère, d'ailleurs honnêtes, justes et pieux; vous l'avouerai-je, Monsieur? quelques discours échappés à mon père . . . m'en ont fait soupçonner une raison qui les excuserait un peu.[15] Peut-être mon père avait-il quelque incertitude sur ma naissance . . . que sais-je. Mais quand ces soupçons seraient mal fondés, que risquerais-je[16] à vous les confier? (83–84)

All the discursive elements (tenses anchored on the here-and-now of communication, the vocative and questions addressed to the narratee, the modals of subjectivity) emphasize the narrating self. Yet a retrospective narrator would of course no longer be ignorant of the circumstances surrounding her birth as she writes her text. The passage cannot be read as self-quoted monologue, without the inquit phrases that serve to distinguish past thoughts from present speech. If it is focalized by SC, it is clearly the speech of SN, whose knowledge remains limited to what she suspected at the moment of event. In other words, there seems to be no difference between SC and SN, no time lag separating them. Recalling our first hypothesis regarding the existence of Suzanne-editor, let us now make a second and suppose that SN wrote these words before learning the truth, in the manner of an epistolary narrator. If we represent Suzanne's story on a time-line (see Fig. 4.1), then this passage appears to have been written during segment 1. The next problem involves the direct address to "Monsieur." If Suzanne recorded her story periodically and as it happened, then either (1) she knew the marquis from the very beginning and was able to address him about her uncertainty, or (2) the second-person references were added later by SE, who

14. See in particular Lizé (1972, 162), and Rustin (1978, 42).
15. OV: "une raison qui les excusait un peu" [a reason that excused them a bit].
16. OV: "que risquais-je" [what was I risking].

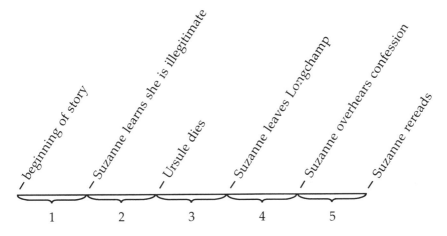

Figure 4.1. Time-line of Suzanne's story

edited the text of SN in view of sending it to the marquis but who allowed the uncertainty to stand.[17] The following passage, even more curious, provides little support for our hypotheses:

> Tant d'inhumanité, tant d'opiniâtreté de la part de mes parents ont achevé de me confirmer ce que je soupçonnais de ma naissance. Je n'ai jamais pu trouver d'autres moyens de les excuser. Ma mère craignait apparemment que je ne revinsse un jour sur le partage des biens . . . mais ce qui n'était qu'une conjecture va se tourner en certitude.[18] (103)

Once again, there is no reason to believe that this discourse ("je n'ai jamais pu trouver") is being filtered through the experiencing self. On the other hand, an epistolary SN, writing during segment 1, would not use the imperfect tense ("je soupçonnais"), which points to retrospection, but the present tense. Only the final proleptic clause, which emanates from a more knowledgeable Suzanne, could be attributed to the

17. Most critics suppose that Suzanne did not know the marquis before her legal proceedings because they identify him with the historical Marquis de Croismare, mentioned in the so-called "préface-annexe" of the novel. Indeed, none of the novels examined in this study has been linked so closely to the historical conditions of authorship and composition as La Religieuse. The readers of most editions, however, approach the text without having read the preface. If we adhere only to the memoir-novel itself, there is no reason to believe that Suzanne could not have known the marquis earlier. This is not a conviction on my part, but it is textually plausible.

18. OV: "se tourna en certitude" [turned into certainty].

correction of SE. With this clause, the editor builds suspense by playing on the future that is shared by both heroine and reader. But the reader, who is also uncertain at this point about what is to come, is unaware of any anomaly. The revelation comes on the following page: "je ne doutai plus de la vérité de ce que j'avais pensé sur ma naissance" (104), and SN takes over again from here. It is only at this point that all the preceding doubts can be perceived as a paralipsis, but chances are good that a rereading will be necessary for this to happen. Most readers will empathize with the experiencing self and fail to notice the infraction.

(2) Chronological confusion also involves Suzanne's knowledge about the death of certain characters. If SN wrote her story in installments, this would explain why she describes Manouri ("Cet homme a le coeur sensible" 190) and the superior of Sainte-Eutrope ("C'est une petite femme toute ronde" 207) in the present, whereas she later learns that these characters have died. These statements would therefore have been written sometime during segment 5, before SE begins to reread. A similar incident occurs during the episode at Longchamp and involves the fate of Ursule (143–44). Suzanne expresses concern for the future safety of her friend, whereas some fifty pages later she will witness her death. Once again, the retrospective stance is not respected:

> Cette jeune personne, Monsieur, est encore dans la maison, son bonheur est entre vos mains; si l'on venait à découvrir ce qu'elle a fait pour moi, il n'y a sorte de tourments auxquels elle ne fût exposée. Je ne voudrais pas lui avoir ouvert la porte d'un cachot, j'aimerais mieux y rentrer. Brûlez donc ces lettres, Monsieur. . . . Voilà ce que je vous disais alors; mais hélas elle n'est plus, et je reste seule.

This passage offers further evidence that Suzanne has edited and corrected her original text. The vocative and the tense system point to SN, who is worried about the fate of Ursule. The passage seems to have been written during segment 2, but the last sentence poses several problems. The proleptic announcement of Ursule's death seems to be an addition by the more knowledgeable SE, and "voilà" points to the previously written letter of SN. But what is the referent of *alors*? When did Suzanne write this to the marquis? The clause "je reste seule" implies that she is still a prisoner at Longchamp (after narrating Ursule's death, SN writes: "Me voilà donc seule dans cette maison" 202), and therefore must have been written during segment 3. All of these things considered, we can say that the focalizer of this sentence is Suzanne, located at some temporal point between the experience of her friend's death and her transferral to Sainte-Eutrope. The sentence constitutes an editorial correction, but not on the part of a retrospective SE rereading her entire text. It is as though we perceive her consciousness at each of several moments, written in a series of letters to the marquis ("ces lettres"), letters that she did not send right away and later had to amend.[19]

If we compare this instance of suppressed information with the one concerning illegitimacy, we can see a certain parallel. The focalization is that of the epistolary narrating self, whose knowledge is limited. The reader receives no dissonant guidance from the cognitive privilege of the retrospective editing self until the latter takes over and makes a proleptic reference to what we and SC are about to learn. Although events are focalized by SC/SN, her perspective is not readily differentiated from that of SE. Shifters are merely elements of surface structure that can point to either the speech act or the narrated event. Without the graphics of quotation, however, there is no indication that shifters and other discursive elements have any deictic field other than the present instance of discourse. We assume that the discourse emanates from the editor, whose words we have read at the outset. We therefore follow the consciousness of SN and her proximal vision of events without being aware of it. I am not suggesting that the concepts of an epistolary SN and a retrospective SE will bring coherence to the novel's many inconsistencies. My point is simply that Suzanne often narrates as though she were temporally close to her story and did not know its outcome. It is perhaps the boldest and most innovative of many techniques used by Diderot to achieve consonant self-narration, to effect a convincing integration of the narrating self and the experiencing self, and to efface the boundary between story and discourse.

(3) Surely the most problematic of the novel's internal contradictions concerns Suzanne's understanding of homosexuality. If we assume that SC does not fully understand her superior until she overhears the latter's confession near the end of the novel, then we should expect SN to yield to her in order to reveal her agitations and her progressive discovery. We must first note that SC is not altogether ignorant of the subject of sexuality. While still at Longchamp, she knows enough to make spurious accusations: "Je m'étais échappée en propos indiscrets sur l'intimité suspecte de quelques-unes des favorites" (131). From the very beginning

19. This concept of the amended letter is not unlike Stewart's (1987) explanation of the famous letter of Mme. Simonin, sent to Suzanne the day before it was written. Stewart points out that Simonin says "Adieu encore une fois" halfway through the letter. This allows for the possibility that she "has had time later to adjoin . . . a second note which will also accompany the package, and which describes what has happened . . . since the first was dictated the day before" (108).

of the Sainte-Eutrope episode, she suspects there is something wrong in her superior's attentions, and she runs to her confessor for moral guidance. As in the matter of her birth, she is not without suspicions of the truth, and these are revealed in various ways: "Réveillée, je m'interrogeai sur ce qui s'était passé entre la supérieure et moi; je m'examinai, je crus entrevoir en m'examinant encore . . . *mais c'étaient des idées si vagues, si folles, si ridicules, que je les rejetai loin de moi*" (230). SC suspects what has happened between her and the superior but refuses to accept the significance of it. She is, however, knowledgeable enough to make a mental comparison between this episode and a previous accusation of lesbian affections: "Je pensai que j'allais devenir l'entretien de la maison, que cette aventure qui n'avait rien en soi que de bien simple serait racontée avec les circonstances les plus défavorables; qu'il en serait ici pis encore qu'à Longchamp où je fus accusée de *je ne sais quoi*" (242). Elsewhere, in a dialogue with her superior, SC stresses her innocence, and her responses include "Je ne sais pas," "Je l'ignore," and "Je n'entends rien à cela." Yet she does admit to knowledge about sins of the flesh: "il y a du péché à cela" (237). She is afraid not only of catching the superior's "illness" but also of the threat to her innocent reputation. SN is willing to admit that SC was bothered by her intimacy with the superior: "Quoique ma conscience ne me reprochât rien, je vous avouerai cependant, Monsieur le marquis, que sa question me troubla" (229). SN, it seems, must overcome her repugnance in order to narrate these scenes: "Elle [the superior] s'arrêta à ce mot et elle eut raison, ce qu'elle avait à me demander n'était pas bien, et peut-être ferai-je beaucoup plus mal de le dire, mais j'ai résolu de ne rien celer" (236).

Interspersed throughout the text, and side by side with these hints of suspected knowledge, there are numerous and persistent denials. These protestations of ignorance are contaminated by discursive elements, so that they appear to emanate from SN. A good example occurs early in the novel and concerns the above-mentioned accusation of Suzanne's misconduct with a young nun at Longchamp. The incident itself is narrated in the historical present, and then we read:

> On accourt à ses cris, on l'emporte,[20] et je ne saurais vous dire comment cette aventure fut travestie. On en fit l'histoire la plus criminelle. . . . [O]n me supposa des desseins, des actions que je n'ose nommer. . . . En vérité, je ne suis pas un homme et je ne sais ce qu'on peut imaginer d'une femme et d'une autre femme, et

20. OV: "On vint à ces cris, on l'emporta" [One rushed to her cries for help, she was taken away].

> moins encore d'une femme seule. . . . [Q]ue vous dirai-je, Mon-
> sieur, il faut qu'avec toute leur retenue extérieure . . . ces femmes
> aient le coeur bien corrompu, elles savent du moins qu'on
> commet seule des actions déshonnêtes, et moi je ne le sais pas;
> aussi n'ai-je jamais bien compris ce dont elles m'accusaient,
> et . . . je n'ai jamais su ce qu'il y avait à leur répondre. (164)

The quantity of discursive elements gives the impression that this affirma-
tion of ignorance belongs to SN, clearly a retrospective narrator, for an
epistolary narrator would not say "aussi n'ai-je jamais bien compris" or
"je n'ai jamais su" if she were close to this event. The historical present of
event becomes the present of discourse, which tends to blur the distinction between their deictic fields. We may remember Suzanne's earlier
reference to the "intimité suspecte" of several nuns and begin to question
the reliability of the speaker. If so, we will notice that Suzanne knows
enough about homosexuality to point an accusing finger, but that she
vehemently denies any such knowledge when she is herself accused.

More protestations of this kind occur in the Sainte-Eutrope episode,
which comprises about one-third of the novel, but something is different. Discursive elements are present, but this time they do not foreground the experiencing self. On the contrary, emphasis is laid on the
temporal distance between SC and SN by means of the grammar of
dissonance:

> Elle me tint cent propos doux et me fit mille caresses qui
> m'embarrassèrent un peu, je ne sais pourquoi, car je n'y enten-
> dais rien, ni elle non plus, et *à présent même que j'y réfléchis,*
> qu'aurions-nous pu y entendre? Cependant j'en parlai à mon di-
> recteur qui traita cette familiarité, qui me *paraissait* innocente et
> qui me le *paraît* encore, d'un ton fort sérieux. (214)

> Je me confessai, je me tus, mais le directeur . . . me fit mille
> demandes singulières auxquelles *je ne comprends rien encore à pré-
> sent que je me les rappelle.* (254)

> [J]e ne *voyais* et ne *vois encore* aucune importance à des choses sur
> lesquelles il se récriait avec le plus de violence. (256)

In consonant self-narration the present–past polarity is usually effaced.
Here, on the contrary, the narrator calls attention to her retrospective
stance, not through the knowledge of hindsight but by a juxtaposition of
past- and present-tense verb forms along with temporal adverbs. In-

deed, it is the knowledge of hindsight that has been effaced. Even if we hypothesize that these passages were written before Suzanne overheard her superior's confession (segment 4 of Fig. 4.1), they undermine what she has already told us. SN *now* knows less than SC knew *then*. By the time we read these denials, we have already seen glimpses of the knowledge of SC, and it becomes difficult to find a causal-chronological relationship between past experience and present ignorance. This difficulty will of course be aggravated in segment 5, after the confession scene in which SC finally learns the whole truth while SN remains in the dark.[21]

In the other cases of suppressed information, we have seen that events are focalized by the experiencing self but foregrounded by discourse and so anchored in the narrator's deictic field. The knowledge of SN is at least partially hidden until the reader discovers the truth along with SC. In this case, however, the situation is quite different. Cognitive privilege is denied even by SN in the here-and-now of her discourse, even after overhearing the superior's confession. The lesbian experience is past, but the ignorance of its significance is projected into the present, beyond the moment of revelation. Rather than confusing the two deictic fields, her discourse serves to differentiate them. Reflecting on her recent confession to Lemoine, SN writes: "Je ne me rappelle, Monsieur, que très imparfaitement tout ce qu'il me dit. A présent que je compare *son discours tel que je viens de vous le rapporter* avec *l'impression terrible qu'il me fit*, je n'y trouve pas de comparaison" (256). Once again she draws attention to her hindsight through grammatical means, separating distinctly the here-and-now from the there-and-then. It is clearly a retrospective SN, rather than the experiencing self, who is emphasizing her ignorance. The reader would expect her to attribute the difference between the effect of Lemoine's speech as she is reporting it now and the impression it made on her at that time to her own acquisition of knowledge between the moment of event and the moment of speech. Instead, SN continues to insist that her superior is merely sensitive to music and that her confessor's admonitions are unnecessary: "Certainement cet

---

21. Mylne (1982) expresses doubt that Suzanne has learned the entire truth by eavesdropping on the superior's confession and states that the narrator still does not fully understand (168). As we have seen, however, there is much evidence to the contrary. Rustin (1978) points to the bad faith of the narrator, whose retrospective innocence can be explained by "the repression of a lesbian tendency" (45). Rex (1983) sees latent homosexuality even in Suzanne's relations with Moni and Ursule (190–94). In a most provocative article, Undank (1986) discusses the novel as "an engagement with representation in the course of which accustomed distinctions and ideologies evaporate; the borders between sexes and between sexual orientations become obscured" (163). It is interesting to note that Marcel Proust also used paralipsis to create suspense by hiding knowledge about homosexuality from his retrospective narrator (Genette 1972, 215–16).

homme est trop sévère."[22] Voice and perspective are at odds: while her speech reflects her temporal distance from the past she recounts, her consciousness follows closely the immediate present of experience. These focal manipulations convey a portrait of Suzanne that is, if not atemporal, at least elusive of logical and chronological progression. As the experiencing self focalizes her confused suspicions, her own sexual awakening, and her struggle to understand the superior's conduct, the narrating self maintains all the while that she, supposedly older and wiser, is ignorant of it all.[23] When the narrator denies what the focalizer presents, the narration becomes unreliable.

Critics are more likely to detect the unreliability of SN than are readers approaching the text for the first time. The latter are more likely to perceive the experiencing self and the narrating self as one, to "naturalize" the text into a coherent whole, and to become caught up in the dramatic present of Suzanne's experience. They are not likely to remember that it was SN and not SC who expressed doubts about her birth, concern for the safety of Ursule, and uncertainty about the behavior of the lesbian superior. Unless forewarned by the narrating self, they discover events along with the experiencing self, with whom they identify because they, too, are unaware of the future. Paradoxically, these readers are quite conscious of the narrator and her protestations of ignorance and at the same time oblivious of the retrospective knowledge that she should possess. A critical reader will find, however, that Suzanne is lying to the marquis. Even if we return to the hypotheses of the epistolary narrator and the editor—which by now seem insufficient—we must realize that SE eventually corrected SN's lack of knowledge about her birth and about the death of certain characters (i.e., SE intervened in segments 1 and 2) but did nothing to alter the impression that SN had no knowledge of homosexuality before segment 5.

The "abrégé."　　We have seen that Suzanne's temporal relation to her text and to her intended reader is ambiguous. In the beginning, as we contextualize her deictic field, she seems to be writing a long letter to the marquis in order to explain who she is, and this is the text we are reading.

22. This sentence was a later addition to the original version, as if to stress a denial of cognitive privilege to the narrating self.

23. One cannot really speak of an "older" Suzanne, as Stewart (1970) has shown that she does not age along the same chronological line as her story (149–56). Once again, the manuscripts reveal that Diderot made his heroine progressively younger and thus prevented her from aging according to narrative time. Suzanne seems to live in an eternal present because it is her experiencing self that dominates the narrative.

Yet this notion is constantly destabilized as we read: she seems to have written a part of her story earlier ("Voilà ce que je vous disais alors") and she has apparently received a response ("vous avez voulu savoir"). What is surely the most destabilizing, the most decontextualizing element of all appears just after she overhears the superior's confession:

> Ici les Mémoires de la soeur Suzanne sont interrompus; ce qui suit ne sont plus que les réclames de ce qu'elle se promettait apparemment d'employer dans le reste de son récit. Il paraît que sa supérieure devint folle et que c'est à son état malheureux qu'il faut rapporter les fragments *que je vais transcrire.* (275)

This startling introduction to the "abrégé" posits the existence of a new deictic field and a new narrative voice, one that is hierarchically superior to that of Suzanne since it transcribes the fragments that follow. Its intrusion gives the sudden impression that what we have been reading is a metadiegetic narrative, an embedded narration presented and focalized by the discourse of a "supereditor" on a higher embedding level. In presenting Suzanne's manuscript, this new voice mediates the transition back to the deictic field of Suzanne and the marquis.[24]

What follows in the "abrégé" is the more or less detailed narration of the progressive madness and death of the superior, of Suzanne's escape from the convent and of her struggle to find asylum in the outside world. Except for the increasing frequency of the historical present, mingled haphazardly with the preterite, much of this narration resembles the earlier part of the text. The narratee is still present ("Quelle mort, Monsieur le marquis!" 280) and the tenses of discourse still refer to the moment of narrative instance ("C'est ici que je peindrai ma scène dans le fiacre" 281). There is one good example of the selective nature of Suzanne's memory: "Je ne dis rien qui ne soit vrai, et tout ce que j'aurais encore à dire de vrai ne me revient pas ou je rougirais d'en souiller ces papiers" (280). Ever mindful of her innocent self-image, she cannot remember what she does not dare to report. The historical present is the dominant tense used to narrate her escape and first days in Paris, until it yields to the discursive present: "J'entre au service d'une blanchisseuse chez laquelle je suis *actuellement*" (284). From this moment on, the deictic

---

24. Some critics find it significant that this new voice intervenes just after the confession scene. For Mylne (1982), "it is precisely here, with Suzanne poised between innocent ignorance and guilty knowledge, that [Diderot] abandoned the detailed narration of her memoirs and fell back on 'l'abrégé qui les termine' " (173). For Pedersen (1978), Suzanne writes her memoirs to understand her experience, and she stops writing at the moment of truth (223).

field of SC joins that of SN. Except for one sentence referring to the death of Manouri in the past, the remainder of the text is unmitigated discourse, ending with a final appeal for help. Then, curiously, we find a postscript, a last paragraph that resembles the first in that Suzanne once again refers to her completed text in the past and to the marquis as a third person, outside of her discourse. In this final passage, says Josephs (1976), we are forewarned by the narrator of the limits of her self-knowledge, and then warned of the doubtful veracity of her account (750). The objective truth of all that we have been told is once again called into question. The narrative has fallen to pieces because the narrator is no longer credible.[25]

Conclusions and interpretations.   In writing her text, Suzanne's goals are to show herself as attractive and innocent, to portray the horrors of monasticism of which she is a victim, and finally to induce the intervention of her narratee. The focalization of her text is manipulated to meet these ends. She never loses sight of her intended reader, and in order to maintain this relationship she relies heavily on discourse. When she cedes the focalization to others, it is usually to reveal snatches of their speech and thoughts that her reader will surely condemn. Quite often, however, she delegates the focalization to her earlier incarnation, in order to better convey her ignorance, her uncertainties, her mental agitations of past experience. In all of this, Suzanne strives to give an impression of objectivity. She allows the longest antimonastic statement of her text to be focalized by her attorney. Her own criticisms of the convent and of her fellow nuns are often disguised as objective aphorisms. She admits to uncertainty about the thoughts and feelings of others and even about her former self. When she presents the speech and thoughts of others, she often couches them in the pseudo-objectivity of narrated monologue.

In view of her appeal for help, it is important to Suzanne to reduce the temporal distance between her own past and the present of her intended reader. Although the knowledge and perspective of hindsight are useful for her self-defense, for intervening and commenting upon her former persecutors, more often she eschews historical detachment completely. She allows the experiencing self to focalize the moment of event as though it were the moment of speech, and she narrates it as such. Focalization shifts back and forth, deictics are used ambiguously, undifferentiated forms of speech blend together, and past thoughts merge

---

25. For an insightful analysis of the "abrégé" as undermining textual authority, see Sherman (1984, 228–29).

with present discourse. The text exploits temporal indeterminacy and tends toward a coincidence of several deictic fields. As a result of these focal manipulations, the narrative stance wavers between retrospection and fusion with the narrator's past self.

Consonant self-narration can require the narrator to suppress vital information that she has obtained subsequently. As she identifies with her earlier self and allows the latter to focalize events, she must renounce all temporal and cognitive privilege. She recognizes that her perceptual experience of certain crucial questions and her earlier reflections about them will be more interesting to her reader than her retrospective memory of them. By surrounding this experience with discourse, she anchors it in the deictic field of her reader, who follows the experiencing consciousness without realizing it is past. Paralipsis thus provides a nonproleptic means of maintaining suspense in the memoir-novel. It also leads to chronological incoherence and infractions of convention, which critics have long attributed to an oversight on the part of a careless author.

It is my contention, which I have argued elsewhere (Edmiston 1985), that the famous *bévues* or internal contradictions form part of a deliberate and self-conscious experimentation with narrative techniques. This view is supported by the fact that many of the author's own additions and corrections to his manuscript, which could have resolved the problems and which I have signaled in the notes to this chapter, merely enhance the confusion. The changes involve an insertion of discursive elements that reduce the distinction between the deictic fields of narrator and character. By means of consonant self-narration, Diderot has added new dimensions to the memoir-novel. He has maintained suspense for the reader by denying retrospective knowledge to his heroine at crucial moments, and he has given her access to her own reflections and self-knowledge at these moments. The appearance of the narrating self coincides with the disappearance of cognitive privilege, making it often difficult to situate Suzanne in a particular temporal perspective. The manuscripts also show that Diderot made his heroine progressively younger and thus prevented her from aging according to narrative time. Her consciousness is captured as an eternal present because she is constantly closer to her experiencing self than to her narrating self, closer in time to the events she is experiencing and to her reaction to them. In short, Diderot has infused the principal advantages of the epistolary form into the memoir-novel format.

Denial of knowledge also fulfills a function directly related to Suzanne's narrative enterprise. She tries desperately to convince the marquis of her innocence. In the first half of the text, her denials concern the vow-taking ceremonies in which she participated physically if not mentally. Loss of memory maintains the innocence of the victim, who is thereby absolved from having taken an active part. In the second half, she vehemently denies all knowledge of homosexuality, but this time her credibility is undermined by her own discourse. It is impossible to reconcile the acquisition of knowledge by the character, which we have witnessed, with the narrator's protestations of ignorance. Always concerned with the self-image she is projecting, Suzanne clings desperately to her innocence, so that the guilt that pursues her will appear, by contrast, all the more odious. Lack of knowledge serves, once again, to exculpate her, to absolve her of all responsibility.

On another level, denial of knowledge fulfills an ideological function. Despite her protestations to the contrary, Suzanne suspects and fears a moral evil, but she does not want to understand it. The problem is that she confuses innocence (lack of guilt) with ignorance (lack of knowledge about guilt). Her confessor has assured her that an innocence based on ignorance is her only defense against evil. Ignorance is thus a Christian virtue, while knowledge is the forbidden fruit, the original sin. In keeping with her Christian teachings, Suzanne rejects all understanding of the superior's desire, believing she will thereby be safe from its contagious influence. Ironically, her purity remains intact precisely because of her forebodings. When the truth is finally revealed to her, she grows even more resolute in her aversion to moral evil, thus proving the priest's theory wrong. The dialectic between ignorance and knowledge is an ideological argument of the text, a less obvious one that has received little critical attention (Edmiston 1978). Diderot demonstrates the weakness in the Christian system of ethics: Suzanne remains pure through her own moral awareness, and not because of the ignorance and submission to authority taught by the Church.

CONCLUSION

Focalization, says Bal (1985), is "the most important, most penetrating, and most subtle means of manipulation" (116). It can provide insight into one character and privilege that character's point of view over those of the others. In personal narration, focalization is subservient to discourse—the narrator's direct communication with the narratee—as a means of persuasion. Through the four memoir-novels that we have studied, we can now make some observations about these narrative devices.

The personal narrator uses discourse to set up the narrative situation and establish a communication with the narratee. Jacob's frequent use of first- and second-person pronouns are elements of an oral style that contribute to his conversational tone as he attempts to draw the reader into the communicative act. His many references to the narrative instance reveal a narrator who is highly conscious of his freedom to pass over details, to abridge the speech of others, and to shift from one scene to another. Des Grieux and Suzanne both have a specified narratee and an obvious rhetorical purpose in telling their story. Each of them desires esteem and sympathy, each wants to provoke a positive reaction, and each makes abundant references to the narratee and to the narrative process. The exception here is Meilcour, who almost never draws attention to his act of communication. Reference to the narratee is virtually absent from his text. Meilcour's discourse is mostly limited to maxims, objective "truths" about women and the social mores that are supported by his own experience and which the reader is intended to recognize. They are expressed in a sententious present that merges with the narrator's discourse and thus acquires the force of authority. Some of these shared truths—like those of Jacob—include "nous" and "vous" because narrator and reader inhabit the same world. Suzanne disguises her criticisms of monasticism as objective aphorisms and uses them to highlight an ideology. Des Grieux's maxims deal with the power of love and with noble and vulgar sentiments, although he is generally less sententious than the other narrators.

Meilcour is also an exception in that he is the most consistently dissonant of our narrators. He maintains a sharp differentiation between the young hero and the older narrator, between the candid ignorance of one and the sophisticated authority of the other. When the hero focalizes, the narrator distances himself from the former's beliefs through modal verbs, and the self-quoted and self-narrated monologues are surrounded by dissonant commentary. Dissonance is less obvious in the other novels. Both Jacob and Des Grieux reveal the duplicity of their younger selves, but unlike Meilcour they use dissonance as a means of self-defense. Des Grieux maintains a certain distance from the hero's sense of security about Manon, but without corroboration the reader remains in doubt. Suzanne uses the grammar of dissonance but fails to keep any sustained distance from the experiencing self. Alternations between *now* and *then* can be observed in all three novels, but there is little or no ironic detachment. On the contrary, Jacob, Des Grieux, and Suzanne strive for consonance in various ways, effacing the distinction between narrating self and experiencing self in order to foreground the latter. With Jacob and Des Grieux it is often difficult to separate the two registers stylistically and ideologically. Des Grieux presents the hero's perceptions through self-quoted and self-narrated monologues, but unlike Meilcour he makes no contrast between these and his own dissonant commentary. There is no double standard by which the hero's conduct can be judged. Jacob's discourse is often contaminated by elements from the hero's perception, while self-narrated monologue sometimes contains the discursive language of the narrator. The lack of clear division between the two selves leads to a fusion of time planes. Like Jacob, Suzanne expresses the perceptions of the experiencing self in the discursive language of the narrator, and both narrators reveal a lack of discrimination in their methods of self-quotation, so that past thoughts merge with present ones and the temporal distance between them is obscured. With Suzanne, the very basis of the present–past polarity is constantly undermined, so that the narrator as well as the reader remain close to the moment of experience. This emphasis on the experiencing self should not surprise us, says Ifry (1987): unlike the narrator of a true autobiography, the narrator of a memoir-novel is a fictional character who is easily effaced behind the protagonist (495).

It is especially with regard to the presentation of other characters that we can see the difference between a true autobiographer and these personal matters. External focalization allows them access to the knowledge of hindsight and affords them a great deal of control over our response to the characters. Meilcour provides information about certain characters that he learned subsequently. Jacob exercises a tight control over the speech of his characters, reporting false quotations, typified speech, and making parenthetical asides. Like Jacob, Des Grieux designates his characters with tendentious epithets and provides essential portraits to condition our response to them. Only Suzanne seems to have no cognitive advantage over her younger self regarding other characters.

Like the autobiographer, the personal narrator can present scenes or events that were spatially distal from the protagonist and therefore not witnessed directly. Whether explicitly justified or not, such scenes are readily attributed to the knowledge of hindsight. Meilcour presents none, Jacob and Des Grieux justify some of theirs by eavesdropping, while Suzanne attributes some of hers to subsequent knowledge. Unlike the autobiographer, however, these narrators can provide insights into the psychology of other characters, and even delegate focalization to them so that they become perceiving subjects. This tendency toward nonfocalization is once again offset by the narrator's retrospective stance, which favors our reception of such information as authentic knowledge acquired subsequently. Meilcour reads the minds of other characters in order to reveal what the hero did not know, and only occasionally does he make an attempt to justify his insights. Jacob uses the techniques of invented monologues and focal delegation to others through FID to give an impression of insight without actually transgressing his perceptual limitations. Des Grieux provides brief but unrestricted insight into others, who thus become spectators of the hero and furnish flattering perspectives of him. Suzanne represents the speech and thought of others by hybrid techniques that background her own intrusive presence, and this delegated focalization is used to evoke censure of the characters. Lanser (1981) states that "the focalizing character also signals an affinity between that character and the narrative voice, and thus constitutes an important index of the narrator's psychological stance" (141, n. 36). If "affinity" means "sympathy," then we have seen that this is not always true in personal narration: Meilcour, Jacob, and Suzanne delegate focalization to others (respectively, to Lursay, to Doucin and the elder Habert, and to the other nuns) for purposes of irony and even censure toward them.

The personal narrator can also use internal focalization, restricting his or her knowledge and perception to that of the experiencing self. Hortense is presented only through the vision of the younger Meilcour, and the narrator provides no authoritative guidance. Des Grieux creates a similar mystery around Manon by remaining silent about her feelings for the hero and he presents certain other characters existentially, just as they appeared to the young protagonist. Suzanne uses internal focalization to present the superior of Sainte-Eutrope, whose behavior seems strange to the experiencing heroine. Only Jacob avoids any consistent use of internal focalization when presenting other characters, about whom there is really no mystery for the reader.

Each of the novels studied offers an interesting case-study for a particular problem that is specific to it. The selective focalization of *Les Egarements* makes use of all three possibilities open to the personal narrator. Hortense is focalized internally, the hero and others externally, and the presentation of Lursay especially seems to be nonfocalized. No one point of view is sufficient in this *Bildungsroman,* and Crébillon has achieved a synthesis of first-person limitations with omniscient psychological incursions, the function of which is to establish irony toward the floundering hero. In *Le Paysan parvenu* the attempt to fuse the moments of event, narration, and reception creates a peculiar case of temporal ambiguity. Discursive elements, and especially the future tense, are used to create metalepsis, in which the extradiegetic narrator and narratee enter the diegetic world of the characters. Marivaux plays on the double temporality of story and narration as though the two were contemporaneous, and exploits the futurity of discovery shared by hero and reader. It is in *Manon Lescaut* that the use of focalization as a device for manipulation is most obvious. Des Grieux allows even minor characters to focalize when they can provide a positive perspective on the hero. Focalization by his principal opponents—his father and Tiberge—serves to foreground their ideological differences with the hero, which are gradually undermined by the narrator's discourse. Manon, the most important character in the novel, is seldom a focalizing subject, and as an object her thoughts remain inaccessible to the narrator after the opening pages. Prévost has increased his narrator's power of persuasion by providing him with the perfect narratee, one who ascribes to his assumptions from the outset. Des Grieux is thus a highly manipulative narrator but not an unreliable one. Suzanne, on the other hand, must be considered unreliable because her discourse is undermined by the focalization of the heroine. An extreme case of temporal indeterminacy and inconsistency may be seen in *La Religieuse,* in which narration, quoted speech, and discourse are often not distinguished graphically and in which the narrative instance can never be anchored on a particular moment. Against every rule of convention, the narrating self denies her cognitive privilege just as she resists aging. Unlike cases of conventional paralipsis, in which the narrator remains silent about facts until the protagonist learns them, Suzanne denies even the knowledge acquired by the heroine. It is to Diderot's credit, however, that her unreliability is not noticed on a first reading of the text. So convincing is Suzanne's psychology that most readers follow her consciousness through her experience and fail to be struck with her infractions. It would be better stated that the reader identifies readily with the experiencing self and ignores the retrospective stance of the narrator.

The eighteenth-century memoir-novel was intended to imitate a true auto-biography, a historical document written by a real person about his or her life. By accepting this imitation of history, the fictional autobiographer found himself constrained by a number of logical rules. Although the four novelists presumably took this principle of narrative authority quite seriously, we have found in their works a great deal more freedom than one might expect. Throughout this study I have pointed out the "infractions" of our narrators each time they transgress the limitations imposed by convention. These limitations offer a convenient standard by which we can measure the reality of contemporary fictional practice. We must not, however, construe the narratological model as an aesthetic ideal, against which all infractions are viewed as technical weaknesses. (A glaring example is *La Religieuse*, long regarded by critics as the clumsy result of a writer's inability to abide by generic rules, whereas to my mind it is the boldest and most innovative example of narrative experimentation in France before *Jacques le fataliste*.) On the contrary, the infractions are creative innovations, striving to overcome the bondage of convention and to attain a narrational freedom not shared by the autobiographer—or at least not by the historian.

The eighteenth-century novel has received little attention from students of point of view, who have perhaps taken memoir-novel logic more seriously than did the novelists themselves. Theorists have tended to focus on post-Jamesian writers who raised point of view to a disciplinary regimen. What I have tried to demonstrate in the present study is that while convention did impose a single point of view—what Genette (1983: 52) calls a "prefocalization"—on the memoir-novelist, it did not close the door on the evolution of fictional technique. Novelists found themselves torn between adherence to the pretense of historical "truth" and the need to expand the conventions, to exploit new methods of creating a convincing illusion. The rigors of logic sent them searching for the least obtrusive ways of penetrating consciousness, of gaining insight, and of attributing it all to hindsight. Let us not forget that our authors were not only the products of intertextual convention. They also contributed to it.

APPENDIX:
THE EVOLUTION OF THE
CONCEPT OF FOCALIZATION

Gérard Genette is generally considered to be the first to have differentiated between the categories of Voice and Mode, between the function of speaking (the narrative instance) and the function of seeing (the narrative vision or focus or point of view). His theory, set forth in his "Discours du récit" (1972), has become a fundamental classic of narratology. A decade later, he made further clarifications and responded to his critics in *Nouveau Discours du récit* (1983). We shall consider the two works together (1972, 183–224; 1983, 28–52).

Genette defines his category Mode as the "regulation of narrative information" (1972, 184) and divides it into two parts, Distance and Perspective. Distance is the quantitative relationship between the narrator and his story. It concerns how much information is provided, as well as the degree of presence of the informant. After discussing the classical dichotomy of mimesis (or the more direct "showing") and diegesis (or the more distant "telling"), Genette concludes that the former is merely a degree of the latter: pure imitation through language is impossible, but an illusion of mimesis can be achieved through diegesis. Genette then renames the dichotomy "narration of events" and "narration of speech." The former can never be mimetic. Its degree of illusion depends upon the relative presence of a speaker (not really a modal problem but one of voice) and upon the quantity of details provided (which is really a temporal problem involving the duration of a narrative). A "narration of speech," however, can exhibit varying degrees of mimesis, depending on whether the discourse is that of a narrator or a character. Genette distinguishes between three types of discourse used to represent speech and thoughts, ranging from the most distant to the most mimetic.

The other modal category, Perspective, is the qualitative relationship between the narrator and his story, governed by his capacity for knowledge and by the point of view, restricted or not, that he adopts. Genette denounces the long-standing confusion between the question of narrative voice ("who speaks?") and that of perspective ("who sees?" [1972, 203]).[1] He later modifies the latter question with a less visual formulation, "who perceives?"; and since the focal position is not always identified with a person, the question becomes "where is the focus of perception?" (1983, 43). In order to avoid prolonging the confusion between vocal and modal classifications often found in studies on point of view, Genette renames this category (and coins the term) Focalization.

Focalization is defined as a restriction imposed on the information provided by a narrator about his characters, and more specifically, on his access to their psychology. Following the triadic typologies of Jean Pouillon (based on vision) and Tzvetan Todorov (based on knowledge), Genette recognizes three types of perspective. The first of these is *zero focalization* (Pouillon: "vision from behind"; Todorov: "narrator > character"). Since the *focal character* is the one whose point of view orients the narrative perspective, a text in which the narrator says more than any character knows is a nonfocalized text. There is no focal character and therefore no focalization, no restriction on the narrator's information. Not only does the narrator have access to the minds of all his characters, but he may also provide information that is not known by any character: "the classical narrative sometimes places its 'focus' in a point so indeterminate, or so distant, in such a panoramic field . . . that it cannot coincide with any character . . ." (1983: 49). In Anglo-American terminology, this kind of text is dominated by an "omniscient" narrator, or rather one who provides complete information by means of which the reader becomes omniscient. Paradigm: Fielding's *Tom Jones*.[2]

The second type is *internal focalization* (Pouillon: "vision along with"; Todorov: "narrator = character"). As opposed to complete information, only a restricted selection of information is provided by the narrator of a focalized text. Internal focalization occurs when the narrator says only what a character knows, thinks, and perceives. This focal character be-

---

1. Genette discusses this confusion in the theories of Brooks and Warren, Stanzel, Friedman, Booth, and Romberg. For an analysis of point of view theories before Genette, see Van Rossum-Guyon (1970).

2. The use of paradigms (provided by Genette 1983, 88) is meant to illustrate ideal types and should not obscure the fact that "the choice of focalization is not necessarily constant throughout the duration of a narrative" (Genette, 1972, 208).

comes the subject of all perceptions. Every character, setting, and event is presented from his point of view. Internal focalization may remain fixed in one character throughout a text, or it may shift between two or more focal characters. Paradigm: Joyce's *Portrait of the Artist as a Young Man.*

The third type is *external focalization* (Pouillon: "vision from outside"; Todorov: "narrator < character"). This type of perceptual restriction occurs when the focus is outside of any character, and "outside" must be understood here in the psychological sense in order to distinguish this type from zero focalization (type 1). A character is presented "objectively" by a narrator who says less than this character knows. He has no information about the character's thoughts, so that his ability to perceive is restricted to that of an anonymous spectator. External focalization is often used in the opening pages of a novel to create mystery or suspense, as the narrator cannot (or rather, will not) penetrate the character's mind. Genette points out, for example, that the narrator of Flaubert's *L'Education sentimentale* begins with initial "ignorance" of Frédéric's mind before becoming "omniscient" (1972, 208, n. 1). The most sustained use of this type is found in the modern detective story. Paradigm: Hemingway's *The Killers.*

To clarify the commentaries of Genette's critics, I offer four observations about his typology. First, a text that is nonfocalized (type 1) can also be called "multifocalized *ad libitum*" (1972, 209). This means that a narrator who is generally omniscient in a text can (and usually does) choose to present different characters in different ways. While telling us every thought of one character, he can impose restrictions on his own ability to perceive the psychology of another character, in order to achieve certain effects.

Second, internal focalization (type 2) contains a paradox: if everything is presented from the point of view of the focal character, then that character cannot be described or designated from the outside by the narrator, nor can his thoughts and perceptions be analyzed by anyone else. Genette points out that for this reason internal focalization is seldom used rigorously, except in interior monologue or in a novel like Robbe-Grillet's *La Jalousie,* in which the speaker must be deduced rigorously from his focal position alone (1972, 209–10). More often, a sustained use of internal focalization allows for three types of perception: (1) "vision along with" or exterior vision, by means of which the world is perceived along with the character (e.g., "The large living room was cool and dark"); (2) interior vision, which presents the character's thoughts (e.g., "She felt relaxed and comfortable at once"); and (3) perception of the character from the outside (e.g., "She walked slowly across the room"). Genette therefore uses the term "internal" to describe what Barthes (1977) calls the "personal mode" of narration, that is, the narrator is so invisible that the text in question can be translated into the first person without necessitating any other changes (40–41). Our examples meet this criterion: "The large living room was cool and dark. I felt relaxed and comfortable at once. I walked slowly across the room."

Third, external focalization (type 3) can be adopted by one character toward another. In Jules Verne's *Le Tour du monde en 80 jours*, the focalization is internal through Passepartout, the puzzled witness-character, and external on Philéas Fogg, the main character whose behavior remains a mystery (1972, 208). This means that we have access to the thoughts of the former but not to those of the latter. This observation in fact forms a corollary—implied but never stated explicitly by Genette—to his concept of a focalized text: internal focalization, the restriction of all perception to that of a character, logically implies external focalization on the others who inhabit his world. The narrator can read the mind of the focal character alone, while perception of other characters must pass through the latter's restricted field of vision.

Fourth, we have seen that the fundamental distinguishing feature of Genette's typology is the ability to perceive psychological activity: the narrator has either unlimited access, or access to the focal character only, or no access at all. It seems clear, however, that a spatial dimension is also involved. The narrator of a nonfocalized text can move freely through diegetic space, from one location to another, while the narrator of a focalized text cannot. The latter is spatially limited either to the locus of the focal character (when internal) or to that of a hypothetical spectator (when external). "Hypothetical" means that the spectator is not a dramatized character (as in internal focalization), but his perceptual vantage point is nonetheless located within the fictional world. The difference between the two involves psychological access to the central character. We may conclude then that Genette's conception of focalization as a restriction, in both its internal and external manifestations, is a function of the intradiegetic location of the "focus."[3]

Genette's concept of focalization has been criticized and thoroughly revised by Bal (1977, 1981, 1985). Bal's most important contribution is her differentiation between the focalizing subject, or *focalizer* (*focalisateur*), and the focalized object (*focalisé*). She contends that Genette's typology of focalization confuses these two different principles of classification.

---

3. The spatial dimension is already evident in one of Genette's models. As Angelet and Herman (1987) correctly observe, Pouillon's "vision from behind" and "vision along with" are based on the position of the subject of perception (187).

The distinction between types 1 and 2 is predicated on the seeing subject, whose perceptual ability is either unlimited as in omniscience or restricted to that of a character. The distinction between types 2 and 3, however, follows a different principle: "In the second type, the 'focalized' character *sees*, in the third he does not see, he *is seen*. The difference this time is not one between the 'seeing' instances but between the objects of their vision" (Bal's emphasis, 1977, 28). Bal thus maintains that Genette's distinction between the internal and external types is a confusion between the subject who sees and the object who is seen. A distinction must be made, she says, between the focalizing subject ("focalization *by* Passepartout") and the focalized object ("focalization *on* Philéas Fogg"). Genette's differentiation between these types, she says, involves our access to the character's mind, which either is or is not revealed. In a narrative with external focalization, characters are also focalized, but we watch them from outside their minds. The distinction then between Genette's types 2 and 3 is predicated on the psychological or mental object, on the degree to which a character's mind is perceived. Bal admits that Genette's typology is valid for measuring the narrator's knowledge: "It is true that from the first to the third type, the 'knowledge' of the narrator decreases, and in this sense the series is homogeneous. But this difference does not concern *point of view* or *focalization*" (Bal's emphasis, 1977, 28). Bal finds Genette's typology incoherent because she redefines the very nature of focalization.

In Bal's system, the narrator's knowledge of the object's mind is irrelevant. Instead she proposes a concept of focalization that is more visual in nature, predicated on the functional difference between the seeing subject and the object seen. She posits the existence of a focalizer and a focalized object for every narrative fragment: every passage is the object of focalization on the part of some subject, hence a nonfocalized passage cannot exist. Bal defines focalization as the "relationship between the 'vision,' the agent that sees, and that which is seen" (1985, 104). Once the cognitive and psychological aspects are deleted in favor of the visual, there is no longer any difference between Genette's type 1 (an omniscient narrator) and type 3 (an ignorant narrator): "The 'knowledge' of the narrator and of the character is a purely metaphorical and thus inoperative concept, and need not be considered" (1977, 37).

For Bal, focalization is an "instance" concerning the presentation of perceptions. A narrative text contains three instances, which are arranged hierarchically: (1) narration—a text consists of linguistic signs produced by a subject, the narrator; (2) focalization—the vision is the content of the narrator's words, presented in a certain order and from one or more points of view by a second subject, the focalizer, whose

identity may or may not coincide with that of the narrator; (3) action—
the story, object of the vision, consists of chronologically ordered actions
performed by the actors, or characters; an actor's identity may coincide
with that of the other two subjects, which is usually the case in autobiography. The hierarchy involved is based on relations of subject and object,
the object of a higher layer being the subject of a lower one. Hierarchy
can also exist within a layer. There can be, for example, a hierarchy of
narrators, and Genette calls them "extradiegetic," "diegetic," and "metadiegetic." Bal extends this concept of embedding to the layer of focalization. The subject–object relation governs shifts in focalization, the result
of which is embedding: "There is embedding when a *narrative object*
becomes the subject of the following level" (Bal's emphasis, 1981, 45).[4]
Just as the narrator can cede his function to a lower-level narrator, pro-
ducing a hyponarration (or what Genette calls a metadiegetic narrative),
so the "primary focalizer" can yield to lower-level focalizers. These embedded focalizations present the perceptions and opinions of a character
and are hierarchically "inferior" to the presentation of the story as a
whole by the primary focalizer. They need not occupy a large amount of
textual space. This may be seen in the following sentence from Brontë's
Wuthering Heights, quoted by Bal: "This time, I remembered I was lying
in the oak closet, and I heard distinctly the gusty wind." The narrator
and primary focalizer here is Lockwood, writing in his diary; the first
embedded focalizer is Lockwood the character, remembering his dream
of the previous night; and the second embedded focalizer is Lockwood
seen in his dream, lying in the closet and hearing the wind.

Bal retains the terms *internal* and *external* to designate the focalizing
subject, but once again she changes Genette's definitions. The terms no
longer refer to access to the psychology of a character, but rather to the
diegetic locus of the focalizer: internal means that a character-focalizer is
the seeing subject, while external means that a narrator-focalizer is the
subject and the character is the object seen. The narrator is the primary
focalizer, external to the diegesis. This primary focalizer can yield his
function to a character, who then becomes an internal focalizer. If a
character is the *object* of a focalization by the narrator, then the functions
of narrator and focalizer merge. If a character is the *subject* of focalization, then the two functions remain distinct. It should be noted that Bal's
reformulation of the internal–external opposition implies an inside–

---

4. Bal uses the term "object" to refer both to the content of a subject's activity, and to the
object of one *layer* that in turn may become the subject of a lower *level*. Following
Berendsen's (1984) suggestion (146), I use *layer* here for the former (narration, focalization,
action) and *level* for the latter (shifts within each layer), by analogy with Genette's "narrative levels." I do so for purposes of clarity, although I do not subscribe to these concepts.

outside opposition concerning the locus of the focalizer relative to the diegetic world (Bal states this explicitly, 1981, 47). She is then led to admit that the location of the focalizer inside the fictional world imposes a restriction on perception. While the focalizing subject is not characterized by his ability to read minds, Bal does not disregard psychological perception. With regard to the *object* of focalization, she uses the term "perceptible" to designate what could be perceived by a hypothetical spectator, and "imperceptible" to designate what could not, such as mental activity. She points out that this distinction characterizes only the focalized object and that it has no direct relationship to the focalizer (1977, 38). It should be obvious that this is not true. If a narrator-focalizer can present imperceptible objects, thoughts, for example, which could not be known to a hypothetical spectator, then clearly this ability says something about his powers of perception. In other words, the focalizer can be characterized by his objects of focalization, despite Bal's efforts to separate them: "Two possibilities exist: if a narrative begins in *external focalization* and then changes to *internal*, it is not necessarily the focalizer who changes, it can also be the focalized object, the character 'seen from within' being the object and not the subject of focalization" (Bal's emphasis, 1977, 37). So, if the focalizer changes, then focalization is yielded to a character inside the fictional world. If the focalized object changes, from perceptible to imperceptible, it seems logical then that the focalizer's power of perception also changes, from that of a spectator to that of a mind-reader. Characterization of the object also characterizes the subject. Moreover, Bal admits that when focalization is yielded to a character, the latter's field of vision is limited: "An imperceptible object can be focalized only by a first-level focalizer [narrator], whereas a perceptible object can be focalized at any level" (1977, 42). What does this mean, if not that a primary focalizer can be "omniscient," whereas a character-focalizer cannot read minds? Genette would surely agree with such a restriction. Subject and object may be analyzed separately, but they cannot be dissociated totally, as though there were no correlation between them.

Bal's reformulation of the internal–external opposition provokes her to realign Genette's triadic typology into a diadic one. Her internal type corresponds to his internal type, while her external type corresponds to his external-plus-zero types. This realignment is based on her reading of Genette (1972). Using only that text, we may schematize Bal's reading of his typology as follows:

(1) zero: subject (narrator-focalizer) is unlimited, characters are objects

(2) internal: subject (character-focalizer) is limited, other characters are objects
(3) external: subject (narrator-focalizer) is limited, characters are objects

Bal is able to combine Genette's types 1 and 3 because both involve a seeing subject (outside any character) who focalizes on the characters, and to oppose this combined category to his type 2 in which the seeing subject is a character. Like Genette, she admits that the internal type is limited in perceptual ability. The essential disagreement lies in the viability of type 3 as a separate category. But Genette (1983) makes a much-needed clarification that serves to further differentiate type 3 from type 1: "In external focalization, the focus is situated at a point in the diegetic world chosen by the narrator, *outside any character*" (Genette's emphasis, 1983, 50).[5] This definition implies a spatial restriction as well as a psychological one. Whereas a nonfocalized text places no spatial limitations on the narrator, the locus of external focalization is always intradiegetic and therefore limited. Events are perceived as though by an anonymous witness, who has no power to read minds and who is no more able than any character to move through diegetic space. Genette's point is that the subject of focalization, even when not identified with a character, *can* have a limited perceptual ability similar to that of a character. Type 3 must now be schematized differently:

(3) external: subject (neither narrator nor character) is limited, characters are objects

Moreover, in Genette's system, internal and external focalization can be adopted by both dramatized and undramatized narrators, whereas a dramatized narrator is not possible in a nonfocalized text since no character can be omniscient and omnipresent. In other words, types 2 and 3 are similar in that the subject is limited, both spatially and psychologically. It should be clear, then, that even if we accept Bal's definitions and

5. In his review of *Nouveau Discours du récit*, Soelberg (1984) points out that Bal's criticisms of Genette (1972) were useful in provoking more explicit definitions from him, particularly those of internal and external focalization (120). Genette (1983) admits that a refinement of his original concept may be found in Jost (1983), who insists on its spatial dimension. Focalization, says Jost, includes two distinct features: "on one hand, the *knowledge* of the narrator with respect to his characters (does he know more, less, or as much as they do?); on the other hand, his *location* with respect to the events he recounts" (Jost's emphasis, 195).

ignore the "knowledge" of the narrator, we cannot combine types 1 and 3 on the basis of focalization by an external narrator. Genette's typology, as it applies to heterodiegetic (third-person) narratives, may now be schematized as follows:

Type	Subject coincides with character	Locus relative to diegesis (spatial)	Access to minds of characters (psychological)
zero	no	outside (unlimited)	inside (unlimited)
internal	yes	inside (limited)	inside own/outside others
external	no (spectator)	inside (limited)	outside (limited)

At the risk of repetition, we may state the comparison in another way. What Bal calls "external" (extradiegetic subject) is what Genette calls "zero," that is, an omniscient narrator who is spatially and temporally unlimited, who has access to the minds of all characters and to information known by no character. What Bal calls "internal" (intradiegetic subject, or character) is divided by Genette into two types of restrictions, both of which involve spatiotemporal limitations: "internal" means the narrator has access to the mind of the focal character, while "external" means the subject is not a character but a hypothetical spectator who has no psychological privilege.

Following Bal, Berendsen (1984) states that Genette's zero type is not a separate category but rather a mixture of internal and external focalization, an alternation between the points of view of narrator and character (141). This formulation is valid only for Bal's definitions of internal and external. It allows for the kinds of cognitive and spatial privilege found in a nonfocalized text by attributing them to an external narrator-focalizer. Yet it does not account for any restrictions that a narrator might choose to adopt. Genette admits to the composite nature of his zero type (my first observation about his typology, above). But as internal and external signify, for him, knowing or not knowing a character's mind, any variation between the two will still allow for a third possibility, the "superior" point of view of an all-seeing and all-knowing narrator. Therefore he concludes that "zero focalization = focalization that is variable and sometimes zero" (1983, 49).

Bal's concept of focalization may be useful for describing textual shifts in perception, but it largely ignores the whole problem of restrictions on point of view. Her differentiation between subjects and objects, however, is a much-needed contribution to Genette's theory.[6] It resolves the paradox of internal focalization (my second observation, above): when a focal subject is designated or described by a narrator, he becomes an object of the latter's presentation, which is not *strictly* limited to the former's field of vision. The subject–object distinction also explains the debate over Passepartout and Philéas Fogg (my third observation, above): the adoption of internal focalization imposes a restriction on the subject, whose view of *other* characters is necessarily external.

The internal–external opposition is one of psychology for Genette, one of diegetic locus for Bal. There is room for both in a theory of focalization. We have seen that Genette's definition of a focalized text implies a spatial limitation within the diegesis (my fourth observation, above). On the other hand, the spatial distinction between Bal's narrator-focalizer and character-focalizer implies, more than she admits, a correlation between a subject's perceptual ability and the nature of the objects perceived. Therefore, the difference can almost be reduced to one of terminology. For Bal, external focalization is performed by a narrator, located outside the fictional world. This narrator has access to the minds of any character, knows information unknown to any character, and is spatially unlimited. For Genette, these are characteristics of a nonfocalized text. Internal focalization, for Bal, is performed by a character, located inside the diegesis and spatially limited. Genette divides this kind of restriction into two parts: internal, involving a character whose mental processes are accessible to the narrator; and external, involving a narrator who acts as a *hypothetical* character, a spectator who cannot read minds. This is not to disguise the fundamental difference between Genette and Bal, the difference between focalization as a restriction on perception and as a narrative instance. It is this difference that explains why every text fragment, for Bal, is the object of focalization on the part of some subject, whereas for Genette some passages are nonfocalized.[7]

6. Genette rejects, as do I, Bal's notion of focalization as a narrative instance and her concept of embedding (the "focus" cannot be located at two points at the same time). While he criticizes her terms "focalizer" and "focalized," he does however speak of the "fictional subject of all perceptions" and of the "object of the narrative" (1983, 49–50).

7. Uspensky's ([1970] 1973) study on point of view in fiction makes use of the internal–external opposition in ways that prefigure both Genette and Bal. Uspensky identifies several planes—ideological, phraseological, spatiotemporal, psychological—which may or may not coincide in a given literary work. On the spatiotemporal plane (similar to Bal's position), external means from a bird's-eye view and a retrospective stance, as though the narrative were being conducted not from a viewpoint in the characters' present but from one in their future. On the psychological plane (similar to Genette's position), the internal–external opposition refers not to a space relative to the described action but to the characters' mental activity (130–33).

Vitoux (1982) develops further some of Bal's conclusions. Starting with her distinction between subject and object, Vitoux points out that Genette's second type, internal focalization, is in fact a double one, in that the character is both the one who sees and the one who is seen. As focalized object (FO), it is opposed to the external type, with the difference being that the focalizer either has or does not have the privilege of psychological penetration, either can or cannot perceive more than could a hypothetical spectator. To characterize these two kinds of objects, Vitoux retains Genette's terms of internal (FO-int) and external (FO-ext). As focalizing subject (FS), Genette's second type is opposed to the first, to the absence of focalization and thus to the absence of any perceptual restrictions. In the latter case, Vitoux says that the power of focalization is retained by the narrative instance, that is, that the separate functions of narration and focalization are superimposed (360).

Vitoux introduces the concept of delegated focalization: the narrator can choose to delegate the function of focalization to a character, who then becomes a delegated subject (FS-d). Following Bal, Vitoux limits the perception of this delegated subject to external objects (FS-d → FO-ext), so that the focal position of FS-d is equivalent to that of any other character, that of a nonprivileged witness. The advantages of this concept, he says, are as follows. On the side of FS, there is no limit to his knowledge and no restriction on his vision. On the side of FO, FS has the *privilege* of penetrating the minds of the characters but is under no obligation to do so. FS can correlate to FO-ext if he chooses to restrict his vision and to remain outside the minds of the characters. On the other hand, FS can correlate to FO-int if he chooses to include their thoughts, and this also means "vision along with," or seeing with the focal character. In this case, FS identifies with the characters, knows what they know but sees only what they see (361). Focalization is rarely consistent throughout a text, and various alternations and shifts can occur, as in the following schematic example (in which X, Y, and Z designate characters): FS → FO-ext on X, then FO-int on X, then FS-d to X → FO-ext on Y, Z, etc. Taking up Genette's reference to Jules Verne, Vitoux shows that the narrator-focalizer's relationship to Philéas Fogg (FS → FO-ext) is no different from that of the delegated focalizer, Passepartout (FS-d → FO-ext), even though the former is not limited except by his own choice. The effect of delegated focalization is generally to organize the narrative with a subjective vision of events, to show the progressive discovery of a situation, to present a process of interpretation at work (362–63).

Vitoux thus presents an admirable synthesis of the theories of Genette and Bal, taking into account the perceptual restrictions of one and the subject–object opposition of the other. On the side of Bal, he recognizes that the "knowledge" of the narrator is not a necessary criterion in the classification of focalizers: "Focalization is defined only by the capacity of the narrative instance to mark its limitations, without going beyond them yet while suggesting something beyond" (365). On the side of Genette, he acknowledges the correlation between the seeing subject and the objects of vision, hence "the double necessity of dissociating FS and FO for analysis, but of studying them together in the interdependence of their functions" (362). The concepts of delegated focalization and privilege without obligation permit us to re-structure Genette's typology along the subject–object axis:

(1) zero: privilege of information (FS → FO-ext and → FO-int)
(2) internal: psychological privilege (FS → FO-int), but also delegated, limited in vision (FS-d → FO-ext)
(3) external: restriction of information (FS or FS-d → FO-ext)

Regarding the second type, Vitoux notes that the privilege of psychological penetration always belongs to FS, while the "vision along with" is delegated to the character (367). This schematization, which I have deduced from Vitoux's theory, would seem to validate Berendsen's claim that type 1 is really a combination of types 2 and 3, but that is only because Vitoux has ignored the dimension of space.[8]

The early work of Stanzel ([1979] 1984) predates that of Genette but was originally published in German and long ignored by other narrative theorists. Stanzel accounts for different forms of "mediacy of presentation" by constructing a typological circle based on a triadic system of "narrative situations," identified by the categories of Person, Mode, and Perspective (4).[9] Within Mode, Stanzel places a narrator or "teller-character" at the diegetic pole and a reflector (a nonnarrating character) at the mimetic pole, with varying possibilities for dominance of one pole or the other. During most narrations there is an oscillation between the overt mediacy of the teller-character and the illusion of immediacy provided by the reflector-character. The category of Perspective is subdivided into a diadic opposition between internal and external, resembling that of Bal. Internal perspective prevails when the point of view is located in the main character or in the center of events, while external perspective occurs when the point from which the narrated world is perceived is located outside the main character or at the periphery of

8. See Angelet and Herman (1987) for an interesting analysis of several passages from Balzac according to the theories of Genette, Bal, and Vitoux (190–93).

9. My presentation of Stanzel is based on the English translation of Goedsche (1984), in which the author has taken account of critical reactions to his earlier work.

events. Stanzel's system, however, also recalls the triadic typology of Genette. Whereas Genette's two noninternal types are distinguished on the basis of knowledge and of a vantage point in space, Stanzel's external perspective varies from the "authorial" narrator, located outside the fictional world (which Genette would call "zero"), to the "peripheral" narrator, a character who is located inside the world but who is not the main character (the difference here is that for Genette, this "peripheral" narrator need not be a dramatized character but his perception of the main character would be just as limited). Stanzel's distinction between internal and external perspective is determined by the degree of mediacy, and he makes a correlation between Mode and Perspective: "There evidently exists a close correspondence between internal perspective and the mode dominated by a reflector-character, on the one hand, and between external perspective and the mode dominated by a teller-character, on the other" (141). Concerning the presentation of consciousness, internal perspective suggests immediacy, the illusion of insight into the character's thoughts with no justification required. External perspective corresponds either to an omniscient narrator, or to a peripheral first-person narrator who will have to "motivate" or justify his knowledge of the thoughts of any character other than himself (127).

Stanzel's perspectival opposition does not depend on the narrator's ability to penetrate a character's mind. He does point out, however, that internal perspective necessarily results in a restriction on the kind and degree of knowledge of the teller-character or the reflector-character. The limitation of knowledge about the narrated world gains in significance for the reader. Internal perspective also exhibits an affinity with the perception of space, whereas spatial relations are less important in external perspective. "In other words, only in the case of internal perspective does perspectivization become semiotically significant" (113). Stanzel's recognition of the limits placed on the possible objects of focalization brings his theory closer to that of Genette.

To summarize, we can say that the internal–external opposition in all these theories applies to limitations imposed on the subject of focalization, despite differences in terminology. For Genette, Bal, and Stanzel, internal focalization means that the point of view is that of the focal character, located inside the world of represented events, while noninternal focalization means that the central character is not the focalizing subject. Genette's zero and external types have the common characteristic that the subject of perception is not the central character. The difference between them is a cognitive one and involves the narrator's privilege of psychological penetration. Bal translates this cognitive difference into perceptible and imperceptible objects, but rigorously separates these from the focalizing subject. Vitoux shows, however, that there is indeed an explicit correlation between the two. Stanzel resembles Genette in his acknowledgment of spatial and psychological limitations, imposed not only in internal perspective but also in external perspective when the subject of perception is a peripheral narrator.

Turning now to our primary concern, the homodiegetic (first-person) text, we find that further refinements of these theories are necessary. Genette deals primarily with Proust as a study example, and he constantly differentiates between the older narrator and the young Marcel.[10] He points out that focalization can be performed either by the narrator or by the hero, but both are called internal ("internal focalization on the narrator," 1972, 214, n. 2). This is presumably because of the psychological dimension, because everything is presented through the mind of one character. Yet Genette has defined internal focalization as a situation in which the narrator says only what the character knows, and a first-person narrator (FPN) usually says *more* than his younger self knew at the moment of event, as Genette himself points out: "The narrator almost always 'knows' more than the hero, even if he is the hero himself" (1972, 210). Evidence of focalization by the narrator may be seen in foreshadowing and other types of prolepsis ("we shall see later," "I have learned since"), which emphasize the subsequent and greater knowledge of the narrator. Thus by Genette's own definition, focalization by a FPN cannot always be regarded as internal.

Nor can it be said to be nonfocalized, for no FPN can be omniscient or omnipresent. Genette states that a FPN is authorized to speak in his own name. While it is true that he can say more than any character knows, he too is subject to restrictions: "The only focalization that he must respect is defined with regard to his present information as a narrator, and not to his past information as a hero" (1972, 214). He can, of course, choose to suppress his subsequent knowledge and allow the hero to focalize, which results in a "hyperrestriction" (1972, 219). Sometimes, however, ignorance is shared by hero and narrator, precisely because some kinds of information are inaccessible to both. Genette's definition of *paralepsis* as an infraction of focalization, by means of which the narrator makes incursions into the consciousness of other characters or describes something he could not have seen, further demonstrates the limits imposed on a FPN, who must justify his knowledge. Focalization becomes zero (omniscience) only when the FPN provides information he could never

10. Bronzwaer (1978) criticizes Genette for not having stressed that these two "I's" are two distinct voices (6). Berendsen (1984) responds that there is only one narrative voice but two focalizers, the narrator and the perceiving character (142).

have known. Otherwise his field of perception is limited, albeit less so than that of the hero. The narrator knows more than the character, but his knowledge is not boundless.[11]

In external focalization, finally, the narrator says less than the character knows. In autobiographical fiction, this would seem to hold true only toward other characters and not toward the narrator's younger self.[12] A FPN could choose to withhold his own earlier thoughts and thus adopt an external focalization—an infraction that Genette calls *paralipsis*—but with respect to other characters in his world he would logically have no choice. This restriction would be imposed by the homodiegetic voice—a phenomenon called "prefocalization" (1983, 52). Genette certainly implies as much about Proust. He points out that modal expressions ("perhaps," "as though," "seen") are often indices of internal focalization that enable the narrator to say hypothetically what he could not otherwise affirm; and that various kinds of indiscretion (eavesdropping, spying) serve a similar function by enabling the hero to acquire knowledge about other characters. Could he not also say that these techniques are necessary devices of justification for the FPN, whose ignorance of others requires the adoption of external focalization? Internal focalization by one character logically implies an external view of the others who inhabit the same world.

The focal possibilities offered to a FPN thus contain elements of all three of Genette's types, but clearly no type alone is adequate to describe

11. Genette's (1983) rather paradoxical statement—that only the information of the hero at the moment of event strictly deserves the term "focalization"—is followed by the admission that a homodiegetic narrator must justify his knowledge, and that this vocal choice implies consequently a modal restriction (51–52). His original position is summed up by Cordesse (1986): "the narrator-character cannot be attributed with all the powers of the author-narrator, as far as focalization is concerned. As a character, he has at his disposal only introspection (self-focalization?) to study himself, and external focalization to study the other characters. Zero focalization, the prerogative of fiction, is of course forbidden to him" (45).

12. Genette (1983) states explicitly that external focalization can occur (albeit rarely) even in homodiegetic narration, i.e., when the narrator is also the hero, so long as his own mental activity is not revealed. As examples of this phenomenon Genette cites the monologue of Benjy in Faulkner's *The Sound and the Fury*, Hammett's *Red Harvest*, and Camus's *L'Etranger* (83–85). Genette's position here presents a contradiction of his own term. A distinction must be made between what the narrator can perceive and what he chooses to reveal, and the latter does not concern focalization. I would respond that the lack of introspection on the part of these narrators represents less a restriction on perception than a refusal to communicate their thoughts (or, in the case of Benjy, an inability to articulate them). I would refer to the theory of Pierre Vitoux: the FPN has the privilege of presenting the mind of the hero but is under no obligation to do so. In such cases, says Cohn, the reader must look for the narrator's motivation for hiding his own mental activity (Cohn and Genette 1985, 106).

them. Such a narrator can limit himself to the perceptions of his younger self (internal). He is not, however, restricted to those perceptions and he enjoys certain spatial and cognitive advantages resulting from his temporal distance. He therefore often says more than his younger self knew at the moment of experience (a characteristic of the nonfocalized type). Finally, toward other characters his perceptions should logically be those of a spectator (external), although here again, his temporal distance allows for a certain psychological privilege.

Genette (1983) abandons the idea that focalization by a FPN is always internal. An attempt to illustrate the focal possibilities of the FPN may be seen in his paradigms of various narrative situations (1983, 88), but these paradigms also reveal certain inadequacies of the typology. He relates homodiegetic narration to zero focalization (Lesage's *Gil Blas*), to internal (Hamsun's *Hunger*), and to external (Camus's *L'Etranger*). Genette does not explain why he places *Gil Blas* under the zero type, as though the narrator of that text were omniscient or unrestricted. How, for example, is Gil Blas different from Proust's narrator, whom Genette earlier identified with internal focalization? How is he different from Des Grieux in *Manon Lescaut*, a text that Genette also places under the internal type? It should be clear that the distinctions here no longer involve the narrator's psychological privilege, as they do in the heterodiegetic paradigms of *Tom Jones, Portrait of the Artist as a Young Man*, and *The Killers*. They are predicated not on what the narrator *knows* but instead on what he chooses to *reveal* to the reader—a choice that does not involve focalization. Genette seems to have lost sight of his own definition of the concept as a restriction on perception.[13]

The focal difference between *Gil Blas* and *Hunger* corresponds to Cohn's (1978) dichotomy of "dissonant self-narration" and "consonant self-narration" (145–61). A dissonant narrator views his younger self retrospectively, often distancing himself from past ignorance and delusions while providing a great deal of subsequent knowledge. A consonant narrator, by contrast, draws no attention to his hindsight and identifies with his younger incarnation by renouncing all cognitive privilege. Cohn (1978) explains the reasons for the relative scarcity of consonant self-narration. Narrators usually like to maintain their distance from the past they are recounting and therefore avoid total consonance. Total annulment of narrative distance, as it is found in *Hunger*, is rare. Moreover, in

---

13. Tamir (1976) agrees that the focalization adopted by a FPN need not be internal: "The personal mode often serves as a convenient excuse for limiting the focus of narration, but this does not mean that it cannot, as a principle, vary in focalization." It is clear, however, that she, too, defines internal and external according to whether the narrator "exposes or does not expose his or someone else's inner life" (417).

autobiographical novels the time of reflection is more often the present than the past, so the dominant consciousness usually belongs to the narrating rather than to the experiencing self. This enables a FPN like Gil Blas to comment, with hindsight, on his past life. Dissonance and consonance are degrees, however, not absolutes. Although a narrator may be largely dissonant, he may choose at times to identify with the experiencing self. When consonance occurs, its characteristics are (1) interrogatives directed to an unknown future, which have long since been answered, (2) effacement of all marks of the present–past polarity, and (3) focus on the experiencing self (167–71). In *L'Etranger*, finally, there is an almost total lack of introspection on the part of the narrator, who gives less information than even the experiencing self knows. We surely cannot say that Meursault "knows" less than Gil Blas. What we can say is that the reader knows less about the former than about the latter. In Genette's typology of homodiegetic narratives, the progression from types 1 to 3 involves a regression, not in the knowledge of the narrator but in the psychological insight allowed to the reader. In all three types, the knowledge of the narrator is equally restricted, and theoretically at least, there can be no omniscient FPN. The all-important spatial dimension has been overlooked.

Genette admits that a FPN is located outside the fictional events that he narrates: "Gil Blas is an extradiegetic narrator because he is not (*as a narrator*) included in any diegesis but is directly on a level, albeit fictional, with the (real) extradiegetic public" (Genette's emphasis, 1983, 56). Moreover, he says, the autobiographical hero is often more of an observer than a participant (1983, 69). Indeed, the extra- and intradiegetic locus of the focalizing subject is the key to distinguishing between dissonant and consonant self-narration. If it appears surprising that Genette does not explicitly take this fact into account, it is even more surprising that Bal does not, since her external–internal dichotomy (a revision of Genette's typology) is predicated solely on the diegetic locus of the *focalizer*, or subject of perception. Instead, Bal links personal narration to internal focalization, and in doing so she changes her definitions. If the focalizing subject has no diegetic name, if his identity is not that of an actor in the story, then he is considered external; if, on the other hand, he bears the name of an actor in the story, he is internal (1981, 47). According to Bal, then, a FPN like Lockwood in *Wuthering Heights* is always an internal focalizer, except when he listens to the embedded "hyponarration" (Genette's "metadiegetic narrative") of Nellie Dean. The distinction between Lockwood-narrator and Lockwood-character is reflected through embedded focalizers (the former seeing the latter who sees Nellie Dean). Unlike Genette, Bal makes no explicit differentiation between the perceptual limitations of narrator and hero.

What Genette and Bal mean to say is surely that any FPN is limited in focalization. Unlike the impersonal narrator whose authority is generally beyond question, the FPN is theoretically limited both spatially and psychologically, to what the hero (a character) has experienced. He has an advantage over his characters only temporally. It is precisely this temporal distance that affords the FPN a broader focalization than that of the hero. It authorizes him to provide spatial and psychological perceptions that the hero could not have provided at the moment of experience, although these perceptions should be justified by knowledge acquired subsequently. If focalization is defined as a restriction on perception, then it makes sense to say that everything presented by the FPN is focalized, or restricted to what this fictional human being could logically know. The knowledge of the FPN is thus an important criterion—though not the only one—in distinguishing focalization.[14]

Like Genette (1972) and Bal, Stanzel ([1979] 1984) maintains that internal perspective prevails in what he calls the "quasi-autobiographical form of first-person narration" (111–12). This is because the point of view is perceived in the main character, whereas omniscience always presupposes the external perspective of an "authorial" narrator ("external" meaning outside the diegesis). Stanzel prepares the way, however, for a different conclusion that he does not make explicitly, that is, that external perspective can be adopted by an autobiographical FPN, just as much as by a peripheral FPN or by an authorial narrator. Internal perspective, he says, depends on a low degree of mediacy, whereas in fact there is often a great deal of mediacy in personal narration. External perspective, on the other hand, is dominated by a teller-character. Stanzel points out that in personal narration, transitions between the teller-character and the reflector-character do not involve a shift from one person to the other but rather a change in the role of the narrator, from teller to reflector (149). In other words, there is a change from external to internal perspective. Stanzel states that as the emphasis on the experiencing self increases there is an increase in internal perspective (225), which logically implies that an increase in emphasis on the

14. Chatman (1986) contends that a narrator cannot have the focus of narration because he is outside the story: "The narrator's comments are not perceptions or conceptions of the same order as a character's and should not be confused with them. . . . A character can literally see (perceive, conceive, etc.) what is happening in a story because he/she is *in* the story. A narrator can only 'see' it imaginatively, or in memory if he/she is homodiegetic, that is, participated in the events of the story 'back then' when they occurred" (Chatman's emphasis, 194). While I agree essentially with Chatman's statement, I would argue that in the case of a FPN, the story is nonetheless "filtered" (Chatman's term) through a human subject with limited perceptual powers.

narrating self means an increase in external perspective. Elsewhere, Stanzel refers to the phenomenon of "authorialization" of the FPN, defined as a striving for "the universality of the authorial narrator with external perspective and omniscience" (208).

While omniscience always implies an external perspective, the reverse is not true. Stanzel rightly points out that the personal narrator is "embodied" in the world of the characters, and that since there is an existential link between him and his younger self, this corporeality characterizes the narrating self as well as the experiencing self.[15] He admits that an increase in the process of embodiment results in a restriction of the horizon of knowledge and perception of the teller-character, as well as that of the reflector-character. A similar restriction can exist in external perspective, when the narrator is embodied but is not the main character whom he describes. This peripheral FPN is an observer of the main character—perhaps as a close friend or admirer—and therefore, says Stanzel, his perspective is external; yet he is also an embodied character, and therefore his ability to perceive is limited. The same could be said of all personal narrators. Like the peripheral FPN, the autobiographical FPN is now extradiegetic, located outside of the story in which he once participated. Stanzel stops short of concluding that perception and knowledge are also limited in the narrating self, as an embodied narrator, and that the perspective is external in that it is not limited to the point of view of the main character, or experiencing self.

Cohn (1981) challenges the view that internal focalization dominates personal narration. She states that when the past space surrounding the experiencing self is presented from the retrospective vantage point of the narrating self, the perspective is essentially external to the diegesis; when space is seen from the vantage point of the experiencing self, who is ignorant of what his future holds for him, the perspective is internal (176). If a FPN says, "I thought she was lying," then the focalization is internal: the thoughts of the experiencing self are revealed, uncorrected by the narrating self, and the reader remains in doubt. If, on the other hand, the FPN says, "I did not yet realize that she was lying," then the focalization is external: the narrating self is calling attention to his retrospective viewpoint and "correcting" his earlier thoughts by revealing a truth he learned subsequently, that is, "she was indeed lying." Essentially, then, the narrating self acts much like an impersonal narrator who relates past events and describes characters. Like Stanzel's peripheral

15. Cohn (1981) contests the term "embodied" because most personal narrators remain disincarnated as *narrators* (164). Stanzel ([1979] 1984) means simply that the FPN and his younger self are one and the same individual.

narrator, however, he is also an embodied character and therefore subject, logically, to certain limitations.

Rimmon-Kenan (1983) presents a synthesis of the theories of Bal and those of Uspensky ([1970] 1973). Like Bal, she identifies external focalization with the "narrating agent," while the locus of internal focalization is inside the represented events. Following Cohn, Rimmon-Kenan states that external focalization occurs in first-person narratives when the perspective is that of the narrating self rather than that of the experiencing self (74). She seems to lose sight of this important criterion, however, when she shows how the external–internal opposition manifests itself on each of Uspensky's planes, or "facets." She divides the perceptual facet into the components of time and space. Concerning time, "external focalization is panchronic in the case of an unpersonified focalizer, and retrospective in the case of a character focalizing his own past. On the other hand, internal focalization is synchronous with the information regulated by the focalizer" (78). This definition is consistent with the alteration found in a first-person narrative. In spatial terms, she says, the opposition takes the form of a bird's-eye view or panoramic view versus that of a limited observer. She divides the psychological facet into a cognitive and an emotive component. In cognitive terms, the external–internal opposition becomes one between unrestricted and restricted knowledge. In emotive terms, it distinguishes between attitudes that are objective, neutral, or uninvolved, on one hand, and attitudes that are subjective or involved, on the other (78–81). All these facets pertain only to the focalizer. Rimmon-Kenan agrees with Bal that focalized human objects can be seen from within or from without, and she makes no correspondence between subject and object. She again points out that a FPN can reveal his perceptions at the time of narration (external) and those at the time of experience (internal), yet her analysis of the various facets does not bear this out. Only the temporal component accommodates the focal possibilities of a FPN. Temporally speaking, he is external to his story and he views it from the future, as Uspensky points out. The other components require an intermediate category for the narrating self. Spatially, he is external to his story, located somewhere between the position of a limited observer and that of a bird's-eye view. Cognitively, he knows more than he did at the time of experience but his knowledge is not unrestricted. Emotively, he may be less involved than he was at the time of experience, but he cannot be totally objective and neutral about the story of his own life. In short, and to return to Genette's terminology, he does not have the same perceptual powers as the narrator of a nonfocalized text, and perhaps we should add, at least theoretically.

Like Uspensky, Chatman insists that the notion of "point of view" must be subdivided into several functions that are often confused. He labels these the perceptual point of view, the conceptual point of view, and the interest point of view (1978, 151–52). He later adds a fourth function and calls these functions "filter" (perceptual), "slant" (conceptual), "interest-focus," and "center" (1986, 196–98). Chatman admits that the term "focalization" is adequate to express the first function, the perceptual point of view, but ultimately rejects the term because it has spawned a proliferation of "wispy beings—*focalisateur, narrateur-focalisateur, focalisé, hypofocalisé, focalisataire*—whose utility has yet to be demonstrated" (1986, 199). Like Genette, he also rejects Bal's concepts of embedding, layers, and levels. Aside from these criticisms, however, Chatman makes a most interesting point. A narrator, he says, does not have a perceptual point of view because he is outside the story and cannot "perceive" anything about it. He reports events but does not "see" them as a character does. Chatman rejects the notion—proposed by Bal and adopted by Berendsen, Vitoux, Rimmon-Kenan, and others—that focalization *always* occurs, that someone always "sees" the events and characters of a story, and that the narrator focalizes if the characters do not. Focalization, he says, should not be used to refer to the narrator's role: "It makes no sense to say that a story is told 'through' the narrator's perception since he/she is precisely *narrating*, which is not an act of perception" (Chatman's emphasis, 1986, 195). This also holds true for a retrospective narrator: "Typically, he is looking back at his own earlier perceptions-as-a-character. But that looking back is a conception, no longer a perception" (1978, 155). In a first-person narrative, the perceptual point of view is that of the younger self, while the conceptual or ideological point of view belongs to the narrator. A FPN, like all narrators, is external to the world of the story, and, Chatman argues, he does not focalize (in Bal's sense of the term). Here he seems to be essentially in agreement with Genette, who writes: "Unlike the cinematographer, the novelist is not required to place his camera somewhere: he has no camera" (1983, 49).[16] Genette does not treat focalization as an instance that occurs in every text fragment. Indeed, if we accept Genette's definition of focalization as a *restriction* on perception,

---

16. Chatman's (1986) criticisms of Genette's typology seem to lose sight of the latter's definition of focalization and to be based instead on Bal's, which he rejects (200–203). He treats the zero type as problematic, for example, because he says it implies a narrator-focalizer. On the contrary, Genette labels this type "nonfocalized," i.e. "no one focalizes": there are no restrictions on the narrator, who can say more than any character could perceive. The term cannot therefore be equated with "variable internal focalization," as Chatman suggests. Moreover, he proposes the need for terms to describe the useful concepts of "access to the mind of any character" and "access to information which no character has"—which are precisely the criteria for Genette's zero type.

then we can agree with Chatman's position and yet still refer to the perspective of the FPN. The FPN does not perceive, but his text is nonetheless focalized because he is a human being who once participated in his story. He is now external to that story, but not so much as an impersonal narrator who never existed within it. Technically, he is external to the diegesis, but not to the fictional world in which he still lives.[17]

To summarize our findings, we have seen that the knowledge of the FPN is an insufficient criterion upon which to construct a typology of focalization. On one hand, such knowledge is *always* limited to what one individual (narrator/hero) has acquired. The entire text is therefore focalized. On the other hand, the narrator *always* has access to the psychology of his younger self (although he may not reveal it), and *never* to that of others. What must also be taken into account is the passage of time, which creates a refraction of the subject into the experiencing self and the narrating self, each with its own deictic field. The knowledge, perceptions, and diegetic locus of one do not equal those of the other.

We can accommodate Genette's typology to the focal possibilities available to a personal narrator by redefining only his type 3. Nonfocalization (type 1) is possible. The FPN may provide spatial and psychological information that neither hero nor narrator could logically possess. Such information may be more or less justifiable, and more or less noticeable to the reader. Internal focalization (type 2) is possible. The FPN may efface all temporal distance and adopt the intradiegetic vision of the hero, who presents his own mental activity and his view of others at the moment of event. Genette's concept of external focalization (type 3), however, must be redefined as extradiegetic, i.e. as a perspective that is midway between a nonrestriction and an internal restriction. When the FPN speaks about past events and characters from his present vantage point, he is temporally and spatially external to his story. He knows more now than he did then, and he is less involved now than he was then. He is perceptually limited nonetheless because he continues to be a part of the same world in which he lived as the hero. His position, in short, is much like that of the true autobiographer.

Following Vitoux's concept of delegated focalization, according to which the narrator either retains the focalizing function or delegates it to a character, I would argue that heterodiegetic (third-person) texts require only two types of focalization. Zero or nonfocalization means that there are no spatial or psychological restrictions on the narrator's infor-

---

17. Bal (1985) changes her position and comes to this conclusion as well: "In a so-called 'first-person narrative' too an external focalizer, usually the 'I' grown older, gives its vision of a fabula in which it participated earlier as an actor, from the outside" (112).

mation. Internal focalization means that the function is delegated to the central character, who is limited spatially and, toward others, psychologically. What Genette calls the external type means that the unlimited narrator has chosen to act as a hypothetical witness, to limit himself intradiegetically although outside the mind of any character. This is still a case of internal (intradiegetic) focalization, but one performed by the narrator rather than delegated to a character. The narrator may have the privilege of "omniscience," but he is not obligated to reveal his knowledge, just as his first-person counterpart need show no signs of dissonance. In homodiegetic narratives, however, since the narrator simulates the role of an autobiographer, the three types (internal, external, and zero) are necessary, even though the last may be considered as a case of infraction.

TRANSLATIONS OF FRENCH TEXTS

Introduction

Page 1
- [1] This idea, which was not without foundation, filled her with sadness: she saw a woman without morals, without youth, without beauty, take from her in one day the fruit of three months of cares: and in what short time, and after what hopes!
- [2] In this way, however, she learned about her husband's infidelity; but she hardly worried about it: it was only a source of amusement for her.
- [3] She could not hope that G…M… would leave her alone all night like a vestal virgin. So it was with him that she intended to spend the night! What an admission for a lover!
- [4] The following night, when everyone was asleep and the house was in silence, she got up.

Chapter 1

Page 16
- I entered into society at the age of seventeen, and with all the advantages that can make one noticed.
- (This plan, I believe, would have occurred to very few women)
- (according to what I have been told / Madame de Meilcour, whom I have not seen flirtatious in her declining years / since then, I have been none the less conceited)

Page 17
- (it is customary, when one thinks in this way, to esteem oneself more than one is worth)
- The idea of pleasure was, upon my entry into society, the only one that preoccupied me. The peace that we were enjoying *then* left me in a dangerous idleness. The lack of occupation, to which people of my rank and my age *are accustomed* . . . led me toward pleasure.

- Without yet knowing how violent was the penchant that led me toward women, I sought them out carefully.
- those sweet errors of the soul / once this choice was determined, how was I to announce it to the woman who had fixed my attention?
- One often becomes attached not so much to the woman who is the most attractive, but to the woman one believes the easiest to attract.
- (respect becomes an insult to women, and an absurdity for *us* / undoubtedly she believed *you*)

Pages 17–18
- I will pass over the feelings that preoccupied me on that night. There is no man on earth unfortunate enough to have never loved, and consequently not one who is not in a position to imagine them.

Page 18
- the way in which women thought *then* / what the two sexes *then* called Love
- love, *once* so respectful, so sincere, so delicate, had become so reckless and easy . . .
- If we are to believe ancient Memoirs, women *in the past* were more flattered when they inspired respect than desire.
- that which, in a century as wise as *ours*, will perhaps be even more surprising.
- those of my time
- It must not be inferred, however, from what I have just said, that they all offered the same ease. I have seen some who, after two weeks of attention paid to them, were still undecided. . . . I admit that these examples are rare.

Pages 18–19
- (I have observed that the easiest women to conquer are those who begin with the foolish hope of never being seduced)

Page 19
- Morals since that time have changed so prodigiously that I would not be surprised if today one treated as a fable what I have just said on this subject. Only with difficulty do we believe that vices and virtues that are no longer before our eyes have ever existed: it is nonetheless true that I am not exaggerating.
- (she believed you)
- (as I have said)

Page 20
- I did not know, among many other things / I could not imagine / I was too young to feel / I did not know enough about it / I did not yet know / I did not know well enough / I had too little experience / I was too young not to believe I was in love.
- I have spoken too much of my lack of experience; one can see too well, by this narrative, how many false ideas I owed to it, for there to be a need to dwell any longer on this subject.
- However little my ignorance allowed me to divine, I understood that she was not so far from answering me as the first time I had spoken to her.
- When giving her my hand to lead her back to her carriage, I thought I felt her squeezing it: without knowing the consequences that this act would lead to with Madame de Lursay, I squeezed her hand in return.
- I thought I could never disguise myself well enough in Germeuil's eyes; and with a

foolishness common in young people, I imagined that people who were the most indifferent to my situation would have guessed it simply by looking at me.

Page 21
- and beginning to form a bad opinion of women as *stupidly* as I had formed a good one, I examined Mademoiselle de Théville.
- *What can I complain about?* I asked myself. *Should I be surprised by Lursay's harshness? Had I expected to find myself loved, and is it not up to me to procure this advantage? What happiness for me, if I can one day make her love me! The more obstacles she puts in my path, the greater my glory will be. Can a heart as valuable as hers be bought too dearly?* I ended up with this idea, and I found it again the next morning. It seemed that it had been strengthened by the illusions of the night.
- I had no sooner left her than this rendezvous . . . came back to mind. *A rendezvous!* Despite my lack of experience, that seemed serious to me. *She was to have few people at her house: in such a case, that means frankly that there will be none.* She had squeezed my hand: I did not know all the importance of this act, but it seemed to me nonetheless that it is a mark of friendship, which carries a unique meaning from one sex to the other, and which is given only in certain situations. *But this virtuous Madame de Lursay, who had just forbidden me even from guessing her intentions, would she have wanted? . . . No, that was not possible.*

Page 22
- With an experienced man, a word . . . a glance, a gesture, even less, alerts him to the fact, if he wants to be loved.
- I had so little experience with society that I believed I had truly angered her. I did not know that a woman rarely pursues an amorous conversation with someone that she wants to become involved with.
- I was pressed to accept, my embarrassment was increasing, and I think that, for lack of knowing what to respond, I would have let myself be taken home, if Madame de Lursay . . . had not come to my aid.
- I do not know what it was, something so touching and so sweet was shining in Hortense's eyes / I cannot express the revolution that was going on in all my senses / I can only feebly express the confusion that this night caused in me.
- From that moment, I probably had in my heart the seed of what I have been since.

Page 23
- Versac, about whom I will have a lot to say later in these Memoirs . . .
- No one could resemble Versac; and I, who have since walked so advantageously in his steps . . .
- Madame de Senanges, to whom, as it will be seen later, I had the misfortune of owing my education . . .
- It did not occur to me that Senanges would be the one to train me.
- Adored by all the women he betrayed and criticized endlessly, vain, haughty, thoughtless, the most audacious young lord that one had ever seen . . .
- Versac, such as he was, had always pleased me a great deal. I never saw him without studying him, and without trying to imitate those ostentatious airs that I admired in him so much.
- Whatever intensity Madame de Lursay used to show Versac to me in such an unfavorable light, she could not persuade me that this portrait resembled him. Versac was for me the finest of men . . . / I never wanted to believe that Versac could have deceived me.

Page 24

- I finally reproached myself for having paid so much attention to someone who defined herself at the first glance. . . . I saw . . . what the most perverse nature and the most condemnable artifice can offer in the way of the lowest and most corrupted.
- She had never known how to mask her opinions, and one cannot say what she appeared to be, in cases where almost all women of her kind have the art of passing only for flirtatious.
- the vision that offered itself / my beautiful unknown girl
- If one imagines all that is most noble in the most perfect beauty . . . one will hardly be able to have an idea of the person I would like to describe.

Page 25

- I do not know what strange and sudden movement agitated me at the sight of her / I do not know what my eyes said to her.
- She had in fact no need of adornment; was there any so brilliant that she would not have outshone it? was there any ornament so modest that she would not have made it beautiful? Her appearance was sweet and reserved; sentiment and wit *seemed* to shine in her eyes. This person *appeared* extremely young to me. . . .
- She looked at Versac with a strange coldness and a kind of scorn that did not fail to reassure me.

Pages 25–26

- Besides, this man, according to her words, was no longer unknown to her; therefore she must have seen him again? Why would it not be Germeuil? Did I know how he knew her, and for how long? Alas, I said to myself, what does it matter to me who the object of her passion is, since it is not I?

Page 26

- Having witnessed Hortense's sadness and her coldness toward me, to what could I better attribute these attitudes than to a secret passion? The first suspicions I had had about Germeuil revived in my mind; as I thought about them, they grew stronger.
- A state as unusual as hers could be attributed only to a secret and unhappy passion; but if it were true, as I had believed that very day, that she loved Germeuil, what could be the cause of her melancholy? When I had left them, no cloud of trouble *seemed* about to rise between them; could her absence have given rise to such a violent sadness? *One grows sad when one loses one's beloved for a long time.* . . . Germeuil was therefore not the cause of her pain.
- Despite the lack of interest that I *supposed* the unknown girl had for me / this unknown girl whom I adored, and who *I believed* had so much aversion for me / I *imagined* that she was thinking of Germeuil without distraction, and that her heart was peacefully delighting in an idea that I *believed* to be dear to her.

Page 27

- It was a rather simple thing, that she should be reserved with someone she knew as little as me; and if I had not loved her, I would not have been alarmed.
- From time to time she spoke softly to Germeuil, leaned toward him in a familiar way; and these things, as simple as they are in themselves, did not seem that way to me then, and added to my despair.
- In truth, by going to see Germeuil the next day, I could have put an end to this worry, *but how would I expose to him the subject of such a strong curiosity; what motives would I give him?* Despite all the disguises I could have employed, *did I not have reason to fear that he would*

discover the source? And if it were true, as I suspected, that he loved the unknown girl, *why should I alert him to take precautions against my feelings?*
- What! I said to myself, I could have thought that I was the one who had smitten Hortense! I dared believe that this unknown man, so dangerous for her heart, was none other than myself! What an error!
- God! I said to myself in anger, I could have believed that I would be loved; I could have forgotten that Germeuil alone could please her!

Page 28
- a worthy woman
- I forgot at *that moment, the dearest of my life,* that I believed she loved someone other than myself; I forgot even myself.
- Versac could not believe that any heart could escape him; but even if this heart that he wanted to attack had not then been filled with *the strongest passion,* it was virtuous.

Pages 28–29
- As for Mademoiselle de Théville, she looked at me, so I believed, with an extreme coldness, and hardly responded to the compliment I paid her. *It is true that I have since thought* that it was not impossible that she understood nothing; the confusion of my senses had spread to my mind, and the confusion of my ideas prevented me from expressing any of them well.

Page 30
- At this precise declaration of the state of my heart, Madame de Lursay sighed, blushed, turned her eyes toward me languidly, stared for some time, lowered them onto her fan, and remained silent.
- I *thought* I saw by her cold attitude that she really wanted me to leave, and that she *probably* intended to devote the evening to the Marquis.
- I have since appreciated all the skill of Madame de Lursay and the pleasure that my ignorance gave her.
- Since the time when she became a widow and reformed her life, the public, which does not need to be well informed in order to talk, had attributed to her some lovers that she had *perhaps* not had.
- While I was thinking these unpleasant ideas, Madame de Lursay was congratulating herself for having undertaken to hide from me how happy she was.
- I pronounced these words with a fearlessness that she would not have suspected in me the day before, and which seemed to her so unlike my character that she did not even think of being shocked by it.

Page 31
- probably she had gayer ideas / She had apparently counted on my presence earlier
- she appeared to be plunged in the most despondent reverie / she must have been indignant with me
- It is not, at least I have had reason to believe, that she wanted to delay the confession of her weakness for a long time. . . . Her heart was then tender and delicate: according to what I have learned since, it had not always been so.

Page 32
- as a reasonable person, she judged that there was nothing left to hope for from me at that moment

- She believed that it was important for her, in order to acquire me and even to hold on to me, to hide her love for me as long as she could. . . . Besides, she knew that *however ardently men pursue victory, they always like to buy it.*
- She was wise enough to have these thoughts, and probably she did.
- Based on the little I had said to her, she had believed my passion was determined: however, I no longer spoke of it; what course should she take? The most decent one was to wait until love, which cannot contain itself for very long, especially in a heart as innocent as mine, would force me again to break the silence; but that was not the surest course. It never occurred to her that I had given her up: she thought only that, sure of never being loved, I was fighting a love that was making me unhappy.
- She judged / She did not doubt / she feared
- (What course of action did I have left to take?)

Page 33
- Lursay's intention, however, was not to remain silent: the insult was too serious. *To have made her wait, to arrive coldly without excusing myself, without appearing to believe that I needed to, to have not even noticed that she was vexed by it, were there any crimes of which I was not guilty?*
- My coldness, for I was concerned with nothing, embarrassed her; *courtesy, respect, a somber attitude; what a prize, both for what she had done for me, and for the rewards that she was still preparing for me! How could one reconcile so little love and eagerness with the passion that I had already shown her?*
- she knew how far I was from thinking her capable of a weakness . . .
- It was as if to tell me that I was to ask her for a rendezvous. She waited a long time for me to do it; but *seeing* finally that it did not enter my mind, she had the generosity to take it upon herself.
- She recognized, *by the tone of my voice,* how moved I was.
- Madame de Lursay . . . knew, *by the coldness of my glances,* that she was not making as vivid an impression on me as she would have liked.

Page 34
- I was aware that she was reproaching me; we were alone, and I had not fallen at her feet! I had not made this the happiest of my moments! I was letting her go, in short! Did I not know the price of a quarrel? I do not know whether she had these thoughts, but she got into her carriage with an air that assured me that she was infinitely annoyed.
- But, either because my behavior in the rendezvous had displeased her, or because she had wanted to make me desire more of them, she had decided that I would be at the mercy of all the importunate people that my fate would bring to her house that day.

Page 35
- I think she wanted to wait, out of meanness, for me to break the silence: finally I decided to do it. So you are tying knots, Madame? I asked her with a trembling voice. At this interesting and witty question, Madame de Lursay looked at me with astonishment. Whatever idea she had had of my shyness and lack of experience in society, it seemed inconceivable to her that I could find only that to say to her.
- (she seemed to have forgotten) / (she felt she was going to grow old)
- women in this situation
- (she was far from being as frightened as she told me she was)
- (she feared / she was persuaded / she wanted)
- (according to what I have learned subsequently)

- Versac did not doubt for a moment . . . that he would promptly seduce Mademoiselle de Théville.

Page 36
- Madame de Senanges who . . . was thinking more about the number of her lovers than about the length of time they had wanted to remain in her chains, was very much persuaded that her charms were acting on me.
- Madame de Mongennes judged by my cold attitude toward Madame de Senanges that I did not love her, and too stupid not to be excessively vain, she did not doubt that I would yield to her as soon as she wished it.
- Madame de Senanges . . . resolved to behave so well that no one would doubt that I belonged to her / Versac, who had resolved to detach me from Madame de Lursay
- These reflections, which *in all likelihood* Versac thought, calmed him down / It is not, as Senanges has admitted to me since, that I had precisely everything I needed to please her
- Senanges remembered at that moment that Versac had told her that Madame de Lursay had designs on me. . . . She imagined that without compromising herself, it would be easy to clear up her doubts.
- Madame de Senanges no sooner noticed the new ideas of Madame de Mongennes than she became alarmed about them: she judged, and *I believe correctly*, that if Mongennes did not wish to please me, she at least wanted people to think she did.
- what angel, what divinity has descended upon your house, Madame? he asked Madame de Lursay softly. . . . Madame de Lursay told him softly who she was.

Page 37
- After these words we got up from the table; Versac beginning to doubt the success of his plans, Madame de Senanges preoccupied with advancing her own, and Madame de Lursay desperate about the improper conduct of Monsieur de Pranzi.

Chapter 2

Page 41
- Let's get back to me.
- Let's begin.
- That was their situation when I came into the world.

Page 42
- Let us leave aside my nephews, who have distracted me a little from my story.
- In the year after my brother's marriage, I arrived in Paris.
- I will describe him here, although that is not really necessary / But I forgot something, it is the description of the young girl, and I must give it / By this speech of Mme. d'Alain that I am reporting . . .
- the pretty blonde about whom I have spoken / the place that was reserved for me, and that I have already mentioned / So I went home, consumed with vanity, as I have said
- I said in the first part of my life story . . . / I said in the last part that I hastened . . .
- I will pass over the consequences of these sad events; the detail of them would be too long.
- I will leave aside the story of what happened after the visit of Mlle. Habert, and proceed to the moment when I appeared before a magistrate.

- That was the first encounter I had with Mme. Catherine, whose words I have shortened by a hundred *God be praised!* and *may Heaven help us!*, expressions that served at times as a refrain and at others as a vehicle for her speech.

Page 43

- When I think about it, I still laugh about the stupendous astonishment they both felt upon seeing us.
- Imagine / note / Judge / see / Remember / think
- Do you know who this man was, whose life I had probably saved? / Had you intended to love her? you will ask me / Now you are putting on airs, you will say to me; not at all.
- But in this world all virtues are out of place, as are all vices.
- I have noticed that gluttons waste half their time worrying about what they will eat / There are however some silent women, but I think they are not that way naturally.
- In love, no matter how involved one already is, the vanity of pleasing someone else makes your soul so unfaithful and gives you a cowardly complacency on such occasions.

Page 44

- One must admit that the devil is very clever, but also that we are very foolish!
- The man she was addressing was a big brute, one of those servants who care about nothing in a house but their wages and profits.
- I paid him a compliment with the emotion one has when one is a little person who comes to ask a favor of someone important.

Page 45

- So that I went away filled with joy, puffed up with glory, and full of my silly exaggerations about the lady's merit. It never came to my mind for one moment that my feelings injured those that I owed to Mlle. Habert.
- since I was naturally lively, and my spontaneity carried me away, and since I was ignorant of the art of deceit, and I put no restraint on my thoughts other than a little clumsy modesty . . . I came forth with some astonishing tenderness.
- I had refused to marry a beautiful girl whom I loved, who loved me and offered me her fortune, because of a proud and modest disgust that could have struck only a good and honorable soul. Wasn't that a most advantageous story to tell her? And I did my best to tell it in a naïve way, as one tells the truth.

Page 46

- I remember well that in speaking to her in this way, I felt nothing in me which might belie my words. I admit however that I tried to appear and sound touching, like a man who is crying, and that I strived to embellish the truth a bit.
- Perhaps I did wrong in taking Genevieve's money; I do not think I was acting by all the rules of honor; for in the end I was leading this girl to believe that I loved her and I was deceiving her. . . . Besides, this money she was offering me was not acquired in a Christian way, I was aware of that . . . but I did not yet know how to think such delicate thoughts, my principles of honesty were still quite limited.
- As for me, I had lost all countenance, and like a real simpleton I bowed to this man at each word he spoke to me.
- I needed to respond in any case, with my little silk outfit and my little bourgeois neatness, which I no longer held in esteem after seeing so much magnificent clothing around me.

- These words, although quite simple, were no longer those of a peasant, as you can see.
- The son of an honest man who resides in the country, I replied. I was telling the truth yet avoiding the word peasant, which seemed harsh to me.

Page 47
- So I went home, consumed with vanity, as I have said, but a vanity that made me cheerful, and not haughty and ridiculous; my self-esteem has always been sociable; I have never been more good-natured or docile than when I've had reason to esteem myself and to be vain; each person has his character, and that was mine.
- I was not ashamed of the foolish things I said, as long as they were pleasing; for through the thickness of my ignorance, I could see that they never harmed a man who was not supposed to know better.
- Until now my speech had always had a rustic turn of phrase; but for over a month I had been correcting myself rather well, when I wanted to be careful, and I had kept this turn of phrase with Mlle. Habert only because it succeeded so well with her . . . but it is certain that I spoke better French when I wanted to.

Page 48
- [1] But, I said to myself, I am running no risk; I'll have only to move out if I'm not happy. . . . Besides, the whole house smiles upon me . . . already I'm assured my four meals, and my heart tells me that all will go well: courage!
- [2] Ah! what good bread! I've never eaten any better, any whiter, any tastier; much attention is needed to make bread like that; only a saintly hand could have kneaded it, and indeed it was made by Catherine. Oh! what an excellent meal I had!
- [3] Damn, what a succulent little dinner! That's what I call soup, not to mention a little dash of roasted meat, cooked with such perfection.

Pages 48–49
- To increase my perplexity, I looked at this purse of money that was on the table, it seemed to me so full! What a pity to lose it!

Page 49
- My stay in Paris had lightened my complexion a bit; and my goodness! when I was dressed up, Jacob looked very good indeed.
- This red silk flattered me; a silk lining, what a pleasure and what magnificence for a peasant!
- [1] Why go back home? I sometimes said to myself. Everything here is filled with people who are well off and who, just like me, [2] had nothing to rely on but Providence. [3] My goodness! let's stay here a few more days . . . for what each meal costs me, I will go far; [4] for I was abstemious, and I had no trouble being so.
- (Everything here was filled with people)

Page 50
- the malicious one / the little rascal / the discreet d'Alain / our officious busybody / the fifty-year-old nymph
- For I confess to you, Jacob, that I do not want Catherine to come with us; she has a rough and difficult nature, she would always be in touch with my sister, who is naturally curious, not to mention that all prudish women are; they compensate for the sins they don't commit with the pleasure of knowing the sins of others; that is better than nothing; and I am the one making that remark, not Mlle. Habert.

Page 51
- Eggs would make me swell up, said the younger woman; and then it was *my sister* here and *my sister* there.
- they would glance indifferently over this good food: I have no appetite today. Me either. Everything seems bland to me. For me it's too salty.
- But what are you telling me, are you not mistaken? is that possible?
- Tell us this and tell us that.
- And thereupon: I'll let you have it for so much, it's a bargain. No, it's too much. It's not enough. In short, they agreed on a price, and the robe was mine.
- Monsieur so-and-so / in a certain street / in such-and-such an inn / the Marquise so-and-so
- There is in a certain suburb (I don't remember which one it was) an old woman . . .

Pages 51–52
- [1] She was the widow of a prosecutor who had left her quite well off, and she lived in proportion to her wealth. A comely woman, about the same age as Mlle. Habert, as fresh as she and fatter; a bit of a gossip but one with a good heart, [2] who befriended you from the start, who opened her heart to you, told you her business, asked about yours, and then came back to her own, and then to you. Talked to you about her daughter, for she had one; informed you that she was eighteen, told you the accidents of her childhood, her illnesses; turned next to the subject of her late husband, recounted the story of his boyhood, then came to their romance, said how long it had lasted, passed on to their marriage, and finally to the life they had lived together; [3] he was the best man in the world! very assiduous in his studies, and indeed he had earned some wealth through his wisdom and thrift: a little jealous by nature, and also because he loved her very much; susceptible to kidney-stones; God knows how he had suffered! the care she had taken of him! Finally, he had died a good Christian.

Page 52
- Does M. Doucin (speaking of the priest) know you? / Do you know, said one of our witnesses, friend of the hostess, what M. Doucin is going to say to Mme. d'Alain (that was the name of our hostess).

Pages 52–53
- I rather like this neighborhood, she said to me (it was near Saint-Gervais) / Besides, if he does not give you another job (he was speaking to me, and about M. de Fécour) . . .

Page 53
- No, Miss, I said to her then, I am afraid of nothing (and that was true) / I have killed my mistress, I saw her die (and in fact, she died when they brought him toward her).
- Genevieve is a likeable girl, I protect her parents, and I had her enter my house only to be in a better position to help her, and to find her a good position. (He was lying). / We are speaking about the young man whom you have retained (this youth was important to him).
- Genevieve had paid more attention to her master's love than she had told me.
- Certain as she was of Jacob's love, and in fear of losing me . . . she thought that the master's proposals . . . would tempt me in turn.
- Gladly, she said to me, charmed by my interest and by the favorable conjectures she was making about the success of her designs.

Page 54
- And what is funny is that this woman . . . did not know that her soul was so wicked, her true feelings escaped her, her skill deceived her, she was caught up in it herself, and because she pretended to be good, she believed that in fact she was.
- As we walked on without speaking, which came, I think, from not knowing where to begin a conversation, I noticed a sign . . . and I seized this pretext to break the silence, which according to all appearances was embarrassing to both of us.
- The president lowered his eyes like a man who wants to remain serious and who is repressing a desire to laugh.
- I think / probably / so it appeared to me
- Nor had I neglected to look at the president's wife, but in a humble and pleading manner. With my eyes I had said to the one: There is pleasure in seeing you, and she had believed me; to the other: Protect me, and she had promised to do so; for it seems to me that they had both heard and answered just as I am telling you.
- I am persuaded that she said to herself: So my taste is not so bad, since everyone is of my opinion.
- Please sit down, she repeated to me, in the tone of a person who would say to you: Forget what I am, and let's live without ceremony.

Page 55
- Agathe's hands and arms were rather comely, and I noticed that the rascal tried hard to keep them in sight as much as she could, as if she had wanted to tell me: Look, does your wife have anything worth this much?
- You will say to me: How did you know about these conversations? It was while clearing the table and putting things away in the room where they were.
- It was not right away that I figured out this character that I am developing here, I came to sense it only through seeing Agathe.
- Besides, it was not then that I came to know Mme. de Fécour as I describe her here, for at that time I did not have a very deep relationship with her, but I met her again a few years later, and I saw her enough to get to know her.
- I noticed it quite well; and this art of reading people's minds and of understanding their secret feelings is a gift that I have always had and which has sometimes been quite useful to me.
- And those are observations that anyone can make, especially in the situation I was in.

Page 56
- [1] The cleric answered nothing to this devout and even tender emotion shown in his favor. [2] To keep only the elder sister was to lose a great deal. [3] It seemed to me that he was extremely embarrassed.
- Lady Catherine had only paid court to the elder sister . . . who in any case had always governed the house. But since all commerce between the two sisters was ending, that changed everything, and it was much more attractive to pass into the service of the younger sister over whom she would have had control.
- All these proofs of the discretion of our good hostess did not encourage Mlle. Habert: but after having promised her a secret, it was perhaps even worse to refuse it than to tell it; so she had to speak.

Pages 56–57
- [1] Imagine the hopes they had built up against me. [2] A man in prison, what has he

done? We had nothing to do with that; nor did the president, who refused to help us; so it must be for some action outside of our affair. [1] How do I know if they didn't go so far as to suspect me of some crime; they both hated me enough to have this charitable opinion of me.

Page 57
- (Remember / think / don't forget)
- [1] And on all these subjects that I have just mentioned, notice the curious revelation of the morals of Mme. de Ferval. [2] The beautiful inner conscience revealed, how many miseries laid bare, and what miseries! [3] those which dishonor a prude the most, which determine that she is a hypocrite, a true scoundrel. For if she were malicious, vindictive, haughty, slanderous . . . none of that contradicts the imperious austerity of her trade. [4] But to be convicted of being in love, to be discovered in a ribald situation, oh! all is lost; [5] now the prude is hissed at, there is no good face that she can put on.

Pages 57–58
- For my part, I didn't know what to say; this name of Jacob that he had called me held me in check, I was still afraid that he would begin to call me that way again; and I thought only about escaping as best I could; [1] for what could be done with a rival who is called only Jacob, in the presence of a woman who was no less humiliated than I by this excessive familiarity? [2] To have a lover was already shameful for her, and to have one with that name was doubly so; there could be no question of a delicate affair of the heart between her and Jacob.

Page 59
- And thereupon she embraces Mme. de Ferval who thanks her, whom she thanks, leans nonchalantly on my arm, leads me away, makes me get into her carriage, calls me sometimes sir, sometimes my boy, speaks to me as though we had known one another for ten years, always with those enormous breasts out in front, and we arrive at her house.

Page 60
- When she liked you, for example, this bosom I've spoken about, it seemed as though she presented it to you, less to tempt your heart than to tell you that you touched hers.
- Oh! get married after thirty years of a life of that kind, find yourself overnight to be a man's wife, that is already a lot; I also add, a man that you will love by inclination, which is still more, and you will then be another Mlle. Habert.
- (our cleric / our three men) / (let's begin / let's come back / let's return)

Page 61
- I will say nothing of *our* conversation on the way; let's arrive in Paris, *we* entered the city rather early.
- I have since seen many objects of this kind which have always pleased me, but never as much as they pleased me then.
- However, I did not make that reflection then; I am making it only now, as I write.
- But let us leave them in their confusion, and let's arrive at the home of the good Mlle. Habert.
- I went out and headed home. Notice, on the way, the inconstancy of things of this world.

Page 62
- The story of my adventures will not be useless / among the facts I have to tell, I think there will be some curious ones / one will perhaps find the stories . . . a bit long / I believe this detail will not be boring
- some people will be able to recognize me / as one will see further on / you will say to me
- I will write them as best I can / I will tell my whole life / I will give the portrait in a moment / I will say no more about him

Page 63
- Let's see what they will become, I said to myself . . . what course will she take?
- (we were going to continue / he was then to found a pension for her) / (one came to tell me that two people were asking for me below, that they would not come up)
- we shall see later / further on
- 1. You *will see* later on where that *will lead* us.
- 2. When my companion had left, I abandoned my robe (*let* me speak about it while it *delights* me, that *will not last;* I *will soon be* accustomed to it), I got dressed.
- 3. That is all *I shall say* about him in this respect. It is enough about a man whom I have hardly seen, and whose wife *will soon be* a widow.

Page 65
- I am anxious to move on to greater events; so let us pass quickly on to our new house.
- The movers came the next day, our furniture has gone, we had dinner standing up.
- Catherine, finally convinced she will not follow us, treated us accordingly.
- she tried to beat me, I who *resemble* her poor departed Baptiste . . .

Pages 65–66
- Mlle. Habert *has written* a little note that she *left* on the table for her sister, in which she *notifies* her that in seven or eight days she *will come* to arrange things with her, and to settle a few little affairs that they *have* to straighten out together.

Page 66
- There we are at the other house; and it's from here that one is going to see my adventures become nobler and more important; it is here that my fortune begins: a servant with the name of Jacob, from now on it will only be a question of Monsieur de La Vallée; a name that I used for some time . . . It is by this other name that I am known in society; it is not necessary for me to say this name, which I took only after the death of Mlle. Habert.

Pages 66–67
- But all these little details *bore* even me; let's skip over them, and let's suppose that evening has come, that we have had supper with our witnesses, that it *is* two o'clock in the morning, and that we *are leaving* for the church. Finally we are there, the mass is said, and there we are, married in spite of our elder sister and her ally the confessor, who *will no longer get* coffee or sweet rolls from Mme. de La Vallée.

Page 67
- It is for the last time that I give these kinds of details; and as for Agathe, I will be able to speak more of her; but of my way of life with Mme. de La Vallée, I will not say another word.

- There we are, married; I know all that I owe her; I will always strive to do what will make her happy; I am in the flower of my youth; she is still fresh, despite her age. . . . Mme. de La Vallée, as tender as she is, is not jealous; I have no annoying account to give her of my actions, which until now, as you see, have been only too unfaithful. . . . If I am absent, Mme. de La Vallée hopes ardently for my return, but awaits it in peace; when she sees me again, there are no questions, she is charmed, as long as I love her, and I will love her.

Page 68
- Let one suppose between us the sweetest and calmest of marriages; [1] and so ours will be; and [2] I will no longer mention her except in matters in which by chance [3] she will be involved. Alas! [4] soon she will no longer be involved in anything that concerns me; the moment that is to take her away from me is not far off, and [5] it will not be long before I come back to her to tell the story of her death and of the pain it caused me.

Chapter 3

Page 72
- I have noticed, throughout my life / I have experienced subsequently
- I plan to have it published, and I'd like to think that the public will be happy with it
- I begged Tiberge to be no more scrupulous than a great number of bishops and other priests, who know quite well how to accommodate a mistress with their office.

Page 73
- Since there was nothing, after all, in the whole of my conduct which could absolutely dishonor me, at least if one compared it to that of young men of a certain social class, and since a mistress does not pass for a scandal in our century, no more than a little skill at winning in games of chance . . .
- Nor was I one of those extravagant libertines who proudly add irreligion to moral depravity.
- Shall I say it, to my shame? / a retreat that I name with horror / I must confess
- (you will see) / (imagine) / (After what you have just heard)
- the state in which you saw me at Pacy / You were a witness to it at Pacy
- O God! how spontaneous and sincere were my wishes! and by what a harsh judgment had you resolved not to grant them!

Page 74
- What makes my despair could have made my happiness. I find myself to be the most unhappy of all men.
- I still find sweetness in a memory that recalls to me her tenderness and the pleasing aspects of her mind.
- Forgive me if I finish in few words a story that kills me. I am telling you of a misfortune that never had any example. My whole life is destined to mourn it.
- This was one of those unique situations, the likes of which one has never experienced. One could never explain them to others, because they have no idea of them.
- There are few people who know the strength of these particular movements of the heart.

The common man is sensitive to only five or six passions. . . . But people of a more noble character can be moved in a thousand different ways . . . and . . . they have a sense of this greatness which raises them above the vulgar herd.

- A barbarian would have been moved upon witnessing my sorrow and my fear / Where could one find a barbarian whom such a lively and tender repentance would not have touched?

Page 75
- I am persuaded that there is no honest man in the world who, in my circumstances, would not have approved my plans. . . . But will anyone accuse my complaints of injustice if I bemoan the intransigeance of Heaven, which rejected a plan I had formed only to please it? Alas! what am I saying, rejected? It was punished like a crime.
- If it is true that celestial support is at all times equal to the strength of passions, then someone should explain to me by what deadly influence one can be swept suddenly away from his duty, without being capable of the least resistance, and without feeling the least remorse.
- Gods! why call the world a place of misery, since one can experience such charming delights in it?
- Heaven . . . enlightened me

Page 76
- not having enough experience to imagine

Page 77
- I had the fault of being excessively timid and easily disconcerted; but far from being stopped by this weakness, I walked up to the mistress of my heart.
- This plan, as extravagant as it was, seemed to us to be rather well arranged.
- Although I had only taken this precaution through an excessive concern and foresight, it turned out to be absolutely necessary.
- I had set the time of my departure from Amiens. Alas! why had I not set it one day earlier! I would have returned to my father's house with all my innocence.
- It is certain that with my tender and constant nature, I would have been happy my whole life if Manon had been faithful to me.
- an unfortunate instant made me fall back into the precipice / an unhappy accident / misfortunes that did not take long to befall me
- During that time our evil genius was working toward our undoing. We were delirious with pleasure, and the dagger was suspended above our heads.
- Fate delivered me from one precipice only to make me fall into another.

Page 78
- Manon was unaware, as was I, that all the wrath of Heaven and the rage of our enemies were about to fall upon her.
- As for me, I felt at that moment that I would have sacrificed for Manon all the bishoprics of Christendom / I would have preferred death, at that moment, to the state into which I believed I was about to fall.
- In fact, I had not yet calmed down enough to control myself at the sight of G...M... / I committed an imprudence by confessing to him that I knew where his son was; but my excessive anger caused me to make this indiscretion.
- I pretended to apply myself to study. . . . I must confess, to my shame, that I played the

role of a hypocrite at Saint-Lazare / I represented things to the superior, it is true, in the most favorable way for us / I opened my heart to Tiberge without reservation, except about my plan to flee.
- Manon had such delicate attentions for me, that I believed I was too perfectly compensated for all my troubles / I believed I was so happy . . . that no one could have made me understand that I had some new misfortune to fear.
- I thought I was absolutely freed from the weaknesses of love
- I was absolutely freed

Page 79
- However, I thought I saw, beneath her joy and caresses, an air of truth that corresponded to appearances
- I saw / I thought I saw
- Show me a lover who does not enter blindly into all the whims of an adored mistress, and I will agree that I was wrong to yield so easily.
- But I would have had to lose all feelings of humanity to harden myself against so many charms. I was so far from having this barbarous strength.

Page 80
- What a fate for such a charming creature, who would have occupied the highest throne in the world if all men had had my eyes and my heart!
- Gods! with what emotions was I not agitated!
- I would have given, to be free for one moment . . . Just Heaven! what wouldn't I have given.
- What a fate for such a charming creature!

Pages 80–81
- [1] It seemed so impossible to me that Manon had betrayed me, that I feared insulting her by suspecting her. [2] I adored her, that was sure; I had not given her any more proofs of love than I had received from her; why would I have accused her of being less sincere and less faithful than I? What reason would she have had to deceive me? Only three hours ago she had covered me with her most tender caresses and had received mine with passion; I did not know my own heart any better than hers. [3] No, no, I said, it is not possible that Manon is betraying me.

Page 81
- [1] I also recalled Manon's little acquisitions, which seemed to surpass our present wealth. That seemed to smell of the generosity of a new lover. [2] And that confidence she had shown me for resources that were unknown to me! [1] I had trouble giving to so many riddles a meaning as favorable as my heart wished. [2] On the other hand, I had almost not lost her from sight since we arrived in Paris. Occupations, excursions, entertainments, we had always been beside one another; my God! a moment's separation would have afflicted us too much. We had to tell each other endlessly that we loved one another; otherwise we would have died from worry. [1] I could therefore not imagine a single moment when Manon could have been occupied with someone other than myself.

Page 82
- I thought I perceived / I noticed / I could not figure out . . . although it seemed to me / I looked at her
- Finally, I saw tears fall from her beautiful eyes: treacherous tears!

- At first everything was so obscure that I did not understand the slightest conjecture. I was cruelly betrayed. But by whom? Tiberge was the first who came to mind. Traitor! I said, your life is over if my suspicions are correct.
- I was credulous enough to imagine
- I went to the parlor immediately. Gods! what a surprising apparition! I found Manon.
- I could not accuse Manon of a crime for being loved. According to all appearances she was unaware of her conquest; and what sort of life was I going to lead if I was capable of opening my heart to jealousy so easily?

Page 83
- I thought . . . about all the places I had lived in innocence. What an immense space separated me from that fortunate state!
- My plan was bizarre and bold; but of what was I not capable, with the motivations that drove me?
- [1] The death of our enemies would have been of little use to Manon, and would have probably taken from me all means of helping her. [2] Besides, would I have resorted to a cowardly murder? [3] What other way could I find for my revenge?
- [1] I had lost, it is true, eveything that other men esteem; but I was master of Manon's heart, the only thing I valued. [2] To live in Europe or in America, what did it matter to me where I lived, if I was sure of being happy and of living with my mistress? [3] Isn't the entire universe the homeland of two faithful lovers?

Page 84
- I knew Manon; why afflict myself so much with a misfortune that I should have foreseen? Why not strive instead to find a remedy? There was still time. . . . To undertake to wrest her violently from the hands of G…M… was a desperate course of action. . . . But it seemed to me that if I could have managed to have the slightest conversation with her, I would not have failed to win over her heart. I knew all the sensitive areas so well! I was so sure of being loved by her!
- She could not hope that G…M… would leave her alone all night long like a vestal virgin. So it was with him that she intended to spend the night. What an admission for a lover!
- the ungrateful Manon
- I shall scorn what common men admire.
- Shall I not be happy? I added; will all my wishes not be fulfilled?

Page 85
- the ungrateful / crudeness of feeling / delicacy
- By means of what fatality, I said, have I become so criminal? Love is an innocent passion; how did it change for me into a source of misery and disorderly conduct? Who prevented me from living happy and virtuous with Manon?
- this fatal tenderness / Fatal passion! / my evil destiny
- O fortune, I cried out, cruel fortune! grant me here, at least, either death or victory.

Page 88
- (I was at the door, where I was listening)
- I did not learn this sad detail until much later.
- I never learned the details of their conversation, but it was only too easy for me to figure out by its deadly consequences.
- he was secretly pining away for her

Page 89
- First he wanted to know from the lackey everything his son had done that afternoon, whether he had quarreled with anyone or had taken part in the quarrel of someone else, or had gone to some house of ill repute. The lackey, who *believed* his master to be in grave danger and who *imagined* he should spare no effort to provide him with aid, revealed all he knew about his master's love for Manon and the expense he had incurred for her. . . . That was enough to make the old man *suspect* that his son's affair was a quarrel over love.
- but a little curiosity, or perhaps some repentance for having betrayed me (I have never been able to figure out which of these two feelings) . . .
- (perhaps / probably / apparently)
- Tiberge knew that I was at Saint-Lazare, and perhaps he had not been unhappy about this disgrace, which he believed capable of bringing me back to my duty.
- I saw Manon tremble, apparently because of her fear.
- My father probably imagined that so many preparations had not been made without a plan of some importance.
- he noticed / he believed / they doubted / they imagined

Page 90
- My father was surprised to see me still so deeply moved. He knew I had principles of honor, and never doubting that Manon's betrayal would make me despise her, he imagined that my constancy came less from this particular passion than from a general penchant for women.
- My sadness seemed so excessive to the superior that, fearing the consequences, he believed he should treat me with a great deal of gentleness and indulgence.
- I showed him some of these feelings, in a way that also persuaded him that I did not have a bad nature.
- this faithful friend / such a generous and constant friend
- He was a brutal man without principles of honor. He came into our room cursing horribly, and . . . he hurled insults and reproaches at Manon.

Page 91
- Lescaut . . . was not lacking in intelligence and prudence. . . . His advice was wise.
- that old libertine / the barbarian / that old tiger
- Five bold and resolute men were enough to frighten those miserable archers, who are incapable of defending themselves honorably when they can avoid the danger of combat through cowardice.
- He was good enough to consider us as different from the common and miserable people with whom we were associated.
- He made a good impression on me by his appearance and his polite conduct.
- He seemed very sensitive to this display of openness and candor. His response was that of a man who has social graces and feelings, which society does not always give and often causes to be lost.
- We embraced one another with tenderness and we became friends, for no other reason than the goodness of our hearts and a simple tendency that leads one tender and generous man to love another man who resembles him.
- You have such a gentle and likeable nature, he said to me one day, that I cannot understand the disorderly conduct of which you are accused.

Pages 91–92
- We do not treat a person with the breeding of M. Chevalier in this way. Besides, he is so

gentle and so honest that I have trouble understanding that he went to such excess without good reasons.

Page 92
- the good Father / the good superior
- (I found him to be very polite) / (The governor is a polite man)
- (He was good enough) / (he had the generosity)
- that barbarian / that opinionated old man, who would have damned himself a thousand times for his nephew

Page 93
- (She repeated to me, weeping bitterly, that she did not intend to justify her treachery)
- She seemed so charming to me / she received my expressions of politeness without appearing embarrassed / without the least sign of being disconcerted / Manon seemed very satisfied with this effect of her charms
- She was much more experienced than I was. It was against her will that she was being sent to the convent, probably to stop her penchant for pleasure, which had already manifested itself and which subsequently caused all her misfortunes and mine.

Page 94
- She wanted to know who I was, and this knowledge increased her affection because, being of lowly birth, she was flattered to have made the conquest of a lover like me.
- As passionately in love as I was with Manon, she knew how to persuade me that she was equally in love with me.
- Because of my consternation she realized the gravity of the danger, and trembling for me more than for herself, this tender girl did not even dare open her mouth to express her fears to me.
- Manon appeared frightened at the sight of such a sad dwelling. It was for my sake that she was grieving, much more than for her own.
- my ungrateful and duplicitous mistress / the faithless Manon / this incomparable lover
- I knew Manon; I had already experienced only too well that, however faithful and attached to me she was in good fortune, I could not count on her in poverty. She loved wealth and pleasure too much to sacrifice them for me: I shall lose her, I cried out.

Page 95
- I have always been persuaded that she was sincere; what reason would she have had to pretend to that extent? But she was even more fickle . . . when, seeing before her eyes women who lived in luxury, she found herself in poverty and in need.
- (I have always been)
- [1] Have I not promised you, she said to me, that I would find resources? I loved her with too much *simplicity* to grow alarmed easily.
- [2] She sins without malice, I said to myself; she is frivolous and imprudent, but she is straightforward and sincere. Add to that, love alone was enough to close my eyes to *all her faults.*
- He had a thousand good qualities. You will see the best of them later in my story, especially a zeal and a generosity in friendship that surpass the most famous examples of antiquity.

Page 96
- I am sure, he said to me without dissimulation, that you are thinking about some plan

that you wish to hide from me; I can tell by your attitude. I answered him rather sharply that I was not obliged to give him an account of all my plans. No, he replied, but you have always treated me as a friend, and that quality presupposes a little confidence and openness.
- He told me . . . that if I did not renounce *this miserable decision,* he would alert some people who could put a stop to it.
- He pitied the *waywardness* into which I had fallen. He congratulated me on *my cure,* which he believed to be in an advanced state; finally he begged me to profit from *this error of youth* and to open my eyes to *the vanity of pleasure.*
- I know the excellence of your heart and mind; there is no good of which you cannot make yourself capable.

Page 97
- I explained my passion to him as one of those particular acts of fate, which devotes itself to the ruin of a miserable individual, and against which it is as impossible for virtue to defend itself as it was impossible for wisdom to foresee it. . . . [F]inally, I moved the good Tiberge so much that he was as filled with the sorrow of compassion as I was filled with the sorrow of my pains.
- virtue, which I know you love, and from which only the violence of your passions has made you stray
- Let me argue in turn
- He agreed that there was something reasonable in my thoughts / He understood that there was more weakness than wickedness in the disorder of my conduct

Page 98
- this fatal tenderness
- He was content to make a few general reprimands to me about *the fault I had committed.* . . . He told me . . . that he hoped *this little adventure* would make me wiser.
- First he asked me if I had always had *the simplicity to believe* that I was loved by my mistress. . . . He added a thousand little jokes of this nature, about what he called *my foolishness* and my *gullibility.*
- You're a silly little fool / You are a child
- [1] He continued to give me reasons that would bring me back to good sense and inspire scorn in me for the faithless Manon. [2] It is certain that I no longer esteemed her; [3] how would I have esteemed the most fickle and perfidious of all creatures?
- I recognized too clearly that he was right. It was an involuntary movement that made me take the part of *my faithless one.*

Page 99
- Sit down, sir, he said to me gravely, sit down.
- scandal of your dissolute and knavish behavior / the disorderly conduct of a depraved son who has lost all sentiments of honor
- Although I was forced to recognize that I deserved a part of *these flagrant insults,* it seemed to me nonetheless that he was pushing them too far.
- Come here, my poor *chevalier,* he said to me, come kiss me; I pity you.
- dry and harsh tone / inflexible heart
- Can one be a barbarian, after having once experienced tenderness and sorrow?
- Go on, run to your ruin. Goodbye, ungrateful and rebellious son. Goodbye, I said to him in my anger, goodbye, barbarous and unnatural father.

Page 101
- it seems to me that she is worth a little more than her companions
- one of the most extraordinary and most touching

Chapter 4

Pages 103–4
- The response of M. the Marquis de C***, if he *grants* me one, *will furnish* me with the first lines of this narrative. Before writing to him, *I have tried* to get to know him. He *is* a man of the world.

Page 104
- (I had not compromised myself)
- (this narrative)
- and it is this motivation that has made me resolve to overcome my pride and my repugnance, by undertaking these Memoirs in which I depict a part of my misfortunes.
- the summary that ends them
- I am far from being able to praise my father in this way / I have wanted to resemble my sisters from my earliest years / Oh, how many times I have cried

Page 105
- shall I admit to you, sir? / what would I risk in confiding in you? You will burn this letter, and I promise to burn your answers.

Page 106
- (Imagine, sir / But let's quickly close our eyes to that subject / for just imagine, sir) / (One question, sir, that I would have to ask you / But what does that mean? / Do you want me to give you . . . ?) / (O foolish nuns! / How long those days seemed to me!)
- You can guess all that she added about society and the cloister / I will let you imagine the murmur that rose up in the community / Will you believe that my breviary was taken from me and I was forbidden to pray to God? You can imagine that I did not obey.
- When all our sisters had withdrawn . . .——So, what did you do?——Can't you guess? . . . No, you're too honest for that. I tiptoed downstairs and I positioned myself quietly at the door of the parlor and listened to what was being said. . . . That is very bad, you will say. . . . Oh, yes, that is very bad; I said it to myself.

Page 107
- (that scandalous applause that is given to your actors)
- You know, sir, that on Thursday the Holy Sacrament is transported
- A great number of people . . . solicited for me. You were among them, and perhaps the story of my legal proceedings is better known to you than to me / So I forgave the attorney Manouri . . . as well as you, Monsieur Marquis
- I made a decision, sir, that you will judge as you please / But you, sir, who know all that has happened up until now, what do you think? / actions that you will call either imprudent or steadfast, depending on how you consider them
- That is the time of my happiness or my misfortune, depending, sir, on the way you treat me / this foreboding, sir, will come true if you abandon me / sir, it depends upon you whether I know where to go or what I shall become

- Here this moment has finally arrived / This is the most terrible moment of my life / it is as you have seen until now
- (I have told you that I had the same confessor as my mother) / (I forgot to tell you that I saw my father and mother)
- (but you're going to learn at what price)

Page 108
- I will not give you the details of my novitiate / I will pass rapidly over these two years
- (it was a summary of all that I have just written to you) / (I thus began to tell my story approximately as I have just written it to you)
- I could not express to you my sorrow / I couldn't tell you the effect it produced on her
- I assure you that a more clever girl than I would have been fooled / for it is sure, sir, that out of a hundred nuns who die before the age of fifty, there are exactly one hundred who are damned / I am saying nothing that is not true
- I hear all of you, you, Monsieur Marquis and most of those who will read these memoirs. . . . That is not plausible, they will say, you will say; and I agree; but that is true.
- I am going to tell you something that will perhaps seem quite strange to you and which is nonetheless true.
- (I don't know / I wouldn't know / what do I know?)

Page 109
- It was, I believe, the Feast of the Ascension / It was Tuesday, as far as I can remember
- I don't know what was going on in the minds of those in attendance / I don't know what she was thinking / I don't know what she had answered
- (I don't know what took place in my soul) / (I don't know how long I remained in that state)
- The date was set, my clothes made, the moment of the ceremony arrived without my perceiving *today* the slightest interval between these things / I remember neither being undressed nor leaving my cell. . . . I have learned these things since then / I was at their disposal during that entire morning, which has been nothing in my life, for I have never known how long it lasted; I know neither what I did nor what I said. I was probably questioned, I probably answered, I pronounced vows, but I have no memory of it.
- I don't know if it was from pleasure or pain / I don't know what was happening within me / I don't know how that happened / I don't know what else we said

Pages 109–10
- I have courage / my mind works quickly / my soul lights up easily, is exalted and moved / I have an interesting face . . . I have a touching voice / my character leans toward indulgence, I can forgive anything / I like to praise / I am naturally compassionate

Page 110
- with the naïveté of a child of my age and the frankness of my character
- I don't know if it's fitting for me to tell you that she loved me tenderly and I was not the least of her favorites. I know I'm giving myself great praise / In truth, I would be quite beautiful if I deserved the smallest part of the praises she gave me.
- much more likeable than I am
- I foresee, Monsieur Marquis, that you are going to form a bad opinion of me. . . . Let's say that I have a rather strange frame of mind; when things can *provoke your esteem or increase your sympathy*, I write well or poorly, but with an unbelievable speed and

ease. . . . It seems to me that you are present, that I see you and that you are listening to me. If I am forced, on the contrary, to reveal myself in an unfavorable way, I have trouble thinking, I can't find expressions, I write poorly . . . and I continue only because I secretly hope you won't read these passages.

Page 111
- Society has its pitfalls, but I don't imagine one falls into them so easily.
- By thinking about something, one begins to feel that it is just and one even believes that it is possible.
- In the convent it is permitted neither to write nor to receive letters without permission of the superior / we carry our vows from one house to another / the choice of a confessor is a major affair for a house of nuns
- The determination to torment and destroy grows tired in society, but not in the cloister / There are weak minds in religious communities, they are even in the majority.
- These women are well avenged for the trouble you cause them; for one must not believe that they are amused by the hypocritical role they play and the foolishness they are forced to repeat to you.
- the numerous lines of jumble / a mummery / the hypocrite / the pious twaddle with which one fills those first moments / the wicked, recluse creatures . . . who believe they serve God by causing your despair!

Pages 111–12
- I was in a state of disorder that cannot be explained. She said to me: What is wrong with you, my dear child? [1] (She knew better than I what was wrong.) Just look at you! She seemed to pity me. . . . She promised me she would pray, argue, solicit on my behalf. [2] O sir, how crafty these monastic superiors are! you have no idea. She did indeed write. She was well aware of the answers she would be given . . . [3] and it is only after quite some time that I have learned to doubt her good faith.

Page 112
- Another added . . . that I trampled the Crucifix under foot and that I no longer wore my rosary (which had been stolen from me); that I pronounced blasphemies which I don't dare repeat to you.

Page 113
- I have never seen anything so hideous.
- this rare woman who has left behind regrets that will never end
- And why did God not take me at that moment? I was going to Him without fear. It is such a great happiness, and who can hope to have it a second time?

Page 114
- While I was sleeping, this holy woman walked through the halls, knocked on each door, awakened the nuns and made them go down to the church in silence. . . . The next morning she came into my cell. I did not hear her, I was not yet awake. She sat down beside my bed . . . and it is thus that she appeared to me when I opened my eyes.
- (one *affected* to believe the opposite)
- We were there when the superior came in. She had gone to my cell, she hadn't found me; she had gone through the whole house, in vain; it never occurred to her that I was with Ste. Therese.

Page 115

- Imagine, sir, that I was absolutely unaware of how I had been portrayed in the eyes of this priest, and that he had come with the curiosity of seeing a girl possessed, or who pretended to be so. It was believed that only a strong terror could show me in that state, and here is how they went about doing it.
- that is what *apparently* hastened the visit of the grand vicar
- I was not aware of all that.
- I saw part of these searches, I suspected the rest

Pages 115–16

- The following night, when everyone was asleep and the house was in silence, the superior got up. . . . She stopped, *apparently* leaning her forehead against my door. . . . While I slept someone came in . . . holding a small candle whose light shone on my face, and the one who was carrying it watched me sleep, or at least that is what I *judged* by her attitude when I opened my eyes.

Page 116

- She examined the blankets . . . they are good. She took the pillow.
- O sir, what a night that was! I did not go to bed, I sat on the bed. I called God to my aid, I raised my hands to Heaven. . . . O God! what will become of me? . . . Upon pronouncing these words I fainted away.

Page 117

- She asked me how I was feeling, that the service had been quite long today; that I had coughed a little, that I seemed unwell to her.
- [1] She asked me only whether I had gone to bed early. [2] I answered her, at the hour you ordered me to do so. [3]——If I had rested. [4]——Thoroughly. [5]——I expected so . . . [6] How I was doing. [7] Quite well. And you, dear Mother? [8]——Alas! she said to me.

Pages 117–18

- If a nun fails in the slightest way, she makes her come into her cell, treats her harshly, orders her to undress and to give herself twenty lashes for discipline; the nun obeys. . . . The superior becomes compassionate, tears the instrument of penance from her, begins to cry; *how unhappy she is to have to punish!* kisses her forehead, eyes, mouth, shoulders, caresses her, praises her; *but how white and soft her skin is! how beautiful her plumpness! her neck! her hair!* Sister St. Augustine, but you're silly to be embarrassed. . . . She kisses her again. . . . One is very uncomfortable with women like that, one never knows what will please or displease them.

Page 118

- when one gives such strict limits to one's defenses
- (one works to discourage us and to make us all resigned to our fate)
- It seems to me, however, that in a well-governed state
- One does not know the history of these asylums, said M. Manouri in his speech for the defense, one does not know it.

Page 119

- [1] She added to these insidious words so many caresses, so many protestations of friendship, so many sweet falsehoods; [2] I knew where I was, I did not know where I would be taken, [3] and I let myself be persuaded.

- Joy spread throughout the house. . . . "God had spoken to my heart; no one was made for the state of perfection more than I. It was impossible for that not to be, everyone had always expected it. One does not fulfill her duties with so much edification and constancy when one is not really destined for it. The mother of novices had never seen in any of her pupils a better characterized vocation; she was quite surprised by the faults I had shown, but she had always told our mother superior to remain firm and that these would pass."

Page 120

- Not one troublesome story happens in society that you are not told about; the true ones are arranged, the false ones invented; and then there are endless praises and thanks given to God *who shelters us from these humiliating adventures.*
- one brought even more obstruction and violence to something that demanded it only because one had provided for it; this priest had to see me obsessed, possessed or mad
- All of this was noticed, and one concluded that the paper I had asked for had been used in a way other than I had said. But if it hadn't been used for my confession, as was evident, what use had I made of it? Without knowing one would have these concerns, I felt . . .

Pages 120–21

- This document that I was proposing to my sisters, drawn up while I was still engaged in religion, became invalid, and it was too uncertain for them whether or not I would ratify it when I was free. [1] And then was it suitable for them to accept my proposals? [2] Will they leave a sister without asylum or fortune? Will they profit from her due property? What will society say? [3] If she comes to ask us for bread, will we refuse her? If she takes a fancy to get married, who knows what sort of man she will marry? And if she has children? . . . We must oppose this dangerous attempt with all our strength. [4] That is what they said and what they did.

Page 121

- I noticed that the suitor singled me out and that my sister would shortly be only the pretext for his attentions / I believed one would think of me and that I would soon be coming out of the convent

Page 122

- They want me to be a nun, perhaps it is also the will of God, very well, I will do it; since I must be unhappy, what does it matter where?
- First I thought about it lightly; alone, abandoned, without support, how could I succeed in such a difficult plan, even with all the help that I lacked? / What was involved? Drafting a legal brief and giving it for consultation; neither one nor the other involved no danger.
- I had no father, scruples had taken my mother from me; precautions had been taken so that I might not claim the rights of my legal birth; a very harsh domestic captivity; no hope, no resources. Perhaps if it had been explained to me sooner . . . someone could have been found for whom my personality, my mind, my face and my talents would have been a sufficient dowry. This was still possible, but the scandal I had caused in the convent made it more difficult. *One can hardly conceive how a girl of seventeen or eighteen years could have gone to such extremes without an uncommonly strong will. Men praise this*

quality a lot, but it seems to me that they willingly forego it in those whom they plan to marry. It was nonetheless a resource to be tried before thinking about another solution.

Page 123
- Sister Therese lowered her eyes, blushed and stuttered; and yet whether my fingers were pretty or not, whether the superior was right or wrong to notice, what difference did that make to this nun?
- Oh, how ill she was! / How I pitied her!
- but how does one refuse things that give such pleasure to someone upon whom one depends entirely, and in which one sees no harm?

Pages 123–24
- I go down; they open the gates for me, after having checked what I was taking with me, I get into a carriage and away I go / when suddenly there were two loud knocks on the door. Terrified, I immediately jump out of the bed on one side, and the superior on the other; we listen, and we hear someone.

Page 124
- I remained in the midst of the flock with which I had just become associated. My companions have surrounded me, they kiss me and say to one another: Just look at her, my sister.

Page 126
- Some sisters have spat in my face / I have been wounded a hundred times, I don't know how I haven't been killed
- The more I think about it, the more I am persuaded that what is happening to me had not yet happened, and would perhaps never happen.

Page 127
- This superior is called Madame***. I cannot deny my desire to portray her for you before going any further.
- (There were days when everything was confused) / (Such is the woman to whom I had made the solemn vow of obedience)
- The favorites of the previous reign are never the favorites of the following one. I was indifferent, to say nothing worse, toward the present superior, because her predecessor had cherished me.
- I saw that after the scandal I had caused, it was impossible for me to stay here a long time, and perhaps they wouldn't dare put me back in a convent.

Page 128
- I have often wondered whence came this bizarre conduct in a father and mother otherwise honest, just, and pious; shall I admit it to you, sir? a few words spoken by my father . . . have made me suspect a reason that would excuse them a bit. Perhaps my father had some doubt about my birth . . . I don't know. But even if these suspicions were ill-founded, what would I risk by confiding in you?

Page 129
- So much inhumanity and so much stubbornness on the part of my parents have finally confirmed what I suspected about my birth. I've never been able to find other reasons to excuse them. My mother apparently feared I would one day come back and claim a share of the property . . . but what was only a conjecture will soon turn into certainty.

Page 130
- I no longer doubted the truth of what I had thought about my birth.
- (That man has a sensitive heart) / (She's a little, round woman)
- This young person, sir, is still in the house, her happiness is in your hands; if anyone discovered what she has done for me, she would be exposed to all sorts of torments. I would not want to have opened the door of a prison cell for her, I would rather go into one myself. So burn these letters, sir. . . . That is what I told you then; but alas she is no more, and I remain alone.
- (So there I am, alone in that house)

Page 131
- I had made some indiscreet comments about the suspicious intimacy of a few of her favorites.

Page 132
- Awake, I questioned myself about what had happened between the superior and me; I examined myself, and in doing so I thought I had an inkling . . . *but these ideas were so vague, so foolish, so ridiculous, that I cast them away from myself.*
- I thought that I was about to become the talk of the house, that this adventure which was really quite simple would be told under the most unfavorable circumstances; that it would be even worse here than at Longchamp, where I was accused of *I don't know what.*
- I don't know / I'm unaware of it / I understand nothing about that
- there is sin in that
- Although my conscience reproached me with nothing, I will admit to you, Monsieur Marquis, that her question troubled me.
- The superior stopped at this point and she was right to do so, what she was about to ask me was not good, and I will perhaps do much more harm by saying it, but I have resolved to hide nothing.

Pages 132–33
- One rushes to her cries for help, she is taken away, and I cannot tell you how this adventure was travestied. The most criminal story was told. . . . I was said to have designs, to have committed acts that I dare not name. . . . In truth, I am not a man and I don't know what can be imagined between a woman and another woman, and even less about a woman alone. . . . What shall I tell you, sir, with all their outward modesty . . . these women must have a corrupt heart, since they know that dishonest acts are committed alone, and I do not; so I have never really understood what they were accusing me of, and . . . I have never known how to answer them.

Page 133
- She said a hundred sweet things to me and gave me a thousand caresses which embarrassed me a little, I don't know why, for I meant nothing by it, nor did she, and *now that I think about it,* what could we have meant? I nonetheless spoke of it to my confessor, who dealt with this familiarity, which *seemed* innocent to me and which still *seems* so, in a most serious tone.
- I said my confession, I fell silent, but the priest . . . asked me a thousand strange questions which *I still do not understand now as I recall them.*
- I *did not see* and still *do not see* any importance in things he protested against most violently.

Page 134
- I recall, sir, very imperfectly everything he said to me. Now that I compare *his words as I have just reported them to you* with *the terrible impression they made on me,* I find there is no comparison.

Pages 134–35
- Certainly that man is too severe.

Page 136
- (That is what I said to you then) / (you wanted to know)
- Here the Memoirs of Sister Suzanne are interrupted; what follow are only the notes that she apparently intended to use in the continuation of her narrative. It appears that her superior went mad, and it is to her unfortunate state that the fragments *that I am going to transcribe* must be related.
- (What a death, Monsieur Marquis!) / (Here I will portray my scene in the cab)
- I say nothing that is not true, and everything else that I might have to say either has escaped me or I would blush to soil this paper with it.
- I enter the service of a laundress, where I am *currently.*

BIBLIOGRAPHY OF WORKS CITED

Texts

Crébillon, Claude Prosper Jolyot de. *Les Egarements du coeur et de l'esprit,* ed. Jean Dagen. Paris: Garnier-Flammarion, 1985.

Diderot, Denis. *La Religieuse,* ed. Georges May et al. Vol. 11 of *Oeuvres complètes.* Paris: Hermann, 1975.

Marivaux, Pierre Carlet de Chamblain de. *Le Paysan parvenu,* ed. Frédéric Deloffe. Paris: Garnier, 1969.

Prévost, Antoine-François, l'abbé. *Manon Lescaut,* ed. Frédéric Deloffre and Raymond Picard. Paris: Garnier, 1965.

Literary Theory and Linguistics

Angelet, C., and J. Herman. 1987. "Narratologie." In *Introduction aux études littéraires,* ed. Maurice Delcroix et al, 168–201. Paris: Duculot.

Bal, Mieke. 1977. *Narratologie: essais sur la signification narrative dans quatre romans modernes.* Paris, Klincksieck.

———. 1981. "Notes on Narrative Embedding." *Poetics Today* 2: 41–59.

———. 1985. *Narratology: Introduction to the Theory of Narrative,* trans. Christine van Boheemen. Toronto: University of Toronto Press.

Barthes, Roland. 1977. "Introduction à l'analyse structurale des récits." In *Poétique du récit,* ed. Gérard Genette and Tzvetan Todorov, 7–57. Paris: Seuil.

Benveniste, Emile. 1966–74. *Problèmes de linguistique générale,* 2 vols. Paris: Gallimard.

Berendsen, Marjet. 1981. "Formal Criteria of Narrative Embedding." *Journal of Literary Semantics* 10: 79–84.

———. 1984. "The Teller and the Observer: Narration and Focalization in Narrative Texts." *Style* 18: 140–58.

Booth, Wayne C. 1983. *The Rhetoric of Fiction.* 2d ed. Chicago: University of Chicago Press.

Bronzwaer, W. J. M. 1976. "A Hypothesis Concerning Deictic Time-Adverbs in Narrative Structure." *Journal of Literary Semantics* 4: 53–73.

——. 1978. "Implied Author, Extradiegetic Narrator and Public Reader: Gérard Genette's Narratological Model and the Reading Version of *Great Expectations.*" *Neophilologus* 62: 1–18.

Casparis, Christian Paul. 1975. *Tense Without Time: The Present Tense in Narration.* Schweizer Anglistische Arbeiten 84. Bern: Francke.

Chatman, Seymour. 1978. *Story and Discourse: Narrative Structure in Fiction and Film.* Ithaca: Cornell University Press.

——. 1986. "Characters and Narrators: Filter, Center, Slant, and Interest-Focus." *Poetics Today* 7: 189–204.

Ci, Jiwei. 1988. "An Alternative to Genette's Theory of Order." *Style* 22: 18–38.

Cohen, Marcel. 1973. *Histoire d'une langue: le français.* Paris: Editions Sociales.

Cohn, Dorrit. 1978. *Transparent Minds: Narrative Modes for Presenting Consciousness in Fiction.* Princeton: Princeton University Press.

——. 1981. "The Encirclement of Narrative: On Franz Stanzel's *Theorie des Erzählens.*" *Poetics Today* 2: 157–82.

Cohn, Dorrit, and Gérard Genette. 1985. "Nouveaux Nouveaux Discours du récit." *Poétique* 61: 101–9.

Cordesse, Gérard. 1986. "Note sur l'énonciation narrative (une présentation systématique)." *Poétique* 65: 43–46.

Doležel, Lubomír. 1967. "The Typology of the Narrator: Point of View in Fiction." In *To Honor Roman Jakobson,* 1: 541–52. Paris: Mouton.

——. 1973. *Narrative Modes in Czech Literature.* Toronto: University of Toronto Press.

Edmiston, William F. 1989. "Focalization and the First-Person Narrator: A Revision of the Theory." *Poetics Today* 10: 729–44.

Fleischman, Suzanne. 1982. *The Future in Thought and Language: Diachronic Evidence from Romance.* Cambridge: Cambridge University Press.

François, Alexis. 1966. *Le Dix-Huitième Siècle.* Vol. 6 of *Histoire de la langue française des origines à nos jours,* ed. Ferdinand Brunot. Paris: Armand Colin.

Genette, Gérard. 1969. *Figures II.* Paris: Seuil.

——. 1972. "Discours du récit." *Figures III.* Paris: Seuil.

——. 1983. *Nouveau Discours du récit.* Paris: Seuil.

Ginsburg, Michal Peled. 1982. "Free Indirect Discourse: A Reconsideration." *Language and Style* 15: 133–49.

Glowinski, Michal. 1977. "On the First-Person Novel." *New Literary History* 9: 103–14.

Hamburger, Käte. [1957] 1973. *The Logic of Literature,* trans. Marilynn J. Rose. 2d ed. Bloomington: Indiana University Press.

Ifri, Pascal A. 1987. "Focalisation et récits autobiographiques: l'exemple de Gide." *Poétique* 72: 483–95.

Imbs, Paul. 1960. *L'Emploi des temps verbaux en français moderne.* Paris: Klincksieck.

Jost, François. 1983. "Narration(s): en deçà et au-delà." *Communications* 38: 192–212.

Kayser, Wolfgang. 1977. "Qui raconte le roman?" In *Poétique du récit,* ed. Gérard Genette and Tzvetan Todorov, 59–84. Paris: Seuil.

Lanser, Susan Sniader. 1981. *The Narrative Act: Point of View in Prose Fiction.* Princeton: Princeton University Press.

Lejeune, Philippe. 1975. *Le Pacte autobiographique.* Paris: Seuil.

McHale, Brian. 1978. "Free Indirect Discourse: A Survey of Recent Accounts." *PTL* 3: 249–87.

Margolin, Uri. 1984. "Narrative and Indexicality: A Tentative Framework." *Journal of Literary Semantics* 13: 181–204.

Morot-Sir, Edouard. 1982. "Texte, référence et déictique." *Texte* 1: 113–42.

Pouillon, Jean. 1946. *Temps et roman.* Paris: Gallimard.

Prince, Gerald. 1982. *Narratology: The Form and Functioning of Narrative.* Berlin: Mouton.

———. 1987. *A Dictionary of Narratology.* Lincoln: University of Nebraska Press.

Rimmon-Kenan, Shlomith. 1983. *Narrative Fiction: Contemporary Poetics.* London: Methuen.

Romberg, Bertil. 1962. *Studies in the Narrative Technique of the First-Person Novel.* Lund: Almquist & Wiksell.

Scholes, Robert, and Robert Kellogg. 1966. *The Nature of Narrative.* London: Oxford University Press.

Simonin-Grumbach, Jenny. 1975. "Pour une typologie des discours." In *Langue, discours, société: pour Emile Benveniste,* ed. Julia Kristeva et al., 85–121. Paris: Seuil.

Soelberg, Nils. 1982. "Du côté de Méséglise: les métamorphoses du regard. Marcel Proust: *Du côté de chez Swann.*" *Revue romane* 17: 89–109.

———. 1984. "La Narratologie: pour quoi faire?" *Revue romane* 19: 117–29.

Stanzel, F. K. [1979] 1984. *A Theory of Narrative,* trans. Charlotte Goedsche. Cambridge. Cambridge University Press.

Starobinski, Jean. 1970. "Le Style de l'autobiographie." *Poétique* 3: 257–65.

Sternberg, Meir. 1982. "Point of View and the Indirections of Direct Speech." *Language and Style* 15: 67–117.

Tamir, Nomi. 1976. "Personal Narrative and Its Linguistic Foundation." *PTL* 1: 403–29.

Todorov, Tzvetan. 1966. "Les Catégories du récit littéraire." *Communications* 8: 125–51.

Uspensky, Boris. [1970] 1973. *A Poetics of Composition: The Structure of the Artistic Text and Typology of a Compositional Form,* trans. Valentina Zavarin and Susan Wittig. Berkeley and Los Angeles: University of California Press.

Van Rossum-Guyon, Françoise. 1970. "Point de vue ou perspective narrative: théories et concepts critiques." *Poétique* 4: 476–97.

Vitoux, Pierre. 1982. "Le Jeu de la focalisation." *Poétique* 51: 359–68.

Literary History and Criticism

Baril, Germaine, and Lloyd R. Free. 1980. "Antithesis and Synthesis in Crébillon's *Les Egarements du coeur et de l'esprit.*" *South Atlantic Review* 45, no. 4: 23–32.

Bennington, Geoffrey. 1985. *Sententiousness and the Novel: Laying Down the Law in Eighteenth-Century French Fiction.* Cambridge: Cambridge University Press.

Blanchard, J. M. 1973. "De la Stylistique à la socio-critique: narration et médiatisation dans *Manon Lescaut.*" *Modern Language Notes* 88: 742–63.

Boothroyd, Ninette. 1980. "La Modernité de Crébillon fils." *Studi Francesi* 24: 234–42.

Bourgeacq, Jacques. 1975. *Art et technique de Marivaux dans* Le Paysan parvenu: *étude de style.* Monte Carlo: Regain.

Brady, Patrick. 1973. "Other-Portrayal and Self-Betrayal in *Manon Lescaut* and *La Vie de Marianne.*" *Romanic Review* 64: 99–110.

———. 1977. "Deceit and Self-Deceit in *Manon Lescaut* and *La Vie de Marianne:* Extrinsic, Rhetorical, and Immanent Perspectives on First-Person Narration." *Modern Language Review* 72: 46–52.

Brooks, Peter. 1969. *The Novel of Worldliness.* Princeton: Princeton University Press.

Champagne, Roland A. 1981. "Words Disguising Desire: Serial Discourse and the Dual Character of Suzanne Simonin." *Kentucky Romance Quarterly* 28: 341–50.

Cherpack, Clifton. 1962. *An Essay on Crébillon Fils.* Durham: Duke University Press.

Conroy, Peter V. 1972. *Crébillon Fils: Techniques of the Novel.* Studies on Voltaire and the Eighteenth Century, no. 99. Banbury: Voltaire Foundation.

Coulet, Henri. 1967. *Le Roman jusqu'à la Révolution.* Vol. 1. Paris: Armand Colin.

———. 1975. *Marivaux romancier: essai sur l'esprit et le coeur dans les romans de Marivaux.* Paris: Armand Colin.

Dagen, Jean. 1985. Introduction to *Les Egarements du coeur et de l'esprit,* by Claude Prosper Jolyot de Crébillon, 5–58. Paris: Garnier-Flammarion.

Delesalle, Simone. 1971. "Lecture d'un chef-d'oeuvre: *Manon Lescaut.*" *Annales: Economies, Sociétés, Civilisations* 26: 723–40.

Deloffre, Frédéric. 1967. *Une Préciosité nouvelle: Marivaux et le marivaudage.* 2d ed. Paris: Armand Colin.

Deloffre, Frédéric, and Raymond Picard. 1965. Introduction to *Manon Lescaut,* by l'abbé Antoine-François Prévost, iii–clxxvii. Paris: Garnier.

Démoris, René. 1975. *Le Roman à la première personne.* Paris: Armand Colin.

Didier, Béatrice. 1980. "Narratrices et narrataires dans *La Vie de Marianne.*" *Saggi e Ricerche di letteratura francese* 19: 153–71.

———. 1981. "Structures temporelles dans la *Vie de Marianne.*" *Revue des Sciences Humaines* 182: 99–113.

Dieckmann, Herbert. 1975. Introduction to *Préface de La Religieuse,* by Denis Diderot. *Oeuvres complètes,* 11:15–23. Paris: Hermann.

Edmiston, William F. 1978. "Sacrifice and Innocence in *La Religieuse.*" *Diderot Studies* 19: 67–84.

———. 1985. "Narrative Voice and Cognitive Privilege in Diderot's *La Religieuse.*" *French Forum* 10: 133–44.

———. 1989. "Selective Focalization and *égarement* in Crébillon's *Les Egarements du coeur et de l'esprit.*" *French Review* 63: 45–56.

Ehrard, Jean. 1975. "L'Avenir de Des Grieux: le héros et le narrateur." *Travaux de linguistique et de littérature romanes de l'Université de Strasbourg* 13: 491–504.

Etiemble, René. 1961. Introduction to *Les Egarements du coeur et de l'esprit,* by Claude Prosper Jolyot de Crébillon, vii–xxxi. Paris: Armand Colin.

Fabre, Jean. 1979. *Idées sur le roman: de Madame de Lafayette au Marquis de Sade.* Paris: Klincksieck.

Fort, Bernadette. 1978. *Le Langage de l'ambiguïté dans l'oeuvre de Crébillon fils*. Paris: Klincksieck.

———. 1985. "Manon's Suppressed Voice: The Uses of Reported Speech." *Romanic Review* 76: 172–91.

Frautschi, Richard L. (with Diana Apostolides). 1972. "Narrative Voice in *Manon Lescaut*: Some Quantitative Observations." *L'Esprit Créateur* 12: 103–17.

Gaubert, Serge. 1975. "Synchronie et diachronie ou la naissance du narrateur." In *Les Paradoxes du romancier: les* Egarements *de Crébillon,* ed. Pierre Rétat, 43–59. Grenoble: Presses Universitaires de Grenoble.

Gossman, Lionel. 1968. "Prévost's *Manon*: Love in the New World." *Yale French Studies* 40: 91–102.

———. 1982. "Male and Female in Two Short Novels by Prévost." *Modern Language Review* 77: 29–37.

Hayes, Julie C. 1986. "Retrospection and Contradiction in Diderot's *La Religieuse.*" *Romanic Review* 77: 233–42.

Ince, Walter. 1968. "L'Unité du double registre chez Marivaux." In *Les Chemins actuels de la critique,* ed. Georges Poulet, 114–27. Paris: Union Générale d'Editions.

Jones, Grahame. 1978. "*Manon Lescaut*: An Exercise in Literary Persuasion." *Romanic Review* 69: 48–59.

Jones, James F., Jr. 1974. "Visual Communication in *Les Egarements du coeur et de l'esprit.*" *Studies on Voltaire and the Eighteenth Century,* no. 120: 319–28.

Josephs, Herbert. 1968. "*Manon Lescaut*: A Rhetoric of Intellectual Evasion." *Romanic Review* 59: 185–97.

———. 1976. "Diderot's *La Religieuse*: Libertinism and the Dark Cave of the Soul." *Modern Language Notes* 91: 734–55.

Knight, Denise Bourassa. 1985. "Diderot's *La Religieuse*: Suzanne Simonin and the 'Youthful' Men Who See Her." *Nottingham French Studies* 24: 15–25.

Labrosse, Claude. 1975. "La Substitution dans les *Egarements.*" In *Les Paradoxes du romancier: les* Egarements *de Crébillon,* ed. Pierre Rétat, 99–127. Grenoble: Presses Universitaires de Grenoble.

Laden, Marie-Paule. 1983. "The Pitfalls of Success: Jacob's Evolution in Marivaux's *Le Paysan parvenu.*" *Romanic Review* 74: 170–82.

———. 1987. *Self-Imitation in the Eighteenth-Century Novel.* Princeton: Princeton University Press.

Lips, Marguerite. 1926. *Le Style indirect libre.* Paris: Payot.

Lizé, Emile. 1972. "*La Religieuse*, un roman épistolaire?" *Studies on Voltaire and the Eighteenth Century,* no. 98: 143–63.

Mat, Michèle. 1977. "L'Intrigue et les voix narratives dans les romans de Marivaux." *Romanische Forschungen* 89: 18–36.

May, Georges. 1963. *Le Dilemme du roman au XVIIIe siècle.* Paris: Presses Universitaires de France.

———. 1975. Introduction to *La Religieuse,* by Denis Diderot. *Oeuvres complètes,* 11:3–12. Paris: Hermann.

Monty, Jeanne R. 1970. *Les Romans de l'abbé Prévost.* Studies on Voltaire and the Eighteenth Century, no. 78. Geneva: Institut et Musée Voltaire.

———. 1979. "Narrative Ambiguity in *Manon Lescaut.*"In *Enlightenment Studies in Honour of Lester G. Crocker,* ed. Alfred J. Bingham and Virgil W. Topazio, 151–61. Oxford: Voltaire Foundation.

Mylne, Vivienne. 1981a. *Diderot: La Religieuse.* London: Grant & Cutler.

————. 1981b. *The Eighteenth-Century French Novel: Techniques of Illusion.* 2d ed. Cambridge: Cambridge University Press.

————. 1982. "What Suzanne Knew: Lesbianism and *La Religieuse.*" *Studies on Voltaire and the Eighteenth Century,* no. 208: 167–73.

Nichols, Stephen G., Jr. 1966. "The Double Register of Time and Character in *Manon Lescaut.*" *Romance Notes* 7: 149–54.

Pedersen, John. 1978. "La Double Communication dans quelques textes de Diderot." *Revue Romane* 13: 206–28.

Proust, Jacques. 1980. "Le 'Jeu du temps et du hasard' dans *Le Paysan parvenu.*" In his *L'Objet et le texte: pour une poétique de la prose française du XVIIIe siècle,* 39–53. Geneva: Droz.

Ray, William. 1976. "Convergence et équilibre dans *Le Paysan parvenu.*" *French Forum* 1: 139–52.

Rex, Walter E. 1983. "Secrets from Suzanne: The Tangled Motives of *La Religieuse.*" *The Eighteenth Century: Theory and Interpretation* 24: 185–98.

Rosbottom, Ronald C. 1977. "A Matter of Competence: The Relationship between Reading and Novel-Making in Eighteenth-Century France." *Studies in Eighteenth-Century Culture* 6: 245–63.

Rousset, Jean. 1962. *Forme et signification: essais sur les structures littéraires de Corneille à Claudel.* Paris: Corti.

————. 1973. *Narcisse romancier: essai sur la première personne dans le roman.* Paris: Corti.

Rustin, Jacques. 1978. "*La Religieuse* de Diderot: mémoires ou journal intime?" In *Le Journal intime et ses formes littéraires,* ed. V. del Litto et al., 27–46. Geneva: Droz.

Segal, Naomi. 1986. *The Unintended Reader: Feminism and* Manon Lescaut. Cambridge: Cambridge University Press.

Sermain, Jean-Paul. 1985a. *Rhétorique et roman au dix-huitième siècle: l'exemple de Prévost et de Marivaux (1728–1742).* Studies on Voltaire and the Eighteenth Century, no. 233. Oxford: Voltaire Foundation.

————. 1985b. "Les Trois Figures du dialogisme dans *Manon Lescaut.*" *Saggi e ricerche di letteratura francese* 24: 375–401.

Sgard, Jean. 1975. "L'Incipit des *Egarements.*" In *Les Paradoxes du romancier: les Egarements de Crébillon,* ed. Pierre Rétat, 17–21. Grenoble: Presses Universitaires de Grenoble.

Sherman, Carol. 1984. "Changing Spaces." *Diderot: Digression and Dispersion,* ed. Jack Undank and Herbert Josephs, 219–30. Lexington, KY: French Forum.

————. 1985. "The Deferral of Textual Authority in *La Religieuse.*" *Postscript* 2: 57–65.

Showalter, English. 1972. *Evolution of the French Novel, 1641–1782.* Princeton: Princeton University Press.

Siemek, Andrzej. 1981. *La Recherche morale et esthétique dans le roman de Crébillon fils.* Studies on Voltaire and the Eighteenth Century, no. 200. Oxford: Voltaire Foundation.

Smith, Peter L. 1978. "Duplicity and Narrative Technique in the *roman libertin.*" *Kentucky Romance Quarterly* 25: 69–79.

Stewart, Philip. 1969. *Imitation and Illusion in the French Memoir-Novel, 1700–1750.* New Haven: Yale University Press.

————. 1970. "A Note on Chronology in *La Religieuse.*" *Romance Notes* 12: 149–56.

————1984. *Rereadings: Eight Early French Novels.* Birmingham: Summa.

———. 1987. *Half-Told Tales: Dilemmas of Meaning in Three French Novels*. North Carolina Studies in the Romance Languages and Literatures, no. 228. Chapel Hill: University of North Carolina Press.

Terrasse, Jean. 1982. "La Rhétorique amoureuse dans *Les Egarements du coeur et de l'esprit*." In *Man and Nature: Proceedings of the Canadian Society for Eighteenth-Century Studies*, ed. Roger L. Emerson et al., 1:21–29. London: University of Western Ontario.

Thomas, Ruth P. 1970. "The Role of the Narrator in the Comic Tone of *Le Paysan parvenu*." *Romance Notes* 12: 134–41.

———. 1973. "The Critical Narrators of Marivaux's Unfinished Novels." *Forum for Modern Language Studies* 9: 363–69.

Undank, Jack. 1986. "Diderot's 'Unnatural' Acts: Lessons from the Convent." *French Forum* 11: 151–67.

Varloot, Jean. 1975. Preface to *La Religieuse*, by Denis Diderot. *Oeuvres complètes*, 11:75–78. Paris: Hermann.

INDEX